SOCIAL WORK
AND THE TRANSFORMATION
OF ADULT SOCIAL CARE
Perpetuating a distorted vision?

Mark Lymbery and Karen Postle

BAKER COLLEGE OF CLINTON TWP

First published in Great Britain in 2015 by

Policy Press
University of Bristol
1-9 Old Park Hill
Bristol BS2 8BB
UK
t: +44 (0)117 954 5940
pp-info@bristol.ac.uk
www.policypress.co.uk

North America office:
Policy Press
c/o The University of Chicago Press
1427 East 60th Street
Chicago, IL 60637, USA
t: +1 773 702 7700
f: +1 773 702 9756
sales@press.uchicago.edu
www.press.uchicago.edu

© Policy Press 2015

British Library Cataloguing in Publication Data
A catalogue record for this book is available from the British Library.

Library of Congress Cataloging-in-Publication Data
A catalog record for this book has been requested.

ISBN 978 1 44731 041 9 paperback
ISBN 978 1 44731 040 2 hardcover

The right of Mark Lymbery and Karen Postle to be identified as authors of this work has
been asserted by them in accordance with the Copyright, Designs and Patents Act 1988.

All rights reserved: no part of this publication may be reproduced, stored in a retrieval
system, or transmitted in any form or by any means, electronic, mechanical, photocopying,
recording, or otherwise without the prior permission of Policy Press.

The statements and opinions contained within this publication are solely those of
the editors and contributors and not of the University of Bristol or Policy Press. The
University of Bristol and Policy Press disclaim responsibility for any injury to persons or
property resulting from any material published in this publication.

Policy Press works to counter discrimination on grounds of gender, race,
disability, age and sexuality.

Cover design by Soapbox Design, London
Front cover: image kindly supplied by istock
Printed and bound in Great Britain by CPI Group (UK) Ltd,
Croydon, CR0 4YY
Policy Press uses environmentally responsible print partners

FSC
www.fsc.org
MIX
Paper from
responsible sources
FSC® C013604

In memory of Heather Clark

(14 August 1949 – 21 October 2014)

Friend, colleague and champion of older people

Dedication

Both of the authors have recently had and/or continue
to experience serious illness. Both of us have immense
gratitude for the care that we have received from skilled and
dedicated staff within the National Health Service. At the
time of writing we see threats to the NHS from increasing
privatisation and marketisation, and so we decided to
dedicate this book to this amazing institution, with our
hope that health care will continue to be provided in the
public sector on a not-for-profit basis.

Contents

Acknowledgements

As is always the case in completing a book of this nature there are a number of acknowledgements that we need to make. First we wish to convey our thanks to Helen Gorman for allowing us to adapt and update the text on which she worked so hard. We also wish to convey our thanks for the patience shown by Isobel Bainton and the team at Policy Press. Finally, our thanks and gratitude go to Tina Eadie and Tony Postle for their support and seemingly inexhaustible patience.

Our thanks go to the following publishers for allowing their work to be used in this text:

Taylor & Francis and the editors of the *Journal of Social Work*:
  Lymbery, M. (2014) 'Understanding personalisation: Implications for social work', *Journal of Social Work*, 14 (3): 295–312 (part of Chapter Five).
Oxford University Press and the editors of the *British Journal of Social Work:*
  Lymbery, M. (2014) 'Social work and personalisation: Fracturing the bureau-professional compact?' *British Journal of Social Work*, 44 (4): 795–811 (part of Chapter Six).
  Lymbery, M. and Postle, K. (2010) 'Social work in the context of adult social care in England and the resultant implications for social work education', *British Journal of Social Work*, 40 (8): 2502–22 (parts of Chapters Seven and Ten).
Taylor & Francis and the editors of *Practice*:
  Postle, K. (2014) 'Classic Text review: *Empowerment, Assessment and the Skilled Worker*', *Practice: Social Work in Action*, 26 (5): 327–31 (part of Chapter Seven).

Preface

The National Health Service and Community Care Act 1990 ushered in a new regime of community care which marked a considerable change in the way in which social workers, who often became termed 'care managers', worked with adults and older people. Helen Gorman and Karen Postle had both completed doctoral studies, based on empirical research, examining the work of care managers/social workers. In 2003 they published *Transforming Community Care: A Distorted Vision* (Venture Press) in which they argued that the rhetoric of community care was not borne out by the practice, and that in fact the version of community care that was being implemented was a distortion of the principles that supposedly characterised it.

The years since 2003 have seen further legislation and policy, and even greater changes in social work with adults and older people. The greatest change has been the 'personalisation agenda', stemming from policy documents in the late 2000s. As with community care previously, the rhetoric of these documents does not appear to match the reality of much social work practice. Indeed, as we will argue, there has also been a distortion of the fundamental principles of personalisation in the process of implementation. This has been an area of ongoing research for Mark Lymbery, continuing beyond his own doctoral studies.

Given the extent of the changes brought about by, first, the new regime of community care and then personalisation, and considering the context of increasing austerity, the time seemed right for a substantially revised edition of the original text. This book therefore uses pertinent material from the original book and updates this to include changes in legislation and policy. It also incorporates recent, relevant research. The current authors, Mark Lymbery and Karen Postle, continue to argue, as Gorman and Postle did, for the continued significance of social work within the context of adult social care, where skilled work can make real differences to the lives of adults and older people.

Mark Lymbery and Karen Postle
October 2014

Introduction

Setting the scene

The first edition of this book began with the story of how the BBC covered the circumstances of Mr Trebus, an obviously troubled man. This was included because it illustrated two things. First, the ways in which 'community', often presented as a simple, unified concept, is actually much more complex than this. Second, the way in which concerns about an individual were presented by the mass media, despite community care having been in existence for several years. Although this documentary, and Gorman and Postle's (2003) comments on it, are over a decade old at the time of writing this, we have retained this material because the two issues it raised at the time remain current. The details of this example were as follows: on 3 May 2001 BBC1 screened a 'Life of Grime Special' about Mr Trebus. This was the trailer in the *Radio Times*:

> This update (of a previous programme screened two years previously) has all the qualities that made the Polish war veteran's battle so fascinating: his anti-authoritarianism, his terrier-like refusal to see reason and his ability to live in squalor without apparently noticing ... (Lass, 2001: 104)

To the accompaniment of lively music and a voice-over by an apparently bemused (now late) John Peel, the programme showed Mr Trebus' continuing conflict with his local authority's environmental health department. He hoarded rubbish to the point where this became a health hazard both for himself and his neighbours and resisted all attempts to clear this or have repairs made to his property. One humane and kind local person, a retired businessman, decided to champion Mr Trebus' cause and help him in his battles with authority but gradually became worn down and frustrated by his attempts. As the trailer concluded:

> After causing an immense amount of aggravation, he [Mr Trebus] turns to the camera with a face in which butter would refuse to melt to say: 'Have I done something wrong?' (Lass, 2001: 104)

Aside from making us wonder what constitutes entertainment and where our boundaries of public/private life lie, what does this programme tell us about how people are cared for within their communities today? Where were the professionals, such as a GP, social worker or district nurse? Perhaps they were 'unable to comment' leaving it to environmental health officers and the police to steal the limelight. Perhaps attempts to portray a more balanced view would not have made good television. Viewers saw a man in his eighties, a survivor of wartime atrocities, living away from his homeland, now reduced to a figure to be belittled and cajoled like a naughty child. While the sundry officials and the helpful businessman spoke of their admiration for his spirit, they all colluded in a display of 'entertainment' which would not have been out of place in 19th-century Bedlam!

As if to demonstrate how little things have changed since the broadcast of this programme, in 2013 the BBC broadcast a series entitled *Britain's Biggest Hoarders*. Again, we were invited – more than a little voyeuristically – to observe how much of a problem compulsive hoarding caused for some people in society. It was hosted by Jasmine Harman, a television personality more commonly known for presenting an overseas property programme. She demonstrated considerable empathy for the people portrayed in the programme, based on her personal experience, but the series of programmes was still consistent with the treatment of Mr Trebus, in that people's serious psychological conditions were laid out in a manipulative way for the entertainment of the masses.

Most social workers who have worked with older people have met someone very like Mr Trebus or any of the people featured in *Britain's Biggest Hoarders*. In such situations there are always issues to explore such as:

- How can I find out what makes this person tick? Who is s/he? What is her/ his story? How has this come to be?
- What are the person's expressed wishes and how far do these conflict with risk to themselves or others?
- How great are those risks and how could they be managed?
- How much insight does the person have into her/his situation? How far is s/he able to make or participate in decisions about what should happen?
- Who else is in her/his support network?
- How could informal networks be maximised and supported?
- What is the medical opinion?

Social work is just one way of dealing with social problems and many, if not most, people would prefer to resolve the problems in their lives without outside intervention. There are, however, situations in which the art of skilled social work intervention can make a difference, and we would suggest that all of the featured situations in the television programmes could have been among them. Perhaps a social worker had been involved over a long period of time but had been unable to make any headway. Maybe, more worryingly, no-one thought it worth contacting social services because nobody fitted neatly into the right category for their help. Perhaps there was an ongoing discussion across social work teams about whether a social worker should be allocated from any of the possible teams that could be deployed – for example, the mental health team, the care of older people team or the community development team. In any of the cases perhaps a social worker had carried out an assessment, informed people of her/his decision for action and closed the case when further help was refused (as is likely in each case). Whatever the reasons that might have explained the individual sets of circumstances, the outcome both in 2001 and 2013 was that we witnessed proud, vulnerable people locked into intolerable situations that could only end badly. This seems a very long way from what was intended either by 'community care' or by 'personalisation'.

This book aims to explore what has become of the rhetoric that heralded the development of social care in the early years of the 21st century. This follows the reputed 'failure' of community care changes to transform adult social care, on which the earlier edition of this book commented (Gorman and Postle, 2003). As successive governments have maintained, the need for the 'transformation' of social care can be located in this 'failure'; however, there is little understanding of what has contributed to the apparent problems of social care in the first place. As the initial examples illustrate, there remain numerous people for whom the policy of personalisation does not work effectively, just as they were failed by community care policies.

The first edition of this book argued that the community care revolution of the late 1980s and early 1990s was conceived from a political conviction that the welfare state was too costly to run in its current form, due to the escalating costs of Social Security benefits for older people in residential care, and that the answer lay in market enterprise. Naturally, it was suggested, this had a huge impact on how individuals experienced welfare services under the disciplines of community care. The book contended that the changes that led to the transformation of community care into care management represented a fundamental distortion of its original vision. The disciplines of 'care management' became the mechanism through which the realities of community care policies were spelt out as the day-to-day actuality of community care – and how this concept was experienced by users, carers, workers and organisations.

One of the core problems with the system of care is the language which has been associated with the changes. If we examine 'community care', it is dependent upon the conjunction of two apparently unconnected terms, 'community' and 'care'. As our examples above illustrate, 'community' is far from being a simple, unified concept. Williams (1975: 76) has suggested that community is used as 'a warmly persuasive word' to which it is difficult to find a critical opposite. Indeed, the more we explore the meaning of 'community', the more we see that it does not necessarily possess the warm fuzzy connotations it may at first have seemed to have. This is similar to the way that, when we unpick notions of 'family' we find abuse, unhappiness and pain threaded through the rosy picture of closeness and love.

There is a risk of harking back to a 'Golden Age' of community which it is assumed has been lost in recent years. This myth persists, despite the tendency for each generation to perceive the past as organic and whole compared to the present (Means et al., 2008). Oral history studies reflect past understandings of community as being as patchy and differentiated as now, rather than demonstrating universal cohesion and mutual support (Bornat, 1997). This leads us to question why, if 'community' is such a contested notion, did it become so popular across the political spectrum as a basis for a system of care? We suggest that the following political reasons contributed to this:

1. community care policies appealed simultaneously to notions of personal responsibility in neoliberal ideology and notions of collectivity in the ideology of the traditional left;
2. moves towards de-institutionalisation;
3. reduction in public expenditure.

Hence politicians and policy makers from a broad spectrum of viewpoints bought into and fed the 'Golden Age' myth of community.

Appending the term 'care' onto community adds another 'warmly persuasive word', which magnifies the rhetorical grip of the concept. Unlike the notion of 'community', the word 'care' does carry some negative connotations – notably the inherently paternalist understandings of it that imply that the carer knows best, particularly when s/he is a professional (Tronto, 2010) or that 'care' is most commonly used for a parent to a child and so 'support' is more relevant for adults (Clark, 2007). Indeed, the concept has been strongly resisted by the disability movement on these grounds (Hughes et al., 2005). While we can understand this resistance, we also need to recognise that a more common use has it that 'care' is an overwhelmingly positive construct; it is rarely deployed in a critical context. It is held to be what people do for people they love, and its interdependent nature has also been stressed as powerful within feminist literature (Hughes et al., 2005). In its customary use, therefore, the language of 'community care' conveys a powerful, positive sense.

We believe that something similar has been happening in the contemporary world of social care. The dominant conceptual term is of 'personalisation', which is – as Ferguson (2007) has presciently observed – another warmly persuasive word, and hence difficult to oppose. The fact that the origins of personalisation can be located in the work of the disabled people's movement (Glasby and Littlechild, 2009) represents another difficulty: it is hard to suggest a line of argument which challenges the essential idea that there should be enhanced choice and control for service users. However, there is a growing body of literature that starts from the basis that personalisation should be criticised from a number of angles – its apparent fit with a neoliberal ideology that valorises the individual and dismisses the possibility of collective responses (Lymbery, 2014a). The theme of distortion – which was the governing feature of the first edition of this book – therefore holds good in relation to personalisation, the focus of this edition.

What emerged from the empirical research that informed the first edition of the book (Gorman, 1999; Postle, 1999) was a picture of service-driven assessment carried out by a largely demoralised work force. The context was rationing (Lewis and Glennerster, 1996), combined with managerial control and audit (Power, 1997). At the heart of this process was the care manager, who was usually a social worker but could also be unqualified or a member of another profession, such as nursing.

The fact that social workers remained at the core of community care is significant, because it has been argued (Lymbery, 2012, 2014d) that qualified social workers are no longer central to the operationalisation of personalisation, the policy that has become the driving force of adult social care as well as many other areas of government (Needham, 2011). (This is discussed in detail in Chapter Three.) Indeed, under the pressures of austerity, many local authorities – who remain the main employers of social workers – have restricted the numbers they employ (a line of argument which is also expanded further in Chapter Three); this is of course a further example of the impact of market principles on their work. Ironically, although this could be argued as being in line with the principles of personalisation as increasing the control that individual service users have over their services (Glasby and Littlechild, 2009), it also represents another form of distortion of the principles underpinning the policy. This is the case at least as far as the more disadvantaged service users are concerned. This book will be devoted to an exploration of this issue, from the particular perspective of an examination of the social work role. As a precursor to a future consideration of the social work role under personalisation, we will first discuss social work under community care and the conditions of care management.

Social work and community care

If we consider the roles of social workers as employees within welfare agencies, the continued application of market principles to their work becomes obvious. Under the policy of community care it is clear that the alteration of focus within their roles formed part of a wider change process. Following the implementation of care management in 1993 a reconfiguration took place in the way that social workers viewed their work and their professional identity. The application of social construction theory (Berger and Luckman, 1966) is helpful in recognising that the priorities of care managers as role performers in a welfare bureaucracy became particularly focused on enforcement. Compliance or non-compliance with socially defined role standards ceased to be optional: indeed, there was a threat of sanction for non-compliance. At times care managers appeared to be skating on thin ice; there was an ever-present awareness of legal threats and sanctions if 'mistakes' were made which led to defensive forms of practice (Harris, 1987). What the care manager learned as part of this process is significant, for:

> By virtue of the roles he [sic] plays the individual is inducted into specific areas of socially objectivated knowledge, not only in the

narrower cognitive sense, but also in the sense of the 'knowledge' of norms, values and even emotions. (Berger and Luckman, 1966: 94)

An example of this 'enforcement' in the research which informed the original text (Gorman and Postle, 2003) was as follows:

> Norah, visiting Mrs Lyndon-Jones, explained that, due to budgetary cutbacks, she would have to reduce the time which a paid carer spent with Mrs Lyndon-Jones, taking her shopping. Norah discussed whether a volunteer could do the shopping for her instead. Mrs Lyndon-Jones was understandably disappointed by this, saying that her shopping trips were one of the few times she left her flat and, by going with a carer, she was able to choose goods herself.

The intense emotional labour of the care manager/social worker in the context of the commodification of welfare (Gorman, 2000) has been a major part of the reality that both users of welfare and care managers experienced, with bitter consequences for both.

Indeed, the influence of the market on welfare and the new public sector management that developed in the 1990s had an impact on the identity and role of the care manager/social worker in terms both of tasks and the way that the labour process developed, thereby influencing their agendas in terms of priorities and consequently their relationships with service users. As a result social workers'/ care managers' narratives bear a strong similarity to those of the 'street-level bureaucrats' identified by Lipsky (1980) in the way that the tensions generated by decision-making processes affected power dynamics between them and the users of services, with a potential for disempowerment all round. As discussed extensively in the first edition of this book (Gorman and Postle, 2003), under community care policy there was ample evidence of inherent conflicts passed down to the level of practice for resolution or irresolution, with social workers/ care managers modifying their roles and their objectives to reduce gaps between available resources and achieving objectives. Resistance to these forces was apparent, with some significant discourses emerging about loss of autonomy and the need to be accountable, defined less in terms of professional than managerial language. As a consequence, practitioners' understanding of the essential nature of their role encountered some unfamiliar pressures – in relation to interprofessional work for example (Gorman and Postle, 2003).

As a result of all of this, professional social work practice (Schön, 1987, 1992) emerged as characterised by complexity, instability, uncertainty, uniqueness and value conflict, where the stakes were high for the service user in terms of the quality of life that they might experience as a result of the decisions of the care manager/social worker. Evidence from care managers and elsewhere (Lymbery, 1998; Postle, 2002; Gorman and Postle, 2003) suggests that there were attempts to fragment the care manager role, although there is also evidence of resistance to such fragmentation. For example, the case studies reported by Goss and Miller (1995) indicated clear possibilities for user involvement and empowerment; more recently the research undertaken by the Standards We Expect research team has uncovered something similar (Beresford et al., 2011). They have demonstrated examples of work moving from a standpoint of 'them and us' to 'us and us', which gave credibility to the least considered variant of the care management/social work role, that of service users acting as their own care managers. Nonetheless, there were concerns inherent in the community care reforms that they would reinforce and perpetuate ageism by routinising the work with older people – the majority of the service user population – while doing little to address the status of social work practice with them (Lymbery, 2005). Hugman (1994), on the other hand, argued optimistically for the potential for the community care reforms to raise the status of social work with older people from its former position of being largely undertaken by unqualified staff.

One deeply etched picture that emerged is of care managers/social workers as welfare bureaucrats, with a role that was increasingly circumscribed by the policy drive to pin down work activity into units that could be audited – typical of managerialism in social work with adults around the turn of the century (Lymbery, 2004). However, rather than being simply uni-dimensional actors, a more complex issue emerged; here the care manager/social worker acted as a professional expert engaging with users in a climate of uncertainty and risk, drawing on a vast repertoire of skills with the aim of meeting users' needs within the boundaries of available resources. The reinforcement of either the managerial or professional perspective in practice therefore depended upon individual perception, attitude and strategy intent. Consequently, the development of care management, a legitimate activity in public welfare, had a significant impact on the professional identity of social workers working with adults in community care.

When care managers described the contribution of social work to their role it was often as if it was a discrete entity which had been lost in the transition to care management (Gorman, 1999; Postle, 1999). It would have been be easy to dismiss their comments as nostalgia but an alternative explanation could be that staff were using what Giddens describes as the *internally referential* development of the self:

> The creation of a personal belief system by means of which the individual acknowledges that 'his first loyalty is to himself [sic].' The key reference points are 'set from the inside' in terms of how the individual constructs/reconstructs his life history. (Giddens, 1991: 80)

Hence staff reflexively constructed their identities as care managers and, when their work became increasingly at odds with this construction, they organised memories of their work congruently with their expectations of what it should have been. The alternative open to them was to try to work with the resultant tensions and ambiguities (Postle, 2002). Practitioners talked about the elements of social work that they thought had been reduced or lost in the transition to care management, describing in particular the loss of therapeutic elements such as counselling, listening and support, which were also aspects of their work which they found rewarding and satisfying (Gorman and Postle, 2003).

These elements became collapsed under the heading 'social work', as if they constituted that role in an uncontested and non-problematic way. Indeed, they only reflect one vision of social work (Payne, 2006); more collective visions of practice were not articulated (Ferguson and Woodward, 2009). Taking such a limited definition of social work as a given failed to problematise and deconstruct its nature, thereby not subjecting it to critical examination. In failing to do this, the diverse elements of social work have not been scrutinised in the context of its societal location. Lacking this critical examination social work, in the move to care management, appeared to adopt the tenets of wider society in a quite uncritical manner. Consequently, care management evolved as a highly individualistic response to problem solving, creating packages of care for individual people within a managerialist and market-driven ethos. In this sense it was typical of neoliberal political thought (Gamble, 2001). For practitioners, operating in less individualistic ways would have necessitated operating in a manner which challenged this prevailing ethos.

The threat that was posed at the time of community care was to the continuation of social work with adults as, in continuing to fail to challenge this ethos, it could consequently become subsumed by managerialist and market-driven agendas (Gorman and Postle, 2003). There were alternatives to this. Within social work there are diverse elements, with underlying theoretical assumptions, all of which can be deconstructed and then reconstructed and assessed for their potential in addressing the social problems of service users. This would go beyond taking a prescriptive stance on 'what works', which lends itself all too readily to a positivist and questionable interpretation of evidence-based practice (Webb, 2001). Rather it would have involved deconstructing social work to ascertain its content, meanings, scope and nature, to include an examination of its essential constituents, its theories, values, knowledge, skills and practices and, as Pease and Fook (1999) suggest, its underlying premises in ways that acknowledge and incorporate tensions between different, even opposing, strands. It would have involved examining where social work practice was flawed, such as in its tendency to lapse into paternalism or its failure to make alliances both with people who use its services and with other bodies who work with them, as well as its strengths. The diverse and eclectic nature of social work practice, encompassing the therapeutic and emotional as well as the radical and political, its ability to work with the individual as well as with the wider networks and communities, and its potential for drawing upon a broad and diverse knowledge base needed to be deconstructed and its elements valued equally rather than seen as vying for position as the best or only form of practice. Instead of any hoped-for transformation, community care appeared to become a distortion of social work.

While social work has tended to be apologetic for and defensive of its eclectic nature, by deconstructing this eclecticism and then reconstructing those elements of social work which can be used to effectively and appropriately meet people's differing needs, care management could have become more assertive about its body of values, knowledge and skills. However, it was apparent that most care managers had a sense that something was wrong with the forms of practice that were dominant but, while they were able to describe this, and to compare it with former practice, they did not articulate it theoretically (Postle, 1999). In a climate in which outcomes of community care policies were defined as those that are easily measurable, success was inferred from the increasing number of people with high levels of personal assistance needs who were maintained in the community. Such outcome measures ignored both the perspectives of those people with lower levels of need and users' opinions about the quality of service received (Nocon and Qureshi, 1996). Hence care managers, lacking the theoretical understanding with which to critique such policies or their operationalisation, appeared to be levelling unfocused criticisms at the system. As has been clearly demonstrated (Gorman and Postle, 2003), a fuller theoretical understanding of the societal conditions in which care management operated, and of how societal characteristics are reflected in care management practice, would have equipped care managers to evaluate and critique their practice and the operation of the agencies within which they work with greater confidence. It would also have made it easier for social workers to articulate their concerns about any subsequent developments in work with adults, the subject of a subsequent section. First, however, we analyse the impact of these changes on the professional status of social work with adults.

Social work and the bureau–professional compact

Bringing this analysis up to date requires an understanding of the centrality of local government to the development of social work in the United Kingdom. It is important to understand the nature of the bureau–professional compact that has emerged in relation to social work. According to Derber (1983), there are two key forms of managerial control to which public services professionals are subject. The first of these concerns the ends to which professional work is put; in Derber's terms, this form of control is 'ideological' in its nature. The second form concerns the means by which professionals operate, which he defined as 'technical' control. Writing in the early 1980s, Derber contended that many occupations – including social work, which he specifically discussed in his analysis – had ceded ideological control of their work to politicians and managers while retaining substantial control of the technical means by which it is carried out.

This can be seen as applicable in the context of social work, care management and community care. There was a clear ideological control in the uses to which care management was put. Under community care there was an influx of social workers into adult social care, largely to carry out the rationing and gatekeeping work that subsequently attracted such criticism. This was logical in relation to what has been characterised as the 'deep normative core' of community care (Lewis and Glennerster, 1996) – the need to control the overall costs of the care budget, which had become unmanageable during the 1980s. However, this rationing and gatekeeping work meant both that social workers were only exercising part of their repertoire of skills and that they were primarily performing tasks that would automatically bring them into conflict with service users; the rationing function that they were required to operate being the starkest example. Indeed, it has been difficult for social workers to act in ways that represent the full extent of their professional abilities (McDonald et al., 2008). While there was an increasing level of technical control – seen through the prescriptive assessment documents that had to be completed – there remained an acceptance that social workers would be central actors within the discourse of community care. In essence, this is how the 'bureau–professional' compact (Harris, 1998) was established. Social workers accepted the limited scope of their practice in exchange for a sense of security that such work would continue to be needed. This protection is now under threat; the element of control that is now most clearly evident in adult services is the decision about the numbers of social workers that are required and the work that such qualified staff should undertake – both of which reflect a more direct intervention. (The 'bureau–professional compact' is discussed further in relation to deprofessionalisation in Chapter Six.)

Social work and personalisation

In the early years of the 21st century, the rhetoric about community care gradually became replaced by a new language, that of 'personalisation'. Simply put, this conveyed a sense that services were now to be shaped around what each individual wanted, rather than the interests of either professionals or managers (Needham, 2011). Nonetheless, throughout the implementation of community care in the early 1990s the bureau–professional compact appeared to be in place: while practitioners were required to carry out a number of tasks that did not fit comfortably within traditional conceptions of social work, there was a marked growth in their numbers. This is the opposite of what has occurred across the United Kingdom as budgetary cuts bite, with particular stress being felt in English local authorities. As has been outlined elsewhere (Lymbery, 2014d) this has had a number of significant consequences. First, social workers' attention has increasingly been placed on tasks related to determining and, indeed, limiting eligibility and to safeguarding. In particular this focus on the disciplines of assessment and safeguarding has represented a further tightening of the ideological control of their work noted by Derber (1983). The greater emphasis on safeguarding is also testimony to the lack of toleration of risk typical of society more generally (Webb, 2006). Second, deriving from the stringent austerity measures put in place by the Conservative-led coalition, in government since 2010, there has been a widening gap between general care needs in the population and the resources required to respond to them. This has had a direct impact on eligibility criteria, negating the focus on prevention and early intervention that the previous government claimed should characterise personalisation (DH, 2005). Clearly, this also limited the capacity for social workers to be engaged in a wider range of activities – such as community development or therapeutic work – and also represented tighter structures in relation both to the ideological and technical control of their practice. Finally, it is clear that local authorities are employing fewer social workers as they try to reduce the burden on their finances. They are also replacing qualified social workers with unqualified staff for many activities (Samuel, 2011). This is the point where the bureau–professional compact is most obviously being threatened.

It is interesting that social work is rarely mentioned in the early attempts to explain what personalisation was and how it should work (see for example HM Government, 2007; DH, 2008). This is not at all surprising, as the focus of the policy was primarily on its impact on people who use services, which, it was argued, would be overwhelmingly positive (Glasby and Littlechild, 2009). However, the early references to social work can be seen as deeply problematic: for example, the occupation received criticism for allowing itself to become 'perceived as a gatekeeper or rationer of services' (DH, 2005: 28), ignoring the nature of the bureau–professional compact which required it to accept the parameters of practice as set by the state (Lymbery, 2014d). As the policy moved through the various stages of implementation, the implications for social work became clearer.

There were three documents published by official sources that sought to put flesh on these skeletal outlines. First to appear was a Department of Health document that considered the implications of personalisation for all staff in social care (DH, 2009). Because social workers only represent a small part of the total workforce, attention is given to their future roles in just two pages of the report, which means that its judgements were only an outline of the work that could be carried out. The document identified social work as a key element of some practice areas – early intervention, promoting social inclusion and safeguarding. It also highlighted the potential for social workers to support self-assessments, confirming the move away from professional assessments that characterised community care. It also suggested that tasks directly related to safeguarding should always be undertaken by a registered social worker, despite this being deeply problematic due to the withdrawal of social workers from the act of assessment (Lymbery and Postle, 2010). (The inherent problems in this are discussed further in Chapter Seven.)

The potential contribution of social work to personalisation has also been explored by the second document, which was from the Social Care Institute for Excellence (SCIE, 2010a) and which provided a little more detailed coverage of the issues. However, the recommendations remain thin: it highlights the specific focus around safeguarding mentioned in the Department of Health document (DH, 2009), but also concentrates its focus on five areas of practice:

- building relationships
- working through conflict
- knowing and applying legislation
- accessing practical support and services
- working with other professionals to achieve best outcomes.

These are similar to the conclusions drawn by Dustin (2006). At a similar time, a collection of organisations active in the field of adult social care (ADASS et al., 2010) produced the third document, which also considered the role of social work under conditions of personalisation, proposing a pattern for social work involvement which narrowed down the potential social work role into three particular areas of activity:

- supporting people in the assessment of their needs, circumstances and options;
- working with families to improve well-being and safeguard vulnerable family members;
- contributing to early intervention and preventative services. (ADASS et al., 2010)

Each report contains similar recommendations for the fuller involvement of social work, but none go into great detail, nor do their recommendations carry any statutory weight, which is important in the light of the austerity measures within which personalisation is being implemented (Lymbery, 2014c). Therefore, even though a range of writers have highlighted the potential for social work to contribute in a fundamental way to personalisation (see, for example, Duffy, 2010; Foster, 2010; Williams and Tyson, 2010; Lymbery, 2012) there seems little prospect of social work successfully arguing its centrality to change. What is happening in numerous local authorities testifies to this problem, as the number of social workers is being rapidly reduced and the work they are required to undertake appears to be more consistent with rationing and limiting access to resources than the promise of personalisation (Hicks, 2013). Consequently, it is proving difficult for social workers to resist the erosion of their roles. As such, this represents another aspect of the distortion of social work to fit policy priorities.

Outline of the book

The above sections outline the broad parameters of this book, which are amplified in the subsequent chapters. The book is divided into three sections, which seek first to chart the dimensions of policy, then to outline how this has led to a degradation of social work, before, finally, identifying possible ways for it to be reconstructed. Chapter Two, the first chapter in section one, seeks to expand further on the way in which the policy of community care was developed, with particular reference to the role of social work. It is this chapter that carries much of the analysis that characterised the first edition of this text. Chapter Three brings this up to date by focusing on the policy of personalisation, tracing its intellectual contours and its outcomes in practice. From both chapters a number of themes appear that inform the rest of the book: a further exploration of these themes and continuities make up Chapter Four.

The second section of the book builds on the notion, expressed in the first edition, that the development of care management represented a distortion of the principles that produced community care. Collectively, the three chapters within this section make the case that the various factors addressed in the previous chapters also represent a degradation of social work. Chapter Five examines the levels of ideological confusion that have characterised policy, and mounts a critique of the individualist character of policy changes as it affects social work. Chapter Six examines the issue of deprofessionalisation in social work with adults, drawing on the extensive sociological literature about the professions. The implications of these two chapters are explored through a focus on assessment in Chapter Seven: as this has traditionally been the area of activity where social workers have been most deployed it serves as a case study of the impact of ideological confusion and an anti-professional bias in policy. It also highlights the impact of the dominance of resource considerations in community care.

The third section of the book offers suggestions as to how social work could be reconstructed to take a more effective role in the provision of care services for adults. Chapter Eight addresses the centrality of values to effective social work practice, arguing that the core of social work values is actually consistent with the direction of personalisation policy. Building on this, Chapter Nine explores the various ways in which social work can be used to ensure a more effective response to people's needs, working with issues such as safeguarding, the management of complex and uncertain situations, and enabling people to come to terms with difficult issues in their lives.

Chapter Ten of the book argues that, while policy has either disregarded or downplayed the potential of social work to play a constructive part in the lives of adults with social care needs, the potential for such an activity does exist and should be recognised. Both authors share a belief in the positive contribution that social work can make to people's lives: the book is intended both to draw attention to what we consider to have been historical flaws in the development of policy and to highlight the ways in which social work can facilitate an improvement in the way in which policy is enacted. This commitment suffuses the text.

TWO

Community care: origins and influences

Introduction

'Those who cannot remember the past are condemned to repeat it.'
(Santayana)

We take this quote as our starting point here because we have a strong belief that it is vital to take a historical view of policy in relation to adult social care. By understanding its history we can begin to understand how we have arrived at the current state of affairs and we can also appreciate the dimensions of any government policy. If we are to mount a coherent critique of policy we need to be able to chart the elements that have characterised its development. In particular, since the community care reforms remain central to current practice, it is necessary to identify their key elements. This is particularly pertinent to a consideration of personalisation as many of the issues that affected the implementation of community care have reappeared in a current form, as we will discuss in subsequent pages. As the quote at the start of the chapter implies, it is arguably the case that a core problem in much contemporary adult social care is the failure to learn the lessons from previous developments and therefore to risk repeating them. In this respect, personalisation is no different from other policy developments: throughout, its advocates have failed to give detailed consideration to the way in which the previous policy of community care was formulated, and consequently it does not incorporate learning from its successes or failures. In addition, given the focus of this book, we need to concentrate on the place that social work has occupied within the various policy changes.

Of course, while the primary policy to be analysed is the shift to community care, we also need to understand what caused this to come into being: we will argue that some similar pressures exist in the present day to those that were highlighted in the 1980s, particularly in relation to financial constraints and hence imperatives to reduce public expenditure. Indeed, the financial situation under austerity is immeasurably worse than it was in the 1990s. The core focus of this chapter is to chart the development of policy for adult social care in the period following the Second World War, setting the scene for a discussion of personalisation in the following chapter. If we accept that the formation of the welfare state in the 1940s represents the starting point in this analysis there are two specific periods that need to be considered. The first focuses on the fragmented welfare system and its uneven growth and development in the decades following the passing of the National Assistance Act 1948. The second examines the implementation of community care changes from the early 1990s: it is the supposed failure of community care that created the pressure to enact the principles of personalisation. In both of these periods the place of social work will also be considered, before a separate section examines the transition from social worker to care manager.

The early years: adult social care before community care

It is worth charting the origins of community care in diagrammatic form, as it makes clear the reality that social care became a priority only at the point when its costs gave rise to major governmental concern (see Table 2.1).

Table 2.1: A brief history of the development of community care policies 1948–93

1948: Passage of the National Assistance Act, giving local authority welfare departments the responsibility to coordinate social care services.
1962: Enoch Powell, Minister of Health, announced his Hospital Plan, which launched the closure programme for large psychiatric hospitals and hospitals for people with learning disabilities. This marked a policy shift towards providing the bulk of care in the community, rather than in hospitals.
1968: Seebohm Report (Seebohm, 1968) mentioned the need for greater emphasis to be placed on community, rather than institutional, care.
1970s: Little movement. Two White Papers in this decade talked about a shift to community care but there was no real political impetus for this.
1980: Changes to supplementary benefit regulations leading to the spiralling cost of residential and nursing home care in the independent sector, which experienced an unprecedented boom.
1982: Barclay Report (Barclay, 1982) focused on the community and the role of community social work.
1986: Audit Commission (1986) emphasised the need for financial constraints on spending on residential care. At this time there was a *perverse incentive* for people to enter residential care because, for many, their fees were paid by the Department of Health and Social Security (DHSS) in Supplementary Benefit and they received much more than if they had remained at home (Audit Commission, 1986: 4). The private care home market was booming and there were also worries about the demographic changes, which pointed to an increase in the ageing population.
1988: The Griffiths Report (1988) made many recommendations about community care and was the final impetus for the legislation. It recommended that Social Services Departments (SSDs) would be the lead agencies in carrying out care management.
1989: White Paper, *Caring for People* (DH, 1989) gave the government's commitment to community care to enable people *affected by problems of ageing, mental illness, mental handicap or physical or sensory disability* to *live as independently as possible in their own homes.*
1990: NHS and Community Care Act, implemented in April 1993.

The early days of welfare in the 19th century are fascinating to study because they illustrate how the growing recognition of a particular social issue – the needs of older people and disabled people – fed into a range of policy responses that gradually started to address the problem (see Means and Smith, 1998). However, this section will focus on the period following the foundation of the welfare state, covering the years from 1948 to 1993. As we will seek to argue that the financial basis of policy has been particularly important, the section will examine factors that have a specific bearing on this, notably the separation of health and social care. However, we also need to explore a range of other policy developments that are not primarily dominated by financial concerns, particularly the move away from residential to community-based resources.

In our view, the split between health and social care has had a critical impact on the way that services have developed. One of the consequences of the establishment of the National Health Act 1946 and National Assistance Act 1948 was the apparently straightforward – but actually deeply troubling – separation of organisational responsibilities for health and social care. The key distinction was that the newly formed National Health Service (NHS) would be responsible for people's health needs, whereas social care needs would be addressed through the welfare departments established in local authorities. This had particular financial consequences, as health services are normally free at the point of use whereas social services potentially attract a charge from the service user. This principle was enshrined in legislation, as Part 3 of the National Assistance Act 1948 required local authorities to extract a contribution from each service user towards the costs of local authority-provided residential care. As a result, one of the effects of the transfer of responsibility for services from health to social care is that the financial burden shifts. Under health care, for example, when someone is receiving NHS treatment in hospital, it is the total responsibility of the state through the NHS to pay for that care. Under social care, such as when someone is then discharged from hospital, it is normally a shared responsibility of the state – through social care budgets – and the individual. As we will argue, this difference is crucially significant, particularly given the issues we outline now.

In principle, there is an apparently clear-cut distinction between health and social care: in reality the actuality is remarkably blurred (Means and Smith, 1998; Lymbery, 2006). As Jane Lewis (2001) has argued, the years since 1948 have featured a 'hidden policy conflict' between health and social care over which body is financially liable for meeting the needs of older people. The driving factors in this, for Lewis, are the facts that the organisations have separate funding arrangements and that their budgets have increasingly been incapable of meeting people's needs adequately. In addition, the fact that people only have 'contingent' rights to social care as opposed to their 'absolute' rights to health care (Salter, 1998) also affects the budgets: crudely put, the more that people are defined as having social care needs, rather than health care needs, the more their financial position is impinged upon.

This is relevant because both health and social care agencies have become very concerned about accepting the financial responsibility that has accompanied the demographic changes that have characterised the post-war years. These changes have meant that increasing sums have to be spent on the large numbers of people who have become old, frail or disabled (Lewis, 2001; Lymbery, 2006). The particular points to be emphasised here are that both health and social care agencies have sought to avoid this responsibility, and that this conflict has occurred in a hidden manner (Lewis, 2001). Consequently, as Jane Lewis has pointed out, health services have proved much more able to transfer costs than social care agencies have proved able to resist accepting the responsibility (Lewis, 2001). This has created a major hurdle for joint working that has yet to be resolved (Hudson and Henwood, 2002), despite the continuing rhetoric that promotes integration between the two bodies. Indeed, it could be argued that relations between health and social care are worsening (Samuel, 2013b). Therefore, we suggest that the separate organisational and budgetary priorities of health and social care agencies has caused problems in joint working between the two, and have materially affected the way in which policy has developed in practice. This has had a considerable impact at frontline level, with both health and social care practitioners spending disproportionate amounts of their time resolving conflicts regarding funding issues (Gorman and Postle, 2003).

Historically, there was little development of joint working between health and social care services in the years immediately following the separation of powers between the two. One reason for this was that relatively little financial incentive existed to encourage organisations to develop far-reaching joint projects. For example, the joint finance that had been introduced to promote partnership working in the 1970s and 1980s was time limited (Webb and Wistow, 1987); consequently, both health and social care agencies were expected to pick up substantial additional costs when this funding lapsed. With a significant worsening of public finances from the mid 1970s – circumstances that were not unlike the current situation – health and social care organisations faced particular pressures (Webb and Wistow, 1987). Consequently, both parties were cautious in their approach to joint planning, naturally reluctant to adopt the ambitious undertakings that were needed to transform the health and social care landscape.

A range of other problems also need to be acknowledged as these had a particular impact on the development of community care. A central problem was that relatively few services for adults existed outside of hospitals and long-stay institutions. Consequently, despite its failings, such care was often presented as the only response to people's needs. When Enoch Powell, the Minister of Health, announced his Hospital Plan in 1962, launching the closure programme for large psychiatric hospitals and hospitals for people with learning disabilities, he was acting in accordance with a growing weight of professional and academic opinion. The plan clearly marked a policy shift towards providing the bulk of care in the community, rather than in hospitals.

Peter Townsend's (1962) survey was influential in affecting the nature of change in that it revealed profound weaknesses in residential care for older people. At the same time, several studies were published that called into question the efficacy and ethical appropriateness of numerous other forms of long-stay care (for example, Goffman, 1961; Barton, 1966). Indeed, as Butler and Drakeford (2005) have outlined, much social policy has developed through the growing scandal caused by the outcomes of poor-quality services. Given that Townsend's research was focused on the actual situation of many residential homes for older people within Britain, its findings are particularly apposite. Indeed, a recent follow-up study that replicates his approach has produced outcomes that justify his line of attack (Johnson et al., 2012). In his research, Townsend suggested that the residential homes fell into three broad categories:

- Homes that had previously existed under the Poor Law, which had transferred to local authority control. As Townsend's study (1962) illustrates, these homes were commonly of execrable quality.
- Homes that were conversions of large properties. As Townsend (1962) recognised, this sort of development encouraged a number of problems – the buildings were often isolated from community facilities, and their layout often compromised their ability to provide a good response.
- A relatively small number of purpose-built homes. As Townsend (1962) noted, although there was considerable potential to improve standards within this group of homes, it was relatively small in number and the benefits compromised by the failure to invest in quality in relation both to the building materials and staffing (see also Means and Smith, 1998).

While Townsend's study focused on services for older people there were also critical issues in relation to the experiences of adults with impairments, where numerous inquiries pointed up the weaknesses and limitations of practice (Butler and Drakeford, 2005). The pattern of developments for various services areas differed – see for example, Jones (1988) in relation to mental health and Malin (1995) in relation to learning disability – but there were various aspects that these developments had in common. One of them was the pressure to move away from institutional to community care, which was the context within which Enoch Powell was working in 1962. This proved problematic for a number of reasons, including lack of political will to change the institutionally based system and concern about the cost of such a change (Means and Smith, 1998). The large hospitals and unsuitable residential homes lingered on for decades, a problem that was exacerbated by the financial difficulties within both the NHS and local authorities, which constrained the attempt to develop viable alternatives. As we have noted, it was primarily the escalating cost of sustaining independent sector residential and nursing homes which forced the policy change.

Indeed, in his research Townsend (1962) was as much concerned with the lack of development of alternatives to residential care as with its overall poor quality; this is particularly problematic as the shift away from institutional care depended upon the existence of sufficient, good-quality community services. While various pieces of legislation provided for the expansion of many home-based services, their development was piecemeal and hampered by the lack of integration noted above. Numerous official reports highlighted that there should be an increase in the amount and quality of community-based services, alongside greater integration between health and social care (see, for example, Audit Commission, 1986).

In professional social work from the 1960s onwards the need for a stronger community focus was emphasised in both the Seebohm Report (1968) and the Barclay Report (1982). The Seebohm Report also suggested that social workers should be generic, focusing on the needs of all people in the community. In reality, soon after the creation of social services departments, following the passage of the Local Authority Social Services Act 1970, the caseloads of social workers tended to prioritise some service areas over others, with a particular focus on child care (Satyamurti, 1981). In relation to social work with adults in the areas of mental health and learning disability, there was a considerable growth in multi-disciplinary teams, with social workers operating alongside community health professionals. In part, this epitomised the ongoing unresolved tension between specialisation and genericism in social work (Stevenson, 2005): it was necessary to create specialist roles in order to maintain a social work focus in particular areas of activity. However, this multi-disciplinary form of practice did not generally extend to work with older people, who were then, as now, the largest single service user group. A substantial reason for this was the slow process of professionalisation of work with older people (Marshall, 1989; Lymbery, 1998). Consequently, the place of social work within the whole panoply of social care was mixed – the strong and secure place of social workers within mental health was not replicated across the board, for example.

Community care

A range of factors led to the passage of the National Health Service and Community Care Act 1990, the legislation which marked a major change in policy for the care of adults/older people since the inception of the welfare state. At the level of principle there was a genuine desire both to put some flesh on the bones of care located in the community, and to end the over-dependence upon institutional care. However, as the Audit Commission (1986) pointed out, the situation went beyond principle into stark financial realities. As we have noted, in emphasising the need for financial constraints on spending on residential care, the Audit Commission also pointed out the *perverse incentive* for people to enter residential care. Importantly, the budget for Supplementary Benefit was not capped and so there was potentially no limit on the number of people whose fees could be paid in this way. By the 1980s, there was a decline in public provision of residential care, accompanied by a boom in private sector homes, fuelled by a change to the Supplementary Benefit regulations in the early years of that decade (Lewis and Glennerster, 1996). Over the years since community care was introduced, while the extent of private provision of residential and nursing home care has multiplied, this has been accompanied by its concentration between fewer providers (Scourfield, 2007a), which are frequently large, national companies often with diverse interests. An example of this is Castlebeck Care, the company which ran Winterbourne View, a home subject to a Serious Case Review following atrocious treatment of its residents (DH, 2012). This company has since, in turn, been bought out by Danshell, a business which now runs 36 residential units (Samuel, 2013d). There have also been inadequate systems of regulation (Kerrison and Pollock, 2001): as we will argue, this has had profound consequences on the quality of such care.

As we noted at the start of this chapter, a useful way of understanding the complexities of community care policy changes is through a glance at the key influences on its development. We have already noted that the Audit Commission

(1986) had made strenuous criticisms of the financial basis of policy; it also raised concerns about the messy and piecemeal nature of the care system, which lacked meaningful levels of coordination. Crucially, its conclusion was that community care only existed as an aspiration, not a reality (hence the title of its report). This led the government of the day to set up a commission, chaired by Sir Roy Griffiths, to examine how to make community care a practical reality. Published in 1988, the Griffiths Report made many recommendations about community care and was the final impetus for the legislation. Griffiths was particularly critical about the lack of coordination of policy: a key recommendation was therefore that social services should be the lead agencies in carrying out care management. In addition, there was an acceptance of the significance of population ageing, which would create significant demographic challenges.

As far as the government was concerned the Audit Commission had identified the core of the problem, and Griffiths had made specific recommendations that would resolve it. This led directly to the next problem: the construction of a policy that would be politically acceptable. However, there were particular issues that neither the Audit Commission nor Griffiths had seen as awkward, but which have created a problem in subsequent years. Unsurprisingly, given the political complexion of the government there was no real consideration of likely difficulties in the expansion of the private sector into the provision of care – this was seen as entirely straightforward and unproblematic. (Indeed, as can be seen in the policies of the Cameron-led coalition government, this pattern of thought retains its power.) In addition, there was little understanding of the genuine complexity underpinning the idea of joint working between health and social care. Finally, only lip service was given to the needs of informal carers (Lymbery, 2005).

However, for the government the next stage – to produce a policy that would address the problems it had identified – was a little more problematic. Part of the reason for the delay in accomplishing this was the core problem of how to construct it in such a way as to be politically acceptable to the then Prime Minister, Margaret Thatcher, who was deeply hostile to local government and hence not at all keen to accept the expansion of its responsibilities envisaged by Griffiths (Lewis and Glennerster, 1996). Finally, 18 months after the publication of the Griffiths Report, sufficient clarity about the way forward was reached and the White Paper on community care could be published (DH, 1989).

As noted in the earlier edition (Gorman and Postle, 2003), there were a number of factors that had influenced this policy shift:

- Large institutions were no longer seen as the best way of caring for people and the money tied up in institutional care was preventing funding of community care services.
- Community care would be a cheaper option.
- Concerns about excessive spending on welfare benefits, which was seen to be a drain on the economy.

- State provision of services was seen to be cumbersome, inflexible and unresponsive to need, fitting people to services which already existed and giving them little or no choice.
- New Right thinking in the 1980s saw the use of market forces as being the best way to operate public services.
- Growth of an increased managerial culture with emphasis on efficiency, economy and effectiveness.
- Growth of movements of people who use services and their carers voicing their views about services.
- Changes in attitudes towards empowering people who used services.
- Models of care management in use in the US.

It can be seen that these factors, which would operate as policy drivers for community care, are a complex and contradictory mixture of:

1. overtly political imperatives, consistent with neoliberal policies;
2. changes in societal attitudes and in the growing, long-overdue recognition of the views of people using services;
3. financial imperatives in a time of increased constraint.

The conflicting nature of these factors raises the question of how policies developed from them could hope to succeed.

The six key objectives for community care, listed below, respond in a variety of ways to the above issues:

- to promote the development of domiciliary, day and respite services to enable people to live in their own homes wherever feasible and sensible ...
- to ensure that service providers make practical support for carers a high priority ...
- to make proper assessment of need and good case management the cornerstone of high quality care ...
- to promote the development of a flourishing independent sector alongside good quality public services ...
- to clarify the responsibilities of agencies and so make it easier to hold them to account for their performance ...
- to secure better value for taxpayers' money by introducing a new funding structure for social care ... (DH, 1989: 5)

The order of these objectives is thoroughly misleading. If one works on the basis that financial thinking predominated – the rate of expansion in financial support from the public purse for people in residential and nursing care during the 1980s had increased uncontrollably, as the White Paper acknowledged (DH, 1989) – it is unusual that this element of the plan was the final declared objective. However, Lewis and Glennerster (1996) are clear that controlling expenditure was in fact the 'deep normative core' of community care. Indeed, Griffiths had this as a key purpose in his review, the primary function of which was to look at 'the way in which public funds are used to support community care' (Griffiths, 1988: iii), so its centrality in practical policy making is unsurprising.

For Lewis and Glennerster (1996) the other critical issue is buried in the fourth objective; they term the creation of a market in social care as a 'near core objective'. The fact that 85% of the budget allocated to local authorities had to be spent in the independent sector made the political imperatives of the legislation absolutely clear (Gorman and Postle, 2003). Certainly the years since the enactment of the National Health Service and Community Care Act in 1993 have witnessed enormous growth in the provision of care on a profit-making basis, initially in residential and nursing home care, but increasingly in home care as well. If we take these two elements as the dominant features of the legislation, the remainder of the objectives assume less significance, even if they – the first two in particular – represent the more principled aspects of policy. Indeed, these two elements highlight the overtly political nature of the community care reforms. They are consistent with that government's reforms in other areas of state provision and evidence a clear prioritisation of market forces and economics in contrast to empowerment of service users (Clarke and Newman, 1997). However, publicity about the policy changes focused on the presumed benefits for service users and their wider involvement, rather than the other drivers.

Recognition of the paramount importance of controlling costs starts to change the very nature of the community care objectives. For example, the costs of community care could only realistically be managed if the level of dependence on institutional care was replaced by an increase in care at home, which was seen as not only being more effective and suitable but also less costly. Realistically, this could only happen if a greater level of recognition and support for informal carers was granted (Lymbery, 2005). While one cannot ignore the fact that other significant policy drivers were in play, they cannot be viewed without reference to the overriding financial requirements.

For social work, the acknowledged importance of care management to community care appeared to be crucial. Poor levels of coordination had characterised much social care (Webb and Wistow, 1987), and the potentially vital role of care management in addressing this problem was evident in the third objective. Although it was not specified, it had been envisaged that this role would be carried out, by and large, by qualified social workers. Indeed, the research that had informed the development of the idea of care management (see Challis and Davies, 1986) had identified it as a professional, highly skilled activity; it was therefore commonly believed that its implementation would be a good thing for social work (Challis and Hugman, 1993). However, the reality of care management practice has largely failed to live up to this promise, as contemporary research outlined (Gorman, 1999; Postle, 1999). It is worth examining this failure in more detail, as the illusory gains for social work need to be properly understood.

At the time of the implementation of community care in 1993, it was widely felt that the incorporation of care management as the governing professional logic of community care would be beneficial for social work. The core principle of 'case management' (the significance of the divergence from 'case management' to 'care management' will be considered below) had been actively pursued in various pilot projects by the Personal Social Services Research Unit (PSSRU) (see Challis and Davies, 1986). These were well-funded demonstration projects, focusing particularly on defined populations, with decentralised responsibility for budgetary management, the ability to commission services from existing or new providers, and staffed by qualified social workers who carried low caseloads (Bauld et al., 2000). This standard of organisation was seen as essential in securing significant savings. Although it only proved to be cost-effective under certain limited conditions (Dant and Gearing, 1990), it was this notion of cost containment and the concept of the management of services that fired the imagination of the policy makers in the UK, and was to make an impact on the UK welfare system in the 1990s. It is important to remember the professional dimensions of this shift. 'Case management' was identified as a highly skilled activity: indeed, it was suggested that people occupying the role would need to be able to respond successfully to the sorts of more complex situation with which social workers would normally engage (Challis et al., 1995). Consequently it was considered that 'case management' would provide a shot in the arm for social work with adults – a neglected area of practice – since the majority of practitioners would indeed be qualified social workers. Therefore, as it was originally envisaged, the introduction of 'case management' would have had an entirely beneficial impact on the role and status of social work.

Instead, the term 'care management' emerged as common parlance in health and welfare settings in the late 1980s, following the publication of *Caring for People* (DH, 1989). In Huxley's view (1993) the switch from 'case' to 'care' management implied a semantic and linguistic re-engineering. The distinction between these two terms is a critical issue for care management in the UK. This distinction may be seen as the difference between the managerial and administrative control of care services and the meeting of the individual care needs of those who require care in the community perhaps through 'casework' intervention. If we trace the origins of case management back to the US – a much wider geographical area with limited public service development – particular emphasis was placed on the role and skills of the case manager, both in coordinating packages of care and in building and sustaining high-quality interpersonal relationships with service users (Lymbery, 2005). Of course, this was also entirely in line with the core principles of social work developed by Biestek (1961). This was a professionalised conception, which was precisely the variant that had been developed in the PSSRU studies (Bauld et al., 2000). By contrast, care management (as defined by the government through *Caring for People* [DH, 1989], the National Health Service and Community Care Act 1990, and subsequent practice and policy guidance) was conceptualised as an administrative model within a consumerist framework. This approach fitted in with the growing emphasis on the 'market' in welfare and the idea that people could choose from a range of services that included those provided by the private and voluntary sectors. For Huxley (1993) there were no empirical and theoretical referents in this transition: policy simply asserted that 'care' management was a process that could straightforwardly be applied to everyone.

The intentions of the government to control care budgets while introducing a marketised version of social care were clear. In order to manage budgets effectively the government argued that, if the service was to respond to need, assessment should be separated from service provision (DH and SSI, 1991). Although different models of operating care management were potentially possible (Hudson, 1993; Øvretveit, 1993), connected to the ways that local authorities embraced the purchaser/provider split, a model was universally selected that enabled organisations to manage their community care budgets – logically, this was consistent with the primary purpose of the legislation, that of reducing public expenditure (Lewis and Glennerster, 1996). Consequently, as was argued in the first edition of this book, the way in which care management was developed represents a distortion of the person–centred ideals of community care (Gorman and Postle, 2003).

Did care management represent a break with the fundamentals of social work or did it presage the development of social work in another direction (Lymbery, 2005)? Some commentators suggested that there is in fact little relationship between the practice of care management and the core nature of social work (see, for example, Carey, 2003); indeed, others have seen care management as a direct shift away from social work (Postle, 2001). By contrast, other observers insisted that there was potential to create something positive for social work out of the care management role (see, for example, Payne, 1995; Lloyd, 2002). Where one stands regarding the debate concerning changes in the nature of social work depends, in large measure, on the extent to which one believes that the principles of community care have been implemented from a social work perspective. It is worth recalling that, in early care management projects (Challis and Davies, 1986), social workers had a core role in the process, with counselling, therapeutic and interpersonal expertise considered as vital to successful outcomes (Payne, 1995). However, as Gorman (2003) has observed, although the 'traditional' relationship skills of social work were defined as central to the successful performance of the care management role, these skills had to be complemented by well-developed administrative abilities that are not so strongly associated with social work. Indeed, a substantial part of the 'distortion' of care management has come from the fact that these administrative skills conclusively dominated the profession (Gorman and Postle, 2003) and have continued to do so, as we shall see. Indeed, contemporary research highlighted the malign influence that the care management changes had on practitioners, and the extent to which they were troubled by the increasing dominance of bureaucratic and administrative requirements (Gorman, 1999; Postle, 1999; Carey, 2003), leaving practitioners both demoralised and stressed, with the likelihood of detrimental effects for the people with whom they worked.

This anti-professional shift in the nature of social work practice under community care was consistent with the theme of the new managerialism in public services (Lymbery, 1998). This involved more than simply shaking up social services to make them more responsive to better management: it required a fundamental change in the way that the work carried out by social workers was configured and shifted the agenda from a notion of professional work to one where the dominating schema was management structures and practices. In this context the concept of the 'new managerialism' is used in a broad sense: as deployed by Pollitt (1990) it operates as a general set of principles, the basis of which is the seldom challenged belief that more effective management in itself should help to resolve a broad range of social problems. It is important to note that this is, at heart, a profoundly ideological notion (Clarke and Newman, 1997). These authors identify its attempt to realign a series of relationships, between the state and the citizen, between the state and the economy, and between the state and its organisational forms, including labour processes. In relation to community care, the new managerialism encapsulated the belief that social problems could be solved by the better management of resources, including human resources (Lymbery, 2004).

There were a number of ways in which the ideas of the new managerialism were made manifest. Certainly, the growth in importance of the principles of audit (Power, 1997) represents a critical element in the managerialist strategy; indeed, performance measurement became a core feature of much public sector work (de Bruin, 2002). The notion of audit and the significance of the monitoring of performance at work through the achievement of targets became part of the Labour government's strategy for the reform of health and social services through its modernising agenda (DH, 1998). At base, the governing ideal of performance measurement is deceptively simple: it rests on the assumption that any organisation can formulate the desired outcomes of its performance, and that these outcomes can easily be measured by the development of a set of indicators (Lymbery, 2007). One such indicator related to the time limits within which assessments should be completed. While it was obviously important to stress that assessments should be managed in a timely fashion, the indicator was rendered much less useful because it contained nothing about the quality of such assessments. There is little doubt that this was one of the key elements that constrained the autonomy of social workers (Harris, 1998).

The development of the market in social care was another critical issue. As Lewis and Glennerster (1996) highlighted, this was a 'near core' objective of the community care reforms. Local authorities were required to use 85% of the additional grant they received towards the implementation of community care within the independent sector. This meant that they had to develop strategies for the purchase of care services. Consequently, they became enablers rather than providers of services: staff in some local authorities were required to elect to work in either the provider side or the purchaser side of the organisation. The idea of 'consumer sovereignty', that is, that users have free choices about the services they can have, was limited within care management because the nature of the relationship with the state is one in which there were controls set by the local authority through eligibility criteria and restrictions in resources (Wistow et al., 1994). Furthermore, these controls were fundamental to the way in which the care manager, who usually defined 'need', had to operate. Consumers may have been able to express their opinions and exercise their bounded rights, yet the discourse with them was predefined by the organisation through its management. Inevitably choice is restricted if a user needs services that s/he cannot purchase on the open market as an independent purchaser. In some respects, consumerist notions such as flexibility and innovation had some relevance, yet the lack of redress for poor-quality service, the lack of overt critical standards and the constraints of working with limited budgets belied notions of consumerism which then appeared superficial. (As we will see, consumerist ideas remain central to personalisation.)

From social worker to care manager: a changed role

It is important to place arguments about the change from social worker to care manager into perspective, as there had been large elements of social work with adults which had not received significant levels of social work input (Marshall, 1989; Lymbery, 2005). As a result, ideas about a 'golden age' of practice when social work values dominated may be ill-conceived. However, there is little doubt that practitioners were able to identify the elements of their job that did not accord with more traditional notions of social work. It was accepted that the introduction of care management would inevitably change the role of social work staff who undertook the task. Following implementation of the National Health Service and Community Care Act 1990, in April 1993, much research focused on the changed role of the social worker and the sense of loss of social work skills (see, for example, Henwood, 1995; Rachman, 1995), even if there was little sense that these skills had actually been practised in the past. The counselling/therapy role which care managers might have undertaken as part of their work was not clearly defined, for example. This resulted in a worrying trend for some social workers, who had to deal with what they perceived as the loss or under-use of their therapeutic skills. Some responded by leaving the profession to work as therapists, which echoed the situation in the US where the growth of individualised therapeutic work, coupled with financial rewards for this and the difficulties of working in a residual welfare state, has caused social workers to leave their profession for the more lucrative work of therapy (Specht and Courteney, 1994). Care management was similarly seen as squeezing out the less quantifiable skills of social workers, such as emotional support and counselling, and replacing them with bureaucratic and mechanistic approaches involving heavy caseloads and increased administrative tasks (Hoyes et al., 1994).

How did care managers describe how they spent their time? This is how one practitioner explained it:

> 'Contracts, paperwork, writing assessments ... writing assessments is
> OK.... If you look at setting a care package up you've got to write
> an assessment, got to work out which agencies you're talking about,
> got to write out an initial service contract. If they're going into respite
> care, into a rest home, then you're talking about residential contracts.
> You can have two initial service contracts if you can't get one agency
> to do the whole lot ...'

His comments typified what most care managers described with regard to dealing
with bureaucratic tasks largely related to contractual arrangements (Postle, 1999).
Much of care managers' time was taken up with paperwork (Lewis and Glennerster,
1996; Lewis et al., 1997).

Care managers attributed the increased bureaucracy to the operation of the
market and increased budgetary constraints. The notion of an internal market
resulting in a purchaser/provider split, however operated (Means and Smith,
1998), introduced new ways of working for care managers. They had previously
used their 'in-house' services, which required little paperwork and only a very
simple means test to calculate the amount which people paid for domiciliary or
residential care. They commented that using the market to purchase domiciliary
and residential care had brought benefits in terms of flexibility of care provision
but also disadvantages, such as wide variety in quality of service provided with
some agencies' standards declining if, for example, they took on too much work.
In terms of the changed nature of the care managers' work, operating in a market
for care involved them in a plethora of procedures and contractual arrangements
with care agencies and residential homes, as shown in the care manager's comments.

Additionally, the care manager quoted above described the charging policy
forms which had to be completed:

> 'You've also got to do the charging policy stuff so you've got to do
> financial assessments for the charging policy. When the package is set
> up you've got to inform the financial department so that they can
> initiate the charging process.... So an assessment and writing up an
> assessment is over half a day ... a maximum two hours with the client,
> then at least half a day ... [the bureaucracy's about] managing finances
> ... as the care manager, you're responsible for the first part of that,
> getting everything into those financial systems.'

Most local authorities were working with very restricted resources and introduced
charging policies to ensure that people contributed to the cost of their care. Care
managers were responsible for obtaining details of finances from their clients
in order to calculate what the person had to pay for their care (Postle, 1999).
Although the finance section arranged for payments to be made, if anomalies or
queries arose, cases were passed back to care managers to clarify or obtain more
information. While there is clearly a need for accountability for public funds, the

result of undertaking extensive financial enquiries was that care managers became further embroiled in bureaucratic tasks. This was in addition to the administration of means testing, which exacerbates poverty and social exclusion (McLeod and Bywaters, 2000).

The health of older people with whom care managers worked most frequently is often precarious, necessitating frequent changes in their care needs. Care was bought on the basis of individual contracts for people and therefore changes, such as admission to hospital, necessitated alterations to care plans and contracts. The care manager quoted below found that she could keep up with initial contracts but was very concerned about coping with the innumerable 'temporary adjustments', which had to be completed whenever a person's care changed:

> 'It's the admin side of it. I think I'm in favour of care management. I think it's good for the client, but it's not social work as such.... I don't like paperwork. I think I've come to not mind filling in contracts and arrangements and all of that, but it's what comes after that which causes me quite a bit of anxiety ... a trivial thing like temporary adjustments! Have I done it? Have I remembered to stop or start care? ... The temporary adjustment is purely administrative but it bothers me whether I've done it or not.'

An increase in the administrative and bureaucratic requirements of care management was a typical organisational response to community care. Attempting to formalise and bureaucratise care management procedures was a clear application of what Blaug described as 'instrumental' reason. This is concerned with control and efficiency, ensuring that tasks are performed in a uniform way and hence well-suited to market transactions. Blaug compared this with 'communicative' reason, concerned with interaction and emotion (Blaug, 1995: 426). He further commented that such concentration on procedures could tend to help bad social workers and hinder good ones. Most care managers were experiencing a de-skilling of their role in terms of their reduced emotional labour and increased bureaucratic tasks. This was happening in a way which appears to be symptomatic of the wider process of casualisation and de-skilling (Simiç, 1995) and, indeed, of the commercialisation and commodification of emotional labour (Gorman, 2000). It became clear that the concern expressed by some care management staff that their work could be done by unqualified staff was realistic. (Again, the potential replacement of qualified social work personnel with unqualified staff has been resurrected with personalisation.)

Furthermore, the use of reductionist IT assessment procedures reduced the likelihood of the development of an 'exchange' model of assessment, which Smale et al. (1993) described as giving scope for a sharing of information between client and worker and hence relying on the client's expertise in their situation. This was contrasted with a 'questioning' model which they demonstrated as one in which the worker, as 'expert', holds all information and expertise. The notion of *thinking under headings*, as staff on a training course were advised to do (Gorman and Postle, 2003), where assessments are restricted and prescribed by forms or computer systems, epitomised a 'procedural' model, derived from the questioning model, and is used to 'fit' clients to agency criteria or services (Smale et al., 1993). Furthermore, staff were being advised to carry out a paradoxical injunction. They were supposed to use professional skills and judgement in carrying out an assessment, but also to ensure their assessment was circumscribed and thereby constrained by the headings on the IT form, the antithesis of professionalism.

The care managers appeared to be required to use IT because it was available, regardless of its suitability for the task. It was as if failure to use it would be seen as a retrogressive step (Loader, 1998). It is questionable whether any IT system, while apparently purporting to be capable of enabling care managers to perform the task of assessment, can provide more than a simulacrum of the assessment itself. It appeared to represent an assessment, while having none of its interactive, tacit, non-linear capacity and was, in fact, serving a different purpose from that which it ostensibly appeared to do.

A key problem was the replacement of more 'traditional' conceptions of the social work role by an increasing number of bureaucratic tasks. The use of self, however described, is widely recognised as an important and integral part of social work (Howe, 1996; Payne, 2006). The care work or 'emotional labour' which staff do lacks a language to describe it adequately (Camilleri, 1996), and care managers used a variety of terms such as "client-centred stuff", "counselling", "listening" and "spending time" to explain how they formed a relationship with people with whom they worked. There is a problem with the lack of descriptive words for this care work, or the use of words borrowed from the language of counselling or psychotherapy yet lacking their concomitant meaning. It meant that social work left itself open for others, operating particularly within the managerialist worldview, to define its task.

The discourse about care is problematic and paradoxical in nature. The feminised nature of care, in the sense of caring 'for', can be seen as derived from that which defines women's roles as 'natural' care-givers and therefore as inherent in the feminised roles of people of either sex who carry out the caring task. As such, it is all too easy not to see this as 'work' but as something done as a matter of course and thereby rendered 'invisible' (Camilleri, 1996; Pithouse, 1998). However, Camilleri described the emotional labour as not simply an addition to the work but rather as the 'real' work which:

> involves a heavy personal interaction and commitment. Engaging the client in terms of its rhetoric is more than just 'face to face work', it implies getting *inside* the person, understanding their feelings and emotions and using these to make sense of who they are and how they came to be here, that is, to be in need of social work help ... (1996: 84; emphasis in original)

The regulated nature of care managers' work is therefore seen as a result of increased managerialist control and loss of autonomy (Gorman, 2000). Hence, as this care manager commented, while practitioners saw the real work of forming a relationship with clients as core to effective social work, this was being eroded by the time spent on bureaucracy and a fast turnover of work:

> 'You feel more remote from the client because you're whizzing in and you're setting up care and you're out and then you review again in three months and you don't build up that layers of knowledge about that person.... In the past, you could use yourself as a resource a bit more in providing that time or that listening ear, or if somebody was bereaved or whatever, it was quite appropriate to spend the time with the client, listening and counselling, not in a formal way … now it's much more identifying the need and then actually contracting in a service.'

A comment from another care manager provides an example of how an older person's concerns may well extend beyond the immediate need to resolve physical problems.

> 'There's no services available to tap into that can buy trust.... Older people have fears about mortality starting to come to the surface that might not have been the case a few years earlier … they need time to talk about these sort of issues. Last week I was talking to a lady of 82 and she said, "Are you frightened of dying?" That came from her, quite unsolicited.'

Pressures of time and the changed nature of their work were squeezing out time for care managers to undertake this essential care work and forcing them to adopt a much more cursory approach. Care work was becoming seen as something which could no longer be afforded or could, in some way, be short-circuited. For example, one of the training staff on an in-house training course advised staff that they should get service users to "tell me the problem sooner", to avoid people telling them something really important right at the end of a visit or several visits. This advice, intended to help staff to reduce their time pressures, relied on a bureaucratic, linear and procedural approach to the work in which the worker can fit the person to her/his schedule. It contrasted with notions of working at the person's pace using tacit knowledge and reflection (Schön, 1991; Eraut, 1994) to enable and empower them to participate on a more equal basis in the assessment process.

Despite constraints of time and the volume of paperwork, most care managers were attempting to do the skilled care work (Gorman, 1999; Postle, 1999) and, in the process, demonstrating considerable skills in their purposeful use of themselves. However, they frequently commented on their loss of opportunity to use themselves skilfully in their work, feeling that such work was being squeezed out by increased bureaucracy. As one care manager indicated, they already regarded their use of themselves as "undercover" work:

> '[done] behind the system's back, if you like. Trying to do some social work in my spare time but I'll have to nip back and get on and do the work on the computer or whatever.'

Another person described it like this:

> 'There seemed to be a lot more time to go out and spend time with people, listening to what's happening and then feeding it back. We even had time for listening as in i.e. counselling. I don't tend to use the word "counselling" because it's not a qualification I have, but I have listening skills.... The care component of care management seems to be slipping as you don't have time to spend with the client with all the other responsibilities as well.'

It would be simplistic and incorrect to imply from care managers' comments that they thought there was a 'golden age' of social work in which staff spent time working on therapeutic relationships with their clients, did little if any paperwork and yet somehow kept such paperwork up to date. As we have indicated, there was no such period in relation to social work with older people, for example. However, care management was characterised by an apparent loss of time spent on direct contact work with people, in which some social workers felt that they were able to use therapeutic or counselling skills and which could be said to constitute 'care'. This loss could also be seen as contributing to a change in the core relationship in which social workers engaged and worked with their clients. Such a fundamental change in the work, from direct work with potential for therapeutic input to considerably increased bureaucracy, leads to a questioning of the future role of social work itself (Simiç, 1995).

Conclusion

A number of issues are highlighted in the preceding pages. One such is the fact that there had long been an acceptance of the limitations of care services for adults, which – in the fullness of time – promoted the community care reforms. In addition, it is significant that there has been little history of social work engagement in the lives of many adults in need. There are also consistent limitations of policy, particularly the failure to accept that since financial imperatives were the 'deep normative core' (Lewis and Glennerster, 1996) of community care, its practical limitations can certainly be traced to this problem. If this analysis is accepted, any judgement about the success or otherwise of community care must start from this: to what extent did the reforms enable effective management of public monies?

Critically, to what extent was it possible for community care to meet its own objectives as well as people's legitimate expectations?

From the perspective of financial management, community care was clearly successful (Lymbery, 2005). The escalation of care costs through the 1980s was halted through the simple mechanism of making local authorities responsible for a capped budget. When financial problems did occur – from the mid 1990s onwards – central government was able to claim that any failure could be attributed to the profligacy of local authorities. The fact that the policy was enacted over decades, without the problems of funding becoming a major concern, testifies to its success. That the overall budgetary position of local authorities was relatively generous through this period undoubtedly helped: there were not the pressures that have been felt since 2010.

However, it is more difficult to claim success on a number of other fronts, notably in relation to the principled commitments of the policy. For example, this is particularly evident in the case of care management and assessment (Lymbery, 2005). As the previous edition of this book demonstrated (Gorman and Postle, 2003) it was clear that the potentially positive contribution that care management could make to people's lives was not in fact occurring. Care managers were primarily placed in charge of the economic management of resources, which denied the capacity for the role to develop in as constructive a manner as had been envisaged (Carey, 2003; Postle, 2002). In addition, they had the responsibility for managing the purchaser/provider split, which directed increasing amounts of work in the direction of the independent sector.

Of course, the priority given to the management of resources has also affected the quality of services. The comparison between directly provided local authority services and those provided by the independent sector has often been on the basis of cost; as a consequence, an increasing proportion of care services have been provided in the independent sector as opposed to the statutory sector, both in relation to residential and nursing home care (Scourfield, 2007a), and care provided in the home (Ware et al., 2001). In particular, the shift in favour of home-based care rather than institutional care has been clear, even though progress in this direction was initially slow (Lymbery, 2005). A feature of community care has been the establishment of eligibility criteria to define those people who may – and by extension, may not – receive a service (DH, 2002). Since local authorities have been *required* to meet the higher levels of need first, fewer people have found themselves eligible for a service. Naturally, this has affected the ability of local authorities to accomplish the preventative goals of policy. As a result, the fact that many people place a high value on relatively low levels of support (Clark et al., 1998) has become unimportant, since the focus for local authorities has had to be placed on those with higher levels of need. This has meant that there has been little investment on preventative work (Bauld et al., 2000), an absence that has helped to shape the move towards personalisation.

BAKER COLLEGE OF CLINTON TWP

THREE

Personalisation

Introduction

In seeking to establish the ideas that have informed personalisation, and its impact on practice, it is important to move away from an uncritical acceptance of its core tenets. It is clear that it has become a highly contested concept (Ferguson, 2007; Glasby and Littlechild, 2009; Duffy, 2010; Lymbery, 2010, 2014a, 2014d; Needham, 2011; Spicker, 2013; West, 2013; Glasby, 2014; Needham and Glasby, 2014a), and it is not our intention here to argue about it at the conceptual level; we take the view that even if it is accepted without argument, there are numerous areas that are problematic in relation to its implementation. As a result we first wish to highlight its core elements, within the context of implementation, as it is this process that is proving to be particularly awkward (West, 2013); indeed, as we will explore further in Chapter Four, there are parallels with the difficulties that accompanied the community care changes.

Given that our primary focus is on implementation, we will first explore the context of austerity within which personalisation is being introduced. This is because the financial situation within local authorities is material to the success of policy implementation (Lymbery, 2014c). This provides a particular continuity with previous policies; however well intentioned, is it practically possible for an ambitious policy such as personalisation to be fully and properly implemented and achieve its goals in straitened financial circumstances? Having established the financial situation within which personalisation is being introduced, the chapter will go on to consider the key elements that characterise the policy. In particular it will analyse the extent to which it can been seen as a positive innovation – reflecting the need for service users to be more in control of the services they receive – rather than a further importation of consumerist values into the provision of care. Following this, the chapter will examine the progress of personalisation in its implementation, in the awareness that practical problems can blow even the best intentioned of policies off course. Finally, the chapter will examine the complex place of social work within the framework of personalisation; here the impact of austerity is particularly strongly felt (Lymbery, 2014c).

The context of austerity

Unquestionably, there have been severe pressures on local government budgets under the Chancellor's austerity programme (HM Treasury, 2010). While various aspects of service delivery have been protected – some health provision, overseas aid – no such protection has been afforded to the work of local authorities. The origins of this austerity can be located in the financial crash of 2008/09, where the consequences of a massive failure of the banks led to a spectacular worsening of public finances (Taylor-Gooby, 2012): a problem with public finances is, of course, typical of such circumstances. Politically, it is fascinating to note how these failures of the financial system were translated by the incoming government in 2010 into an alternative view: that the cause of the problem was excessive public spending, for which the previous administration was held liable. In turn, this placing of blame has justified the need for what appears to be permanent austerity. It is fair to point out that the previous Labour government was also committed to substantial savings – it had pledged to find £52 billion in cuts in response to the financial crisis, which was substantially more than the avowedly cost-cutting Conservative government led by Margaret Thatcher had achieved in the 1980s (Elliott, 2010). This already eye-watering sum was more than doubled by the incoming Conservative-led coalition, which set out the detail of how the cuts were to be made in the spending review of late 2010 (HM Treasury, 2010). Subsequently, since the plans to revive the economy failed to take effect as quickly as had been hoped, the duration and extent of austerity measures are forecast to be both longer and deeper than originally put forward (HM Treasury, 2013). When he was Shadow Chancellor of the Exchequer, George Osborne had stated that, in relation to proposed cuts, "we're all in this together" but, with the austerity plans in place, it soon became apparent that certain sectors, such as local authorities, would bear the brunt of those cuts.

There are four specific points that have to be made in relation to this, given the significance of the context of austerity on the implementation of public policy (Lymbery, 2014c). First, we need to note that the devastating cuts to public expenditure have never been achieved in any country, not just in Britain (Taylor-Gooby, 2012). This casts critical doubt on the achievability of the coalition's aims. Second, despite the coalition's claims that 'we're all in this together', the austerity measures are disproportionately reducing spending as opposed to increasing tax: this is a political choice which is different in kind from previous responses to recessions (Taylor-Gooby and Stoker, 2011). Third, and this is critical, the impact of spending cuts on local government has been particularly striking: somehow, despite the increase in numbers of those who require their services, local authorities should have accommodated a reduction of 27% in their budgets by 2014/15 (HM Treasury, 2010). As local authorities are where responsibility rests for the response to adult social care needs, it is clear that this is presenting an intolerable burden in at least some of them (Morris, 2013). The financial situation is unlikely to improve under current circumstances:

> Evidence drawn from the real budgets of councils across the country undermines the government's claim that there is no current funding crisis in adult social care. Many local authorities forecast a critical divergence of resource and demand by 2015. (Carr-West, 2012: 15)

In addition, the cuts are falling hardest on those local authorities that serve the most deprived areas (Watt, 2014). Finally, the sense that local authorities are able to find these savings from the more efficient exercise of their duties is common, but may well have limited applicability. There is evidence that local authorities have found various resourceful ways of carrying out their business in recent years (LGA, 2014); however, it is clear that the scale of the savings that still confront them is beyond the scope of efficiency savings:

> Councils argue that a combination of increasing demographic pressures, which they can manage down no further, and rising costs, which have been held down for too long, added to the fact that they have been relentless in implementing the efficiency approaches that they believe to be possible locally, means that it is unlikely that councils can continue to make cuts of this scale without putting services for vulnerable people at risk. (LGA, 2014: 7)

At the very least, this warning should cause concern both centrally and locally.

Consequently, however the principles that informed personalisation are to be understood, the nature of the financial climate within which it is being implemented is important. At the very least, this climate will limit the extent to which the more progressive visions of policy can be implemented. To follow this through in practical terms, it has been claimed that personalisation can be more cost-effective than existing policy (Leadbeater, 2004). Indeed, when applying this policy to social care Leadbeater and colleagues felt able to make bold claims that personalised services could provide both a better response to people's care needs, and to do so at lower cost:

> What started as a solution to the intense needs of a small group of social service users has the *potential* to transform public services used by millions of people, with budgets worth tens of billions of pounds. (Leadbeater et al., 2008: 10; our emphasis)

This enabled the then (Labour) government to state that personalisation would be introduced at no additional cost to the public purse. Despite this, the question of whether there are adequate funds to implement personalisation is critical, a point which the Local Government Association report (LGA, 2014) makes clear. Even in the early stages of implementation, before the financial crash, concern was expressed that the restrictive nature of eligibility criteria was substantially at odds with the intentions of policy (CSCI, 2008; Henwood and Hudson, 2008). By comparison with the current situation, this feels like a time where resources were not a major issue, yet the policy was to be implemented only within the context of existing funds (DH, 2008, 2010a). Indeed, there were clear statements that resource constraints would always exist:

> Public funding for social care will always be limited in the face of demand and such resources as are available should therefore be allocated according to individual need in a way that is as fair and transparent as possible.... To broaden their focus beyond those with the highest needs, councils should ensure that the application of eligibility criteria is firmly situated in the wider context of personalisation, including a strong emphasis on prevention, early intervention and support for carers. (DH, 2010a: 6–7)

This important quotation contains two principles, which are potentially mutually exclusive. The first is that there remains a need to retain eligibility criteria to determine the allocation of scarce resources fairly and transparently. The second contains a clear nod to the principles of prevention and early intervention characteristic of personalisation. There is no consideration at all of the feasibility of managing both of these principles in harmony with each other.

In addition, as we have seen earlier, financial circumstances are significantly worse for local government now than they were at that time (the circular was one of the last to be issued by the outgoing Labour administration). It is an open question whether it was possible to achieve both of these principles then: it is certainly difficult, at the very least, for this to be accommodated in the circumstances that prevail at the time of writing (summer 2014), particularly given the various challenging factors that place pressure on the available budgets (Lymbery, 2014b). Indeed, an authoritative source has concluded that 'it is highly likely that reduced spending on social care for older adults is having a negative effect on the health and wellbeing of users and carers' (Ismail et al., 2014: 7; see also LGA, 2014). However, as we will see, the effective implementation of personalisation rests (in resource terms) on an important principle – that it is possible to do more with less.

The principles of personalisation

The starting point for the personalisation narrative in social care can be found in the then (Labour) government's desire to formulate a 'new vision' for social care (DH, 2005). Simply put, this sought to enhance service users' well-being by enhancing the levels of control that they would have over the provision available to support their needs, including the extent of the choice they should have over the nature and type of services that would be available. As the Green Paper stated:

> social care should be about helping people maintain their independence, leaving them with control over their lives, and giving them real choice over those lives. (DH, 2005: 8)

This theme surfaced in numerous subsequent documents, all making use of the rhetoric of 'choice' and 'control', the questionable nature of which is further highlighted in Chapter Five. Of particular moment is the following statement in the *Putting People First* concordat (HM Government, 2007) which set out the then government's overarching vision for social care:

> The time has now come to build on best practice and replace paternalistic, reactive care of variable quality with a mainstream system focussed on prevention, early intervention, enablement and high quality personally tailored services. (HM Government, 2007: 2)

What is focused upon here is a sense of discontinuity between the past and the present, emphasising the presumed differences between the two (du Gay, 2003; Lymbery, 2010) and the failings of past systems. In reality, there are many continuities between the two eras – for example, the focus on limited resources, heightened managerial control, partial evidence that would justify the shift (Means, 2012) – particularly in relation to the problems that care services seek to address. (We will address these in more depth in Chapter Four.) However, the government sought to deny this by continually emphasising the radical nature of the change that it was seeking to introduce: this had the consequence of making the changes appear desirable and inevitable, the outcome of great social forces. By contrast, there were alternative possible directions that were not considered.

There are two forms of development that characterise personalisation. First, there is the principle of direct payments, whereby resources are directed to individuals so that they have direct control over the use of resources (Glasby and Littlechild, 2009). This is an extension of a radical policy, first developed in the 1990s and particularly taken up by disabled people. Importantly, the development of direct payments came about from initiatives promoted by service users themselves, who put pressure on local authorities to develop more flexible systems of funding their care (Slasberg et al., 2012b). Consequently, it can be seen as a bottom-up policy, in contrast to the 'top-down' nature of much of the implementation of personalisation (Beresford, 2014). While the intention has been to extend direct payments to all service user groups, there has been a slow adoption of these changes, for a variety of reasons, including some concerning professionals' reluctance to adopt the scheme (Clark et al., 2004; Ellis, 2007) and some focusing on their appropriateness for all (Lymbery, 2010; Lloyd, 2014).

Second is the idea that every person should be allocated a personal budget which would specify clearly and transparently the resources that are available to them. This requires the establishment of a new resource allocation system (RAS) that would (at least in theory) ensure that people were in receipt of resources at an appropriate level in relation to their needs. In recent times, Duffy (2012) has been critical of how the RAS has been introduced, noting that it has become bureaucratically dominated, and often used as a vehicle to introduce cuts (see also Series and Clements, 2013). However, in a significant document that specified how important personalisation was to the reform of social care, the government set out the parameters of the intentions of individual budgets:

> In the future, all individuals eligible for publicly funded adult social care will have a personal budget ... a clear, upfront allocation of funding to enable them to make informed choices about how best to meet their needs, including their broader health and well-being. (DH, 2008: 5)

All of this sounds unproblematic, except for the fact that personal budgets grew out of the idea of individual budgets, which were meant to cover both health and social care (Glasby and Littlechild, 2009): their restriction pointed to limitations in the possibilities of personalisation. In addition, when the context of austerity is factored in, more fault lines appear in the policy (West, 2013). It is interesting that, when personalisation was introduced, it was supported by all the major Westminster parties, thus furnishing an unusual level of political consensus (Lymbery, 2014a). It seems, however, that this level of political agreement about the benefits of personalisation is not helpful to a full analysis of its impact in practice. There is a failure to understand that the concept has been subjected to strong critique, on both ideological and practical grounds. In relation to the former, Ferguson (2007) noted a problematic connection between personalisation and marketisation (see Chapter Four); Houston (2010) extended this by casting doubt on the viability – for social care in particular – of the concept of the rational, individualistic perception of the individual in the marketplace (see also Lymbery, 2010). On a different level, Scourfield (2007b) has pointed out that an important fact underpinning the foundation of the welfare state in the late 1940s was that many people were deemed to require support to enable them to live in a secure, dignified manner, and were therefore more than simply consumers (see Chapter Four for more on this). This points to a key fact in relation to social care which is often underestimated in relation to personalisation: that when people need such support they may well be least capable of acting in accordance with consumerist ideals (Lymbery, 2010).

While there are trenchant arguments in favour of personalisation (see Glasby, 2014), and it retains popularity within, for example, the UK's main organisation for older people (Poldervaart and Malenczuk, 2013), judgements about its overall success are difficult to make. Spicker (2013) has suggested that, on a variety of readings, it must be judged to fall short of the claims made on its behalf. At the very least, there needs to be a clearer understanding that there are two contradictory approaches to understanding its origins and hence its impact (Ferguson, 2012a; Lymbery, 2014a). First, while there is an element of its history that draws on the gains made by the disability movement from the 1980s onwards – the aspect that is often cited in support of personalisation (Glasby and Littlechild, 2009) – the opposing view is that there is also a strong consumerist basis to the development of personalisation and it is a policy deriving from government and policy makers, not from people using services themselves (Slasberg et al., 2012b). As we will see in a forthcoming section, one cannot possibly explain personalisation fully unless both of these perspectives are taken into account.

Indeed, it is also important to consider the financial circumstance of austerity when looking at its introduction. Even in the most positive of interpretations of its origins there are significant changes to be considered from a financial perspective. As West has observed, there are major concerns here:

> It provides ideological cover for the most draconian of austerity measures ... to the point where there appears to be a total disconnection between the discourse of personalization-transformation and the policies that are implemented in its name. (2013: 646)

This has led to some influential commentators becoming perhaps surprisingly critical of the direction of policy (Duffy, 2014b). However the various ways in which the principles of personalisation can be analysed, it is what happens to these principles in the process of their implementation that is particularly noteworthy.

Personalisation in practice

It is difficult to identify the impact of personalisation in practice, not least because its intentions have become affected by the austerity that has gripped all local government services since 2010 (Duffy, 2014b). As a consequence, one cannot analyse personalisation as if there is a vacuum in resource allocation: it is hugely complex to separate the changes that personalisation has wrought from the effects of the financial crisis of local authorities. This is a particular challenge for this section: is it possible to reach a sensible conclusion about the impact of personalisation, given the testing context within which it is being put forward? We believe that it is possible to draw some conclusions, but these must necessarily be tentative. In practice, however, the lack of resources of many local authorities is critical: the implication of some reports is that a number of local authorities will run out of money even to accommodate their statutory responsibilities (Morris, 2013).

Needham (2011) has outlined how personalisation has become a driving force for much of public services, with particular emphasis on its grip on adult social care. As she points out, it was first introduced in the context of social care, which is ironic given the Cinderella status of social care in relation to other areas of service, notably health. West (2013) has emphasised how the pursuit of the concept is ideological in nature, and how it has consequently proved difficult for critics to mount any sustained critique of the tenets of personalisation, even though these are often hotly contested (see also Lymbery, 2010). Indeed, the debate about personalisation has often been constructed on a simplistic 'for and against' basis, without consideration of the possibility that, while it may work in certain circumstances it may also be problematic in others (West, 2013; Needham and Glasby, 2014a).

What seems particularly apparent to us is the fact that there has been a strong form of managerial domination of the implementation of personalisation (West,

2013) – a point which is expanded upon in Chapter Four: this is consistent with the managerialist control of care management, to which we referred earlier and, as we noted, served to distort the policy's intentions. A particular change here is that the principles that first informed personalisation appeared from the disability/service user movement, thereby apparently giving the policy additional moral force (Needham, 2011; Slasberg et al., 2012b; Gray and Birrell, 2013; Beresford, 2014). Developing a critique of these principles has often been interpreted as being a critique of the very ideals of the service user movement – to be critical of personalisation was therefore seen as representing a wish to restrict the level of choice and control that it is a moral imperative to grant to those people who use services. Also, since personalisation has been set up as the future, and is in opposition to the current apparently failed system, a voice against personalisation is often taken as a voice that wishes to perpetuate the failed status quo.

A phalanx of policy entrepreneurs have combined to give their imprimatur to personalisation (Needham, 2011). Many of these – for example, Simon Duffy, formerly the Chief Executive of In Control and currently an influential policy commentator – demonstrated a deep commitment to the goals of disabled people and had been active for many years in challenging the essential pattern of services available for them. In addition, the ideal of personalisation was given political respectability through its adoption by writers associated with the left-leaning think tank, Demos (Leadbeater, 2004; Leadbeater et al., 2008). Consequently, when the themes that underpinned personalisation were picked up by the Labour administration (HM Government, 2007; DH, 2008), they were accompanied by substantial encouragement from these other sources. Less publicised was the extent to which personalisation drew on consumerist models of welfare (Ferguson, 2012a; Lymbery 2014a). Even though these are at least equally as important, they do not feature in the official interpretations of the thinking behind the policy shift. This absence has created a significant imbalance in the way in which personalisation has been conceptualised.

The following quotation exemplifies the way in which the official thinking about personalisation came directly from disabled people themselves:

> it involves a shift from viewing disabled people as a group deserving of welfare, to fellow citizens with full rights to participate socially, economically and politically in society. (Oliver and Sapey, 2006: ix–x)

This sort of writing exemplified the way in which disabled people thought of the policy of personalisation. Indeed, there is little with which committed practitioners would disagree in this statement, which helps to explain its clear-cut and apparently unproblematic acceptance. People did not want to be perceived as opposed to personalisation, and held fast to its stated ideas (Ferguson, 2007; Needham, 2011; West, 2013). The policy was buttressed by a plethora of stories about its powerful, transformational effects (Boxall et al., 2009), where individual successes were publicised as if they were in some way typical of the totality of the care population. Interestingly, many of these success stories mirrored accounts regarding the use of direct payments. The essential problem with this approach was picked up earlier and represents a key area of continuity with previous policies (which is further expanded upon in Chapter Four). The way in which it was presented appeared to accomplish a magical feat: the improvement of the outcomes of social care services at no additional expense. Indeed, there was some support – albeit of a rather limited nature – for the veracity of this contention (Duffy et al., 2010). For policy makers this was 'holy grail' territory!

However, in pushing for a universalist approach to personalisation, the Labour administration appeared to ignore several issues while simultaneously underestimating the significance of others. As Clements (2008) put it, the government was demonstrating a form of 'irrational exuberance' characterised by wildly inflated rhetoric. If the claims of personalisation were accompanied by a cool study of issues that characterised older people, for example, this enthusiasm was clearly unjustified (see Lymbery, 2010; Lloyd, 2014). For example, the introduction of direct payments and individual budgets is much more problematic for older people than for other groups (Glendinning et al., 2008). When one factors in the reality that many older people, when they require care services, are likely to be cognitively impaired due to dementia, this conclusion is hardly surprising. In this sense, the purported impact of personalisation – its ability to maximise the ability of all people to increase their control over services that they require – is fatally flawed (Needham, 2011; Lymbery, 2014d). When one sets this in the critically relevant context of austerity, with the implication that services will become less freely available, it is even harder to see how the strategy of universalist personalisation could feasibly be delivered (West, 2013).

However, as Karen West's (2013) paper demonstrates, some local authorities are holding fast to the transformative potential of personalisation, despite the financial picture becoming increasingly bleak. In her case example, the council concerned is seeking to present its new world of adult social care as being entirely within the context of the liberation and empowerment of service users. This is even though it faces the deepest cuts in living memory, which at the very least restrict the ability of the council to act in ways that provide concrete support for the ideals of personalisation. In sticking to the rhetoric of personalisation in this context, this particular council is clearly acting as West has suggested (2013: 646; see also Duffy, 2014b). It is put forward as if there is no alternative to the policies being presented, following the 'epochal' logic that accompanied the shift towards personalisation (Cutler et al., 2007). West takes the view that the role of 'institutional actors' in perpetuating this is understandable, given the intolerable pressures that are placed upon them. She sees local authorities' espousal of the tenets of personalisation as part of a complex coping strategy; essentially, they have been placed in an impossible situation by the government's rush to implement the policy in the context of major austerity. However, she excoriates them for their flawed pursuit of what appears to be, in current circumstances, a fantasy objective.

The action of successive governments in hastening the policy of personalisation in advance of the evidence is discussed in more detail in Chapter Four. For Simon Duffy, the essential problems in personalisation stem from implementation, a failing that he attributes more to the Cameron-led coalition government than its predecessor (Duffy, 2012). However, we believe that the essential limitations of the policy had been evidenced at an earlier stage, as some of the critical literature – written when the previous government was still in power (Ferguson, 2007; Houston, 2010; Lymbery, 2010) – makes clear. Notwithstanding this, Duffy's central point retains substantial force: there was a rush to implement the policy without allowing for the time that was needed to reflect on its various elements and to construct legislative frameworks that would better support them (Duffy, 2012).

Perhaps unsurprisingly, Duffy (2012, 2014b) still takes the view that since personalisation is based on the principles of citizenship it should not therefore be discarded as an ideal – rather, he suggests that we should seek to ensure that it can be properly introduced, backed by research and learning from the developments that have taken place. Elsewhere, Duffy (2011) has been keen to ensure that he communicated a message that personalisation did have limits, and that it could not – in itself – put right the systematic injustices of society. However, in an earlier paper (Duffy, 2010) he appeared to suggest that it could have a radical impact on the practice of social work – arguing that it constituted a full theory about citizenship that was particularly applicable to social work. The full implications of this will be discussed in the following section; at this stage it is appropriate to point out that the 'technologies' of personalisation (Duffy's term) cannot in themselves accomplish such a change (Ferguson, 2012a). It is evident that the limitations of the resource base are radically changing the impact of the changes, demonstrating that 'technologies' can be used either for benign or malign purposes.

Clements (2011a, 2011b) has cited a case which brings this to life in the most appalling way. He discusses the situation of Elaine McDonald, a 68-year-old former ballerina who had originally been assessed by a representative of Kensington and Chelsea local authority as needing assistance at night to use the commode, because her mobility was impaired as a consequence of a stroke. Initially the local authority provided this support, but later changed its package of care so that she was provided with incontinence pads rather than physical assistance overnight. Significantly, Ms McDonald was not incontinent, her difficulties related purely to her mobility. The fact that this was considerably less expensive (to the tune of £22,000 p.a.) is of course material to their decision. Clements (2011b) observed that this decision is immediately problematic because the authority was failing – as a direct consequence of this change – to respond to Elaine McDonald's assessed need, which it has a statutory obligation to do.

Following a High Court review, the council reassessed her circumstances, changing its decision so that in its judgement Ms McDonald now required more general support at night (even though her actual needs had not changed) – deciding that this could, of course, be met by the provision of incontinence pads. Clements (2011a) is scathing about the process that the council undertook, arguing that it was seeking only to provide legal cover for its financially driven decision rather than responding to Ms McDonald's need for self-respect. In this context, Elaine McDonald was unequivocal that using the incontinence pads was a clear affront to her dignity – a view supported by a range of organisations, including the Stroke Association, Age UK and the Equality and Human Rights Commission. However, when the case came to the Court of Appeal the decision of the council was upheld. By a clear majority, the Court of Appeal judges ruled that the argument that focused on personal dignity – implicitly reflecting back to the Human Rights Act 1998 – would not carry the day. The council was able to take action that had been clearly financially driven (Clements, 2011b). In the process they were able to claim, in Clements' terms, that Elaine McDonald did not, in effect, understand her own dignity (Clements, 2011a)!

While we should be careful not to draw hard and fast conclusions from a single case, there are nevertheless important lessons to be taken from it, which torpedo some of the more optimistic elements of personalisation. Clearly it is difficult to read the Court's judgment – which had the perverse effect of rendering a continent person incontinent (Clements, 2011a) – as being in any way consistent with the ideals of personalisation. What we can see, however, is a decision that was made largely, if not solely, for financial reasons. Of course, to have acted in accordance with the original assessment would have been very costly for the local authority, reinforcing our point about the impact of austerity. There seems little doubt that the question of resources weighed heavily both with the council and the Court of Appeal. In addition, from a legalistic point of view, the Court of Appeal's judgment effectively meant that decisions about personalisation could not be taken to be the outcome that a civilised society would expect, which was the basis of the dissenting opinion that failed to carry the day legally (Clements, 2011b). We suspect that precisely this standard would be fully supported by the vast majority of service users; consequently, the Court of Appeal's judgment rips a substantial hole in the ideals that purportedly should accompany the introduction of personalisation.

Social work and personalisation

It has been suggested that there is a ready fit between personalisation and social work (Williams and Tyson, 2010). Indeed, the centrality of social work has been highlighted by no less influential a figure than Simon Duffy, who has commented that:

> Social workers have a better understanding than most of the enormous difficulties that assail millions in our society today. Social workers also have to believe in the power of people to bring about positive change.... Social workers must, in order to live up to their responsibilities, embrace the technologies of personalisation and find

> ways to make them work – and improve them when they break.
> (Duffy, 2010: 265–6)

However, this positive assertion of the potential of social workers has been challenged by many within the disability movement (Oliver, 2004; Harris and Roulstone, 2011) who claim that social work should no longer be involved in the lives of disabled people (the former) or that it must reform urgently to respond to the new challenges (the latter). In addition, to talk of personalisation as a set of 'technologies' is reductive, as we have argued. Another core problem with such formulations is that they accord social work too much agency to shape its own practices. An acceptance of the status of social work as a state-mediated profession (Harris, 1998; Lymbery, 2014c) is needed to understand its genuine limitations.

This becomes clear when one examines the position of social work in personalisation, as interpreted through both official and influential bodies that have been involved. If we examine first the official papers and chart the status of social work within them, it becomes clear that a consideration of the position of social work was far from the top of the reform agenda. In addition, there was scant understanding of the limits to the profession's autonomy. For example, social work had been criticised for allowing itself to be seen as 'a gatekeeper or rationer of services' (DH, 2005: 28), despite the fact that these had been precisely the functions demanded under community care legislation (Lymbery, 2014c). While it was suggested that more imaginative and creative forms of practice could be formulated – in person-centred planning, care management, brokerage or facilitation (DH, 2005) – there was precious little further detail about what precisely this would entail. Subsequent documents, while furthering the general principles of personalisation, failed to put flesh on these bones (see HM Government, 2007; DH, 2008), continuing to mention social work only in passing and in the most general terms.

This pattern was amended slightly when the government published its workforce strategy for adult social care (DH, 2009). However, since it examined the implications for the entire workforce (reasonably enough, as qualified social workers are only a small minority of it), only a relatively small proportion of the report focused on the specific implications for social work. It suggested that social workers were potentially vital in specific roles – early intervention, promoting social inclusion and safeguarding. In relation to the former, this reinforced ideas that had been promoted earlier: social workers could in effect be moved from their rationing responsibilities to more constructive work, recognising that they 'are skilled at identifying models of intervention, some therapeutic, some task-centred and working through with people the outcomes to be achieved' (DH, 2009: 34). However, subsequent experience indicates that many authorities are reducing the numbers of social workers they employ (Samuel, 2011) and are pursuing a limited conception of personalisation (Hicks, 2013) under the greatest of financial pressures. This demonstrates the importance of the context of austerity, discussed earlier.

There have been other papers from organisations/bodies that are influential in social care. For example, the Social Care Institute for Excellence (SCIE, 2010a) suggested that there would be social work engagement in five separate areas of practice:

- building relationships
- working through conflict
- knowing and applying legislation
- accessing practical support and services
- working with other professionals to achieve best outcomes.

Of course, a critical distinction is that SCIE is only an advisory body, and its suggestions therefore have less force. A similar point can be made in relation to a grouping of a number of agencies who have addressed the problem (ADASS et al., 2010), although they have more authority in that they represent the body that commissions social care (the Department of Health) and the representative body of employers (the Association of Directors of Adult Social Services) alongside a quango (Skills for Care) and two professional bodies (the Social Care Association and the British Association of Social Workers). Their conclusions are quite similar in that they suggest that there are three broad areas in which social workers could operate:

- supporting people in the assessment of their needs, circumstances and options;
- working with families to improve well-being and safeguard vulnerable family members;
- contributing to early intervention and preventative services. (ADASS et al., 2010)

The precise elements that social workers could provide are arguably less important than the influential nature of the organisations from which the recommendations emanated. If one were to examine this without an awareness of the impact of austerity – highlighted earlier – it could be suggested that there were many areas of activity that would be opened up. This perception is encouraged by some of the early academic papers to examine personalisation. For example, Williams and Tyson (2010) explore the capability of social work to rediscover its potential to work in depth with people who need adult social care services. While these authors acknowledge that a restricted, managerially defined form of practice exists, echoing the conclusions of others (Postle, 2002; Carey, 2003; Gorman and Postle, 2003), they argue for the potential of social work to accomplish far more meaningful work, that would be much more satisfying to practitioners. They build on the idea – evident in the quotation from Duffy (2010) cited earlier – that personalisation is entirely compatible with the core tenets of social work. In the same period, Foster (2010) argued that personalisation would provide social workers with more opportunities to act creatively in relation to service users: the focus on individual responses to need argued strongly for this. Indeed, the Professional Capabilities Framework that governs social work education has now included the element of social justice as central to social workers' practice (TCSW, 2013). Both authors make a strong case for the extension of practice away from the rigidities that had characterised social work under the discipline of care management (Gorman and Postle, 2003).

There seems to be a clear agreement that this had been damaging to the development of social work. As a result, as Ferguson (2012a) suggests, few insiders would disagree with the principle that social work is in need of renewal; indeed, it could be argued that this is a general view applicable to all areas of practice. From the perspective of social work with adults this is particularly true: the previous edition of this book was unambiguous about the way in which care management practice had acted to degrade and distort social work (Gorman and Postle, 2003). However, to suggest that this can in reality be made good by personalisation is a perversion of reality on at least two counts. First, personalisation is based – at least in part – on neoliberal underpinnings (Ferguson, 2007; Houston, 2010; Lymbery, 2014a), which imply that the individual service user is reduced to the status of a consumer (Ferguson, 2012a). If such an ideology is pursued to its logical conclusion, there is little need for any form of social worker – the assumption is that the consumer will act in accordance with the logic of the market, ignoring the fundamental issue of the social problems which led people to use social work services in the first place. Second, it fails to take account of the budgetary crisis within which it is being implemented. Consequently, as suggested several years ago, the conflict between some of the core principles of personalisation – prevention and early intervention – and the financial climate of cuts is having a major impact and affecting many of the principles on which personalisation depends (Henwood and Hudson, 2008). Certainly, in times of extreme financial pressure, when local authorities are seeking to balance apparently incompatible goals, the employment of social workers is not a top priority.

Events subsequent to the general election of 2010 confirm many of these suspicions about the financial climate. While the Conservative-led coalition was careful to signal a sense of continuity in the delivery of personalisation (DH, 2010b), it has also acted in such a way as to change radically the financial settlement within which it is delivered (as noted above). In such a context, the actions of local authorities in substituting costly social workers with cheaper, unqualified alternatives are at least understandable, if regrettable (Samuel, 2011).

Duffy (2010) refers to personalisation in relation to the 'technologies' through which it is delivered. As we have already argued, these technologies are by no means neutral, given the context within which they are being introduced. As Ferguson points out:

> in a context of austerity and ever tighter eligibility criteria, far from promoting social justice the 'technologies of personalisation' can

quickly become mechanisms for reducing spending and in some cases,
for reducing choice and control. (2012a: 69)

The case of Elaine McDonald, cited earlier in this chapter (Clements 2011b),
exemplifies this: the response to her needs was pitched within the context of
personalisation, but bears no relation to the maximisation of her choice and
control, its purported principles. Clearly, the financial situation within which
personalisation is being enacted is having a major impact on its operationalisation,
and directly affecting the practice of social workers. Consequently, many of the
statements that argued for the extension of social work into personalisation are
now proving to be incorrect.

Conclusion

This brief review of how personalisation is working out in reality therefore can
draw conclusions on a number of points:

- The economic context in which it is being introduced is restricting many
  of its potential benefits, such that it is hard to be optimistic about its future.
- In particular, lack of resources is effectively choking off the opportunity to
  put many people in control of their care. In addition, these reduced resources
  obstruct the capability of social workers to be more generally involved in the
  implementation of personalisation.
- Despite the rhetoric which claims personalisation as an unambiguously positive
  policy shift, there are also indications that it originates in part from consumerist
  thinking, which is much more problematic. It also differs from direct payments
  in being a top-down policy, designed by government and policy makers, rather
  than a bottom-up policy, designed by people using services.
- If we examine the implementation of personalisation these issues become
  evident, and there are clear examples where decisions have been taken which
  are antithetical to its purported principles.

What we can conclude, therefore, is that this is a fundamentally flawed policy, just
as community care proved to be. Indeed, as the following chapter will indicate,
there are numerous elements of the current situation that provide a form of
continuity with the introduction of care management. Many of the issues that
were problematic then have reappeared in a different form. It is to an analysis of
these areas of continuity that the book will now turn.

FOUR

Themes and continuities

Introduction

Since one of the key contentions of this book is that there are (often unrecognised) themes and continuities between the twin driving forces of care management and personalisation, the key purpose of this chapter is to highlight what these are. The overall impression we wish to convey is that, despite the rhetorical commitment that personalisation represents a complete break with the flawed past (Lymbery, 2010), there are in fact clear continuities underpinning the approaches that have driven both policies. The detail of each policy may demonstrate significant other changes, but this should not obstruct our view of the themes and continuities that exist.

As a consequence, we will consider several issues where there is a clear connection between the worlds of personalisation today and care management over 20 years ago. The first is the issue of resources, which largely shaped the thinking of the Conservative government in establishing community care (Lewis and Glennerster, 1996). Indeed, it has been suggested that the community care reforms would not have happened were it not for the overwhelming need to manage the soaring cost of independent sector residential and nursing home care (Gorman and Postle, 2003; Lymbery, 2005). Although the management of resources has not been advanced as such a central theme in the implementation of personalisation, resources still remain a critical factor in its implementation, as the first section will make clear.

Another key contextual issue has been the lack of robust empirical evidence to support the proposed changes. As we will discuss, there was little convincing proof that care management, as a process, could be rolled out to everyone receiving adult social care (Bauld et al., 2000). Instead, there were confident assertions that it was absolutely transferable (DH, 1989). Similarly, while there has been good evidential support that personalisation can work for disabled people (see, for example, Leece and Peace, 2010), there has also been evidence that casts doubt on the overall effectiveness of the policy in relation to every service user group, particularly in relation to older people (Glendinning et al., 2008). However, as with community care, there remain confident assertions that personalisation is applicable for all and that it will bring about major benefits as a result (Lymbery, 2010). In order to gain a full understanding of the impact of policy it is therefore important that some of these assertions are subject to critique.

Other themes cluster around the general issues that have characterised the development of public services over the past 25 years, under the influence of the new public management (Hood, 1991). The first of these is the issue of managerialism, the sense that control has been shifted from professionals to managers (Pollitt, 1990). This was a feature of the first edition of this text and remains a core issue in the delivery of social welfare to the present day (Healy, 2009). One of the key manifestations of this has been in the 'fetishisation' of issues around quality, audit and outcomes, an argument that was also a feature of the first edition. That is not to argue that there is anything intrinsically wrong with taking these issues seriously, but they are not entirely what they seem: they are also not at all as defined by service users. There has also been parallel shift towards a more explicitly consumerist view of social care policy (Lymbery, 2014a); while this was an apparent underpinning of community care, its implications have now been made progressively more clear, as we will illustrate. In addition, we also explore the creeping commitment to audit within public services, questioning some of the ways in which it has become manifest. We also consider how the question of quality – ironically perhaps – has not led to an improvement in the overall value of services to users. Underpinning all of the changes has been a notion of consumerism, which has worked in a variety of different ways but needs to be clearly distinguished from involvement, although it often masquerades as this (Beresford et al., 2011).

Finally, we highlight the particular consequences of the shift from care management to personalisation and the potential deprofessionalisation of the workforce. In a book which focuses on the practice of social work this is a vital consideration; it is introduced at this point, with further development of the theme in Chapter Six. We argue that although both community care and personalisation have, in different ways, appeared to promise a healthy future for social work, the reality has been – and is – a long way from this idealised future. It is suggested that these problems have, in large measure, led to the degradation of social work – the theme of the next section of the book.

Resources

The importance of being aware of the implications of restricted resources for the implementation of community care has been long understood (Lewis and Glennerster, 1996). It has been argued that the final motivating factor for the reforms derived from the need to control the escalating costs of residential and nursing home care provided in the private sector (Lymbery, 2005). The unintended consequences of benefit changes in 1980 had sparked this, and the costs of private sector care subsequently grew in an uncontrolled manner (Lewis and Glennerster, 1996). While there was considerable resistance to allocating the responsibility for managing substantial budgets to local authorities (Lewis and Glennerster, 1996), this was indeed the outcome when community care legislation was enacted.

In order to ensure that care monies continued to be spent largely within the independent sector, the government hit upon a scheme that would in effect compel this. To enable local authorities to implement their new responsibilities, it organised a Special Transitional Grant that came to authorities sequentially from 1993, when the community care legislation came into force. This was far from a nugatory amount: £399 million was made available in 1993/4, with an additional £651 million in 1994/5, and an extra £518 million in 1995/6. While each instalment was only ring-fenced for the first year of its allocation, because much of it was spent on new placements starting from April 2003, it continued to be spent in community care (Lymbery, 2005).

While, on the face of it, this appeared to be a generous settlement, it was significant that it was still substantially less than would otherwise have been spent from the Social Security budget (Lewis and Glennerster, 1996). Indeed, it has been argued that the grant was carefully calculated to ensure that the government could safely claim that the policy had been adequately funded (Lymbery, 2005). Indeed, although some local authorities did run into financial problems after a couple of years, this was a sufficiently long time after the launch of community care to ensure that central government was not held to account: by contrast, individual local authorities that ran into difficulties were castigated for a combination of profligacy and inadequate systems of financial management (Lymbery, 2005). Consequently a conflict was introduced between the principles of the legislation and the financial realities of the authorities trying to implement it. This presented clear problems for the social workers who worked at the front line – they had simultaneously to respond to the needs of individuals while ensuring that their decisions remained affordable within the limited funds that had been allocated (Gorman and Postle, 2003). Unsurprisingly, this led to different approaches to meeting needs across the country – another example of the 'postcode lottery' that has often bedevilled health and social care provision.[1]

In this light, the establishment of the *Fair Access to Care Services* guidance (DH, 2002) can be viewed as an attempt to construct a more equitable approach to the knotty problem of eligibility criteria. In theory this would free each separate authority from the problem of having to create its own scale of eligibility, and therefore was intended to bring about an enhanced level of consistency. However, there were critical limitations in the formulation of *Fair Access to Care Services* that constrained its effectiveness. Above all, resource constraints were critical to its implementation. For example, the general framework within which local authorities had to operate confirmed that authorities retained a responsibility to take resources into account when making eligibility decisions (DH, 2002). The guidance specified that:

> it is not the intention of the Department of Health that individuals with similar needs receive similar services up and down the country....
> What is important is for people with similar needs to be assured of

[1] This means that where a person lives determines the services they receive. There have been numerous examples of people living on either side of the same street who receive different levels of service because their addresses are within the boundaries of different local authorities!

similar care outcomes, if they are eligible for help, irrespective of the services that are provided to meet eligible needs. (DH, 2002: 3)

What is promised here is related to parity of outcomes, rather than parity of services. However, this is a rhetorical trick: it is extremely difficult to assure similar care outcomes unless a similar sort of service is provided, regardless of where a person lives (Lymbery, 2005). In addition, given that there was no national direction on what each authority was required to offer, the scope for local interpretation was strong. The eligibility criteria framework featured four service bands for people whose needs were determined to be in one of the following:

- low
- moderate
- substantial
- critical.

Local authorities were required to meet the needs of people in these bands in descending order of need, so would meet critical needs before substantial, substantial before moderate and so on. This meant they would only ever meet low levels of need if they had managed – and this was very unlikely – to meet all the others. This was intended to be applied by each authority in accordance with its financial situation: where resources were tight the eligibility criteria could be made more restrictive. Consequently, without additional resources it would become difficult for local authorities to act in ways that were other than restrictive (Tanner, 2003): this became the core outcome of the review of eligibility criteria. This illustrates a crucial element of care policy: that the element of resources is critical. Looked at in this way, there is an ongoing battle between the availability of resources and the appropriate response to care needs. However, the way in which this debate is framed often overplays the principled aspects of reform while downplaying the need for additional resources. We note again that the key words regarding the intentions of personalisation are 'choice' and 'control', which represent the principled aims of policy. However, the contention that it would also lead to a more efficient use of scarce resources was significant too, given the overwhelming assertion that resources would always be limited (HM Government, 2007; DH, 2008; ODI, 2008).

Personalisation works most effectively when service users are enabled to receive an early form of intervention (Henwood and Hudson, 2008). Hence, of course, as we have outlined, it was always inevitable that major problems would be encountered in seeking to introduce personalisation into a system characterised by intense forms of rationing. While the government recognised that the system of eligibility criteria needed to be revised in order to support the proposed changes (DH, 2010a), it also alluded to the importance of ensuring that personalisation and eligibility criteria fitted together neatly:

Public funding for social care will always be limited in the face of demand and such resources as are available should therefore be allocated according to individual need in a way that is as fair and transparent as possible.... To broaden their focus beyond those with the highest needs, councils should ensure that the application of eligibility criteria is firmly situated in the wider context of personalisation, including a strong emphasis on prevention, early intervention and support for carers. (DH, 2010a: 6–7)

This recognises that the principles of prevention and early intervention underpin personalisation; however, it is hard to see how these principles can be met with tightly cash-limited budgets, a problem foreseen by Henwood and Hudson (2008) in the better economic circumstances preceding the crash. Indeed, at a similar time the Commission for Social Care Inspection (CSCI) was clear that the problem was not the way in which eligibility criteria were managed, it was the fact that there were inadequate resources in the system (CSCI, 2008). However, in the government's review of eligibility criteria nowhere is this critical conclusion mentioned, even though the CSCI document is generously referenced in many other respects (DH, 2010a). The government goes on to suggest that the problem of limited levels of funding can be resolved by councils thinking more broadly about the way in which they prioritise their funding arrangements:

At a time when resources are tight it is recognised that it will not be possible for councils to invest large amounts in prevention and early intervention schemes. Rather it is hoped that that [sic] councils and those applying this eligibility guidance will be prompted to think about prevention and early intervention beyond just adult social services. (DH, 2010a: 7)

That this is a weak formulation, riven with contradictions, is clear and, given the stringent levels of austerity that were coming (outlined in Chapter Three), its recommendations appear particularly flimsy and unrealistic. Even in times of relative plenty there were stark contradictions in the thinking of government. For example, when making the case that the entire system for care and support should be changed, the government confirmed the idea, which was explicit in the whole principle of eligibility criteria, that state funding should be 'targeted at those most in need' (HM Government, 2008: 9). However, later in the same document it stated that: 'A new care system should help people to be independent for as long as possible by focusing on prevention and early intervention' (HM Government, 2008: 34). There seems to be no recognition that these two principles are clearly in opposition: that this was the situation even in 2008 when the case was first made is one thing, but in 2014 – the point at which this chapter is being written – it appears patently absurd, particularly given the extent to which local government is carrying the burden of cuts (Duffy, 2013). Indeed, within the social care field there is clear unease that English local authorities are acting more in response to their budgetary crisis than the principles of personalisation, and that some of the most vulnerable people are missing out as a result (Samuel, 2013a; BBC, 2014a).

Consequently, we can observe that the theme of resources has been significant both in relation to community care and personalisation. In particular, their adequacy or otherwise represents a direct line of continuity. Another element of continuity rests in the ways in which the cuts are being introduced, with the responsibility being passed to 'profligate' local authorities rather than remaining with central government, which is therefore held at arm's length from the decisions. The coverage of the imposition of cuts in Nottinghamshire for 2014/15 makes this point well. Here, in the words of the newspaper report, 'The authority has to find £154 million of savings over the next three years and says the 21 per cent reduction in grants it gets from the Government to pay for its services is a huge problem' (*Nottingham Post*, 2014). In the debate that preceded the council's announcement, a Conservative spokesperson made the following observation: "Forget Labour's smoke and mirrors campaign claiming the Government is to blame. The reality is that Labour mismanaged this council's finances over three decades and shows no sign of changing" (*Nottingham Post*, 2014). In other words, the cuts in 2014 have not primarily been caused by an inadequate financial settlement, but the profligacy and mismanagement of the council. This is a direct descendant of the financial trick played in the late 1990s and indicates how useful it can be to have a range of bodies – local authorities – which can carry the can for the cuts, rather than the government.

The reality is that additional resources *were* needed at the time when community care was implemented, a point that also holds good in relation to personalisation (Lymbery, 2014c). Indeed, we would suggest that an adequate level of resourcing for social care ought to be one of the characteristics of a civilised society: the failure of successive governments to ensure this – while simultaneously protesting that those resources are more than adequate (DH, 2010b) – is little short of shameful.

Evidence

The way in which evidence from research has been misused is another line of continuity. In the case of community care it was clearly demonstrated that care management could be effective in particular, limited sets of circumstances (Challis and Davies, 1986). Although it was not obvious that this success could be readily transferred to all of adult social care, this is precisely what happened. In order to understand this we have to disentangle the various threads of care management. As Payne (1995) has outlined, the British variant of care management that came to dominate community care included a number of important issues.

First, it was initially developed in the US, where services are often uncoordinated and where there are particular geographical problems to overcome (Payne, 1995). Case management – the original term used in its American context – was promoted as a way to improve the coordination of services. Second, the principles of case management – which had become known as 'care management' by the time community care was established – were first applied in Britain in projects fostered and developed by the Personal Social Services Research Unit (Challis and Davies, 1986). One of the elements that characterised such schemes was that they were well-funded demonstration projects, which focused on defined, selected populations and which featured a decentralised responsibility for budgetary management. They were also staffed by qualified social workers who typically carried low caseloads (Bauld et al., 2000). Third, when these pilot arrangements were translated into frameworks that could be applied within community care, several of these crucial distinctive features were lost. As Payne (1995) has argued, these documents define care management as the essential process of assessment, followed by the design, implementation and monitoring of the resultant care plan (DH and SSI, 1991). Although there is mention of the need to maintain strong interpersonal relationships, this element of the guidance is secondary to the preoccupation with care management as a primarily 'administrative' task.

Finally, the guidance on care management defined it as containing seven stages, with stages three to seven representing a circular process (DH and SSI, 1991). In principle, the cyclical nature of care management was important to its conceptualisation: the stages of monitoring and review are necessary to ensure a sense of continuity for people receiving services, and to ensure that the type and level of services remain appropriate for their needs, given likely changes in the nature and level of these needs. The lack of development of these stages was prefigured in the guidance, which focused overwhelmingly on assessment (DH and SS1, 1991); this had major consequences for the nature of practice. An important aspect of the guidance, and a significant departure from the pilot projects, is that the process of care management would be applied to all people seeking assistance from social services, not the tightly targeted populations served by the pilot projects (Challis and Davies, 1986). It became an 'all or nothing' policy, in that people either received care management or may simply have been signposted elsewhere. As eligibility criteria have tightened, so the balance between 'all' and 'nothing' has tipped (Ismail et al., 2014), with fewer people meeting the higher eligibility bands and assessment being geared entirely to determining which band people can be fitted into, rather than the original intention of a holistic assessment. A further concern is that people 'signposted' elsewhere are not followed up and so may well not have been able to access any support (Henwood and Hudson, 2008). Therefore, in the process of its transition to become a central plank of community care policy, care management ignored some of the elements that had made it work in given sets of circumstances. Indeed, the flaws that have later been observed in community care can be traced back to the decisions taken about its range and scope.

If we examine the claims made in respect of personalisation, similar issues appear. It was reported that specific projects had achieved remarkable levels of success, on the basis of which successive governments felt able to develop a system that could apply to all, not taking fully into account the specific issues that had made particular projects a success. For example, Leadbeater et al. (2008) reported the successes of pilot projects under the auspices of In Control, where 2,300 people were in receipt of individual budgets. That this represents only a fragment of the total numbers of service users is clearly a problem; according to figures cited by Leadbeater et al. (2008), there were in the region of 1.7 million people then receiving social care services, over 1 million of whom were over the age of 65. The numbers receiving a service from In Control therefore represented only 0.135% of the total population receiving community-based social care services. The overall uptake of direct payments at that time was estimated as being somewhat higher – 54,000 people: however, this only represented 3.176% of the total social care population. Both of these figures are highly problematic as a basis on which to organise an entire system; given the enormous scope of social care the available research at the point of implementation was surely too limited to justify the entire reorganisation of social care services (Clements, 2008).

In addition, the research evidence base is a lot more nuanced than is reported. For example, there is little doubt that the evidence of Glendinning et al. (2008), while largely positive about the success of individual budgets, is not all equally conclusive. For example, problems are reported that cast some doubt on the widespread adoption of the principles of individual budgets so far as older people are concerned. While the research made it clear that there needed to be further work to determine the approaches that do or do not work in any given set of circumstances, this has not been taken into account in the development of policy. Therefore, to take re-ablement[2] as an example, it has assumed a key role in the development of policy, particularly in relation to older people; however, a sense of what needs to be done and the specific circumstances in which it should take place (outlined in detail by Rabiee and Glendinning, 2011) is not necessarily present in policy. Arguably, a major part of the problem is the assumption that pilot projects can simply be rolled out across a wider population, and that this will automatically guarantee success (Smale, 1998; Gorman and Postle, 2003). In this respect, personalisation seems to be operating on the same basis as care management, and the evidence base is being used selectively:

> uneasiness about the evidence base comes from a sense that formal evidence is being used opportunistically and partially to substantiate a pre-determined policy position … (Needham and Glasby, 2014b: 17)

Managerialism

One aspect of public services that coincided with the implementation of community care was the introduction of the techniques of the new public management into the work of social services, as with other areas of public life

---

[2] The principle of re-ablement is that individuals are supported to recover abilities that they had lost, either through illness or aspects of the ageing process.

(Hood, 1991). There have been two connected effects of this. On the one hand, social welfare organisations have sought to constrain the power of professionals by subjecting them to a variety of forms of regulation. One of the main elements of this was that of managerialism, loosely defined as an ideology whereby the visions of managers are viewed as being of more merit than those of practitioners (Pollitt, 1990). On the other, the embedding of managerialist values into the public sector has been accompanied by wide-ranging sets of performance indicators and financial targets imposed by central government, all of which assert the state-mediated nature of social work and social services organisations (Munro, 2004) – these are discussed in the following section.

'New managerialism' represented more than simply shaking up social services to make them more responsive to better management. It involved a fundamental change in the way that the work carried out by social workers was configured; it shifted the agenda from a notion of professional work to one where the dominating agenda became management structures and practices (Pollitt, 1990). Those working across all of the public services have experienced a continuous period of change since the early 1980s. Some writers have argued that social work takes place in a context of postmodernity (Parton, 1996; Postle, 1999) and, although this is a contentious conclusion to draw, there is nonetheless some indication that the nature of 'change' itself has altered. It is now frequently experienced as random and directionless (Bauman, 1992). This process has been captured in various discourses ranging from the macro to the micro, such as globalisation, post-Fordism, the post-bureaucratic organisation, the new public management, the mixed economy of welfare, plus a variety of terms that relate to the role of the state itself, such as the contracting state, the enabling state and the managerial state (Clarke and Newman, 1997).

To understand the impact of managerialism, we need to set this development in a historical and societal context. It is important to clarify what the core assumptions were for people living through the changes to the welfare state. Most of the post-war generation of citizens grew up with the notion that the welfare state was a 'safety net', a reassurance that we would be cared for in old age or in bad times despite the reality that care was dispensed through a bureaucracy that had, since the Poor Law days, distinguished between the 'deserving' and the 'undeserving'. The realities of the welfare state were inextricably tied up with welfare bureaucracy and the notion of public service. Stewart and Walsh (1992) identified several assumptions which underpinned the culture of public service:

1. an assumption of self-sufficiency: a public organisation responsible for a function will carry out the function directly;
2. direct control is exercised via supervision through a hierarchy;
3. an assumption of uniformity: a service provided should be on a uniform basis within the jurisdiction of the organisation;

4. accountability of a public servant to those who receive a service is through the political process;
5. standardised recruitment and staffing policies.
6. The emphasis was on the traditions of administration, hierarchy and professionalism, bound up with collectivised notions of equity, justice and impartiality. This traditional notion of welfare bureaucracy was to change with the development of the 'new managerialism'.

If we focus purely on social care, until the passage of the National Health Service and Community Care Act 1990, the vast majority of its services had been both funded and directly provided by local government (Means and Smith, 1998). The concept of the 'quasi-market' that formed part of the new managerialist agenda meant the separation of state finance from state provision and the introduction of competition for provision from independent agencies (Le Grand and Bartlett, 1993). The state could be conceived as 'contracting' in the sense that it was no longer a sole provider while at the same time 'contracting' with the voluntary and private sector in agreements to provide services for those deemed to be in need of services; it had become a 'contracting state' (Harden, 1992). (It is also worth noting the irony that it has also been 'contracting' in the sense of shrinking!) All of this was entirely consistent with a neoliberal ideology that seeks to insert the market into all aspects of life (Clarke, 2004b). The reform of community care exemplified the split between purchasing and providing responsibilities, the development of forms of contract between purchasers and providers, a concern for services to be based on need rather than available resources, the delegation of authority for budget control, and the pursuit of choice through provider competition. (In the latter sense one can see that managerialism is also closely related to consumerism.) Clarke and Newman (1997) identify the impact of the new managerialism in terms of attempts to realign a series of relationships, between the state and the citizen, between the state and the economy and between the state and its organisational forms including labour processes. New managerialism encapsulated the belief that social problems embodied in the need for community care could be resolved by the better management of resources, including human resources. This continued to be a valid discourse in a critical evaluation of the new Labour government's 'third way' (Giddens, 1994) and in terms of the development of the concept of 'best value'. In theory the delivery by local authorities of the local services that people want, to the quality they want and at the price they are prepared to pay was the hallmark of the 'best value' strategy. The market and the notion of competition remained a central part of the strategy, linked to the belief that through competition and comparing performance better quality services will emerge.

While many years have passed since the first analysis of the impact of managerialism on social welfare services, this explanation for the operation of social care remains highly relevant. Given the equation between the growth of managerialism and the interests of managers (Clarke, 1998), the way in which personalisation has been introduced is significant. Certainly, in relation to personalisation, it is important to grasp the idea that it has often been promoted by managers as a top-down policy, alongside and in conflict with the bottom-up approach of members of the disability movement (Roulstone and Morgan, 2009).

If we focus on the following three areas of activity (Lymbery, 2001), we can see the extent to which managerialism has persisted and become stronger:

1. Financial management: this has long been central to social welfare, in community care arguably more than in any other area of service (Lewis and Glennerster, 1996). The numerous mechanisms that have been adopted over the years – for example, quotas for admission into institutional care, cash limits for complex care packages, panels to make decisions about funding (Lymbery 2001) – have become normalised. Indeed, with the impact of austerity and its disproportionate impact on local government (Duffy, 2013), there is little doubt that the problem of financial management is becoming more intense.
2. Bureaucratisation: this has been experienced within all aspects of social work, but it had a particular impact on community care. In respect of care management, an 'administrative model' has predominated, with a focus on routinised ways of working and large caseloads, largely as ways of managing the difficulties of the role (Lymbery, 1998; Gorman and Postle, 2003). There is an intensely bureaucratised process underpinning personalisation, as the following critique of self-directed support makes clear:

> Available evidence presented above points to the likelihood of a significant increase in bureaucratisation since self directed support was formally introduced resulting in major losses of efficiency, directly contradicting the predictions of its advocates. (Slasberg et al., 2012a: 170)

This is not at all what many of the supporters of personalisation envisaged as being the case following its introduction, and it is this aspect which practitioners have long found demoralising and demotivating because it detracts from direct work with people (Postle, 1999).
3. Proceduralism: in general terms, social work practice has been governed by ever more detailed procedures, and arguably this has affected adult social care more than any other area of activity. Although procedures can be useful in that they ensure adherence to a basic minimum standard, they are limited in their value and, importantly, cannot replace core social work skills. Certainly, critics have suggested that procedures are much less concerned with the promotion of quality than they are about serving the primary purpose of monitoring and disciplining the workforce (Harris, 1998). It seems that the spread of proceduralism has not been curtailed by the advent of personalisation, although it was hoped that this would be one of its aims (Evans, 2013): rather, workers have had to deploy an increasing range of tactics to maintain their discretion to act in accordance with the principles of personalisation. Evans (2013: 739) terms adult social care departments as being 'rule saturated', conveying a clear

sense of the problems that this creates for professional social workers who can find their creativity and autonomy severely constrained.

The core features of a managerially dominated organisation still remain, therefore; while they may have been amended by the advent of personalisation, there has been no reduction in the grip of managerialism on adult social care.

Audit and quality

A range of other themes are closely linked to the thesis of managerialism; indeed, they are part of the full panoply of the new public management (Healy, 2009). The linked issues of audit and quality come into this category. For example, the market changes that came hand in hand with increased managerialism in health and social care agencies had value for money auditing as one of their main characteristics; as McDonald (2006) has argued, there are close and indissoluble links between neoliberal organisational change, managerialism and performance measurement. Increased scrutiny given to issues such as audit and quality appears, on the surface, to be perfectly reasonable, but we need to look in more detail at what this meant in practice. Power (1997) describes four possible operationalisations of the concept of accountability – fiscal regularity, economy (value for money), efficiency and effectiveness, introduced by the Audit Commission through the Local Government Act 1992 (Munro, 2004). This required all public bodies to institute patterns of audit across the full range of their services; indeed, the concept of the '3Es' (Economy, Efficiency, Effectiveness) rapidly became a mantra across all public services (Boyne, 2002). Very soon the audit explosion became accepted as part of the quality control processes in health settings, with procedures in social care settings being a little slower to get off the ground (Swinkels et al., 2002). In order to effect such changes, standards had to be defined and practice observed, and such observations compared with defined standards, so that activity could be evaluated with the aim of improvement. Within social care organisations the control of quality through audit tended to be confined initially to certain areas of activity, such as the registration and inspection of residential care. However, with the growth of care management stimulated by the purchaser/provider split and the development of an administrative/managerial culture, the scene was set for a further intensification of the 'quality' process and the need for evaluation of practice as part of that overall strategy. The notion of audit and the significance of the monitoring of performance at work through the achievement of targets became part of the Labour government's strategy for the reform of health and social services through its modernising agenda (DH, 1998, 2000a). Inevitably, there are numerous problems with the issue of performance measurement. For example, the more that services are broken down and their outputs separately measured, the less the performance of the service as a whole can be measured (Adcroft and Willis, 2005). In a context that privileges inter-agency and interprofessional work, the measures applied to individual agencies are often actively unhelpful to the task of improving the performance of a larger task (Lymbery, 2007). Because the whole notion of measurement implies a positivistic judgement, it has to be recognised that public services work cannot always sensibly be measured in that way due to the quality of human interaction that is at its heart (Lymbery, 2007). There is also a significant question about what is measured; it is a truism to assert that the things that are measured are always going to be the things that are measurable – this can imply a distorting factor on the part of the inspecting body, the agency that is being inspected, or both (Adcroft and Willis, 2005). This has not stopped the seemingly inexorable spread of the disciplines of audit, and their dominance over those people who work in such heavily monitored fields. This has led to concern over the deprofessionalisation of particular areas of activity, notably social work – our key concern here.

Of course, there are also countervailing pressures at work. For example, the demonstration of a commitment to the quality process depends upon creating attitudes of creativity, independence and autonomy in the workforce (Townsend and Gebhardt, 1990), characteristics that had become subsumed within a new managerialist agenda that embraced a market approach to welfare and contested previously held notions of professionalism. The disciplines of audit affected relationships between both the manager and the professional worker and the consumer and the professional worker. The notion of health and social care as commodities that could be purchased and chosen from a range of alternatives can be critiqued as a chimera that concealed a reality that incorporated risk management and the balance between autonomy and control. Various dichotomies existed relating to the balance between care and control in the exercise of care management, one of those being the balance of power between the welfare professional and the user of the service, the other being autonomy of the welfare professional in his or her role within the bureaucracy. As we shall see in Chapter Six, this has had a major impact on the professional status of social workers operating in adult social care.

Around the turn of the century several policy themes were outlined in various contemporary government documents (DH, 2000a, 2000b) that affect a discussion of quality in community care. These can be summarised as:

- a policy drive to review services;
- the promotion of relationships (both between service users and service providers and between agencies and workers charged with the task of providing planned care in the community);
- the need to develop a skilled workforce.

There are numerous contradictions and tensions inherent in these themes that are interlinked. Policy and practice within local government and health care has become increasingly bounded by the audit and monitoring of work activity; there has been no reduction in this trend in recent years, as witnessed by numerous critical reports in various aspects of health and social care (the most highly publicised being Francis, 2013). This also links to the promotion of evidence-based practice, where the conception of evidence is prescriptive and narrow (Webb, 2001). While the underlying aim of finding ways to improve outcomes for service users is laudable and would be shared by the vast majority of people, both as citizens and workers in the public sector, the means being used to justify the ends require some critique.

While it may be acceptable at certain levels of work for a judgement of competence to be the 'gold standard' to allow workers to practice in certain contexts and settings, an assumption that the existence of basic standards of technical competence necessarily means that quality work has been delivered is erroneous. This is particularly so in work that requires interpersonal interaction and the demonstration of care and respect for individuals (Dissenbacher, 1989). A baseline that emphasises technical skills and denies the realities of emotional labour, rather than setting a gold standard can be influential in encouraging poor-quality work (Gorman, 2000). The job can be done to standards, but the carrying out of the work may not necessarily improve outcomes as perceived by the recipients of those services.

Much of the previous discussion is linked to interpretations of the notion of quality and this is a theme that is developed throughout this book. The concept of total quality management aims to improve the effectiveness of organisations through involving everyone in a process of improvement (Oakland, 1989). The emphasis in this approach is on holism and the importance of recognising both process and outcome. However, as Gaster (1995) has pointed out, in the context of public welfare there will generally be a gap between what is desirable if all aspects of quality were to be measured and the reality of what can actually be achieved within existing resources and levels of commitment. Given the context of austerity, this is a point that bears consistent repetition. There is nothing wrong with trying to measure quality, the problem comes in the acceptance that any measure is unlikely to be perfect and is subject to a number of constraints. In addition, the use of performance measures as tools of censure rather than as aids to development compounds the problem (Lymbery, 2007).

Consumerism

One of the key effects of the development of the market in health and social care in the form of the purchaser/provider split under community care meant that local authorities became enablers rather than providers of services, thereby fracturing one of the core tenets of the public service culture (Stewart and Walsh, 1992). The idea of 'consumer sovereignty' accompanied this: there was a sense, which was relatively little developed at the time, that service users would have free choices about the services they could have. In reality this was limited because of the development of the quasi-market (Le Grand and Bartlett, 1993) in social care, where local authorities – normally through the actions of care managers – managed the relationship between the individual service user and the care provider.

Furthermore, quasi-market controls were fundamental to the way in which the care manager who usually defined 'the need' had to operate. Service users could express their opinions as consumers and exercise their bounded rights, yet the discourse with each individual was predefined by the organisation through its management. Inevitably, choice was restricted if a user needed services that s/he could not purchase on the open market as an independent purchaser. In some respects, therefore, while consumerist notions such as flexibility and innovation had some relevance, the lack of redress for poor-quality service, the lack of overt critical standards and the constraints of working with limited budgets appeared fundamentally to belie notions of consumerism, which then appeared superficial as a result.

If we view personalisation through the lens of consumerism we can see how it has been portrayed as such a desirable concept. Indeed, it resonates with wider political perceptions of neoliberalism, where 'the state increasingly comes to endorse a politics of individual recognition over the politics of collective redistribution' (Webb, 2006: 38). This involves an inherently consumerist notion of the relationship between the individual and state-organised services. Consequently, the disciplines of the marketplace have now penetrated much more deeply into the provision of public services, thereby fundamentally changing the ways in which they are managed. It can be argued that personalisation fits particularly neatly with consumerist ideals. (This issue is addressed in more detail in Chapter Five.)

We see consumerism as a particularly tricky concept within the context of public services. There are a number of ways in which this difficulty can be manifested. For example, there are obvious problems in treating public bodies as if they are the same as private agencies, including questions about the extent to which the idea of consumerism can be readily transferred from a private to a public sector setting. As we will explore more deeply in Chapter Eight, there are contradictions between consumerism and the deeper values of social work. In addition, 'choice' is a deeply problematic concept, particularly when seeking to apply it to public services (Jung, 2010), as we will explore further in Chapter Five. As a consequence, it is important to reflect on the contested nature of consumerism, well exemplified in the following quote:

> It is possible to see consumerist approaches to public service reform as a progressive challenge to producer domination and bureau-professional paternalism: or as a regressive individualisation narrowing collective democratic engagement (and a front for marketisation/privatisation). (Clarke et al., 2005: 178)

Deprofessionalisation

There is an often asserted link between the growth of managerialism and the deprofessionalisation of social work (see, for example, Hugman, 1998). Indeed, it has been claimed that it is the most likely consequence of the increased use of performance management regimes, which we have highlighted in this chapter (Adcroft and Willis, 2005). The deprofessionalisation thesis argues that a range of policy shifts have required a different way of working on the part of professionals, which include the following:

- reduced opportunity to choose broad objectives;
- reduced discretion in how they treat individual cases;
- welfare workers may be required to act in ways that are opposed to their professional opinion of the client's best interest;
- professionals may also be required to enforce policies and objectives that are not of their choosing;
- professionals are increasingly likely to be replaced by workers without a professional qualification. (Clark, 2005)

While there is disagreement about the extent to which there has been a process of deprofessionalisation in social care (Hugman, 1998; Gorman and Postle, 2003; Clark, 2005), at least some of the above characteristics can be seen to apply both in the era of community care and – in even more pronounced form – in the context of personalisation. For example, while one can find evidence for the impact of the first four of the points going back many years, the final one is becoming much more real under the impact of austerity within local government (Lombard, 2011). Consequently, the subject of deprofessionalisation is worthy of detailed consideration (see Chapter Six).

Conclusion

This chapter has illustrated the numerous themes and continuities that characterise the progression from community care to personalisation. Rather than representing a clear break with the past, as some official statements have implied (Cutler et al., 2007; Lymbery, 2010), the chapter makes it clear that – in many areas at least – there are clear areas of continuity. It is also notable that many of them lead directly to the deprofessionalisation of social work and fit with moves that appear to be attempts to undermine social work in other areas of activity (Jones, 2013).

Indeed, there is one particular element of continuity that is particularly affecting both the overall success of personalisation and the professional status of social workers within it. This is the adequacy of the resource base for adult social care. As we have indicated, concern about money was the main reason why the community care reforms were instigated. While influential reports have argued that more resources needed to be pumped into social care just to maintain standards at the same level (see, for example, Wanless, 2006), there seems little doubt that one of the original attractions of personalisation was that it appeared to hold out the hope of improved services while requiring no additional investment (HM Government, 2008). However, since the accession of the Conservative-led coalition in 2010 there have been swingeing cuts that have affected (in particular) local government and disabled people (Duffy, 2013). This means that the vital professional elements of personalisation have not been enabled, despite calls for this to be part of the way in which the policy was implemented (DH, 2009; ADASS et al., 2010). This has major implications for the operations of social workers, the primary professional group to be affected by these changes. The latter chapters of the book will analyse what we consider are the specific contributions that social work could make to the system. Before then we will explore further the dynamics of personalisation: if social workers are to be successful in influencing the direction of policy and its implementation they need to be fully aware of the points at which they can affect it.

FIVE

Ideological confusion

Introduction

This chapter will focus on linked areas, the foundation of the welfare state and the development of social work within it. In the process, we will highlight unresolved areas of confusion or contention. In a book that focuses on the possibilities for social work with adults, it is important to be clear about the ways in which social work's history is inextricably linked with the way in which the welfare state has come to be formed. Indeed, it could be suggested (Ferguson and Lavalette, 2014) that the changes to social welfare since 1990 are part of a plan to tear up the overarching systems of support that have characterised the welfare state. From that point of view, we need to understand the influences that have informed the changes to adult social care in the past.

In order to undertake this task we first need to discuss, briefly, the factors which led to the foundation of the welfare state. While this is a contested area of study (see Harris, 2004), we believe that there are critical factors that can help to explain the formation of policy and the subsequent shape of social work. This leads to the second section in this chapter, the development of social work. Having established the main elements of the welfare state, we will examine the areas of ideological confusion that characterise first the community care era, then the period of personalisation. While they take somewhat different forms, the shape of each policy change embodies the ideological confusion that is the title of the chapter. As a consequence of all of this, we will conclude by arguing that social care policy for adults continues to be characterised by ideological confusion or even, as some would argue, incoherence (Needham, 2011; Needham and Glasby, 2014a).

The origins of the welfare state

Numerous books focus on the origins and development of the welfare state (see, for example, Spicker, 2000; Harris, 2004). To take these two books in isolation, they encapsulate different ways of approaching the same problem: whereas Spicker seeks a way of understanding the conceptual elements that combine to form the welfare state, Harris takes a more chronological approach to focus on the key moments of its development. In this brief section we wish to highlight both the main issues that affected the progress of the welfare state and the ways in which it was organised, with specific reference to social care for adults.

As Harris (2004) indicates, there were numerous periods in the advance of British society when the welfare of communities and of people within them gave particular concern to rulers and governments. The establishment of the Poor Law in 1601 gave responsibility for both the 'impotent' and 'able-bodied' 'poor' to parishes (the 'idle poor' were dealt with more harshly). This consolidated a sheaf of prior legislation and was key in the development of welfare provision (Harris, 2004). This is because it marked the change to forms of public provision for people's welfare. Prior to this, the provision of welfare had largely been seen as a Christian duty, but the exercise of this duty was no longer equal to the task of providing for the increasing numbers of people who required assistance and, importantly, government increasingly saw a need to regulate the poor by imposing conditions on the receipt of relief. The Poor Law of 1601 established poor relief as being the responsibility of each parish; a key element of this was a compulsory rate to be levied on each parish, collected from property owners (Bloy, 2002). Both 'indoor' and 'outdoor' relief were part of this system, largely without the stigma that attached to later versions of the Poor Law. The fact that such a law existed indicated that an interest in poverty and poor people was a legitimate concern for government (Harris, 2004). However, it was inconsistently implemented, with few sanctions actually applied to those parishes that were dilatory in their actions (Bloy, 2002). Consequently, it was often ineffective in practice. So, even at this early stage in the development of welfare provision, we can note some important and often conflicting key themes that will prevail throughout history, remaining with us now:

- a concern, at the level of the state, to provide for people who are seen as in need of help by reasons of, for example, age, impairment or inability to work;
- the funding of such schemes to come from forms of taxation/public funds;
- avoiding the cost of such schemes escalating;
- a concern to ensure that only people who 'deserve' help receive it;
- regulation of people receiving assistance by the imposition of conditions;
- concern about geographical variation across the country.

As time passed there was an increasing recognition of the ineffectiveness of the Poor Law, which led to the establishment of a commission to review its operation (Midwinter, 1994). The 1834 Poor Law Amendment Act was informed by the growing conviction that many people were poor through their own actions or inactions, and that they could change their circumstances if they so desired. In addition, there was a great concern that the previous system was costly to run while being utterly inefficient (Harris, 2004).

One of the main features of the Poor Law Amendment Act was the hardening of the notions of the 'deserving' and the 'undeserving' poor, a separation that became commonplace within much social work thinking in the latter part of the 19th century (Woodroofe, 1962). Because there was particular concern about those who were felt to be 'undeserving' – who could, in theory and with the proper encouragement, work and become self-sufficient if they wished to – the Act was governed by linked principles that, it was felt, would achieve this end. The first of these was that of 'less eligibility', which ensured that conditions within workhouses should be made worse than the most unpleasant conditions outside the workhouse, thereby actively discouraging people from seeking poor relief (Crowther, 1981). While never intended to be deliberately cruel, it is important to note that the conditions in the workhouse were consciously stigmatising, with a boring, monotonous diet and an uncomfortable uniform. A painful example of stigma was that unmarried mothers in the workhouse were often made to wear a yellow dress. The significance of this is that, in the 'language' of flags flown by ships, yellow flags symbolise contagion (Longmate, 1974). It has echoes in Jews having to wear yellow stars in Nazi Germany. The other principle was the 'workhouse test', specifying that relief should only be available in the workhouse. In reality, outdoor relief was still needed both because workhouses could not accommodate all those who required assistance and – as labour was often seasonal, particularly in rural farming areas – having able-bodied workers living in the workhouse was inefficient when their labour was needed on farms (Digby, 1978). Hence this principle was never fully implemented. By the latter part of the 19th century, changes to the structure of society had highlighted the limitations of this system and directly affected the development of social work, as we shall explore in the following section.

In the early years of the 20th century, the provision of benefits was enhanced by the gradual introduction of measures such as old age pensions – calculated to be minimal in its impact, being limited to those over the age of 70 (at a time when life expectancy was 48!) and with the pension itself a pittance (Midwinter, 1994). At a similar time, insurance schemes for ill-health and unemployment were also introduced (Harris, 2004), typical of the creeping collectivism of the time (Seed, 1973). However, these were small and fragmented attempts to improve the lot of poor people, and they proved utterly ineffective in addressing the appalling levels of poverty unleashed by the Great Depression of the early 1930s (Midwinter, 1994). Significantly, however, they marked the beginning of the end of the Poor Law system, with workhouses gradually taking on new uses, such as becoming hospitals, and relief being in the form of cash payments, rather than as food and/ or accommodation.

In 1941, with the country embroiled in the Second World War, a committee chaired by Sir William Beveridge was set up to investigate social insurance and allied services; the subsequent report (Beveridge, 1942) and its enactment in the early post-war years established the contours of the welfare state. The focus of the report was on what were called the 'five giants' – squalor, ignorance, want, idleness and disease. Aspects of the report addressed each of these giants in turn. While the report could not be implemented at the time (as Britain was in the grip of the Second World War), the landslide victory of the Labour Party in the election of 1945 provided a clear opportunity to put many of the proposals into effect (Timmins, 1996). Although Beveridge was a Liberal, elements of the report appealed greatly to supporters of the Labour Party, and the six years of the Labour government represented a massive leap into a much more collectivist vision of government. As well as launching the NHS, introducing a range of universal benefits, abolishing the Poor Law – replacing it with a more comprehensive system of National Assistance – and fundamentally reforming education, the government also took many elements of industrial production (coal and steel, for example) into public ownership (Timmins, 1996).

The contours of the contemporary welfare state could clearly be seen through all the changes; however, in retrospect it is highly significant that there were different arrangements that governed the provision of the two elements that most directly concern this book – health care and social care. While health care was introduced as a universal service, paid for out of general taxation, the funding basis of social care was quite different, always involving a means-tested contribution on the part of the service user (Salter, 1998). This has established problems about the boundaries between health and social care that remain today (Lewis, 2001; Lymbery, 2006). In addition, it is worth noting that Beveridge struggled with the notion of 'desert'. Some financial benefits – for example, unemployment pay – were predicated both on the existence of full employment and the presumption that people were willing and able to work. The first of these issues has been problematic since the mid 1970s: the second has consistently been presented as a difficult problem, particularly by the current Conservative-led coalition government.

It is worth noting that the introduction of the welfare state happened during a time when the country's financial position was desperate, given the expense of fighting on a global scale for six years. Somehow – arguably supported by the sense of collective spirit engendered by the war (Timmins, 1996) – resources were found to implement some extraordinarily wide-ranging policies. Commitment to the continuation of the welfare state was shared by all parts of the political spectrum until the election of the Conservative government under the leadership of Margaret Thatcher in 1979 signalled a break with the past. However, the historical idea of the welfare state, complete with the often conflicting themes we identified earlier in this chapter, still exerts a strong pressure on governments; therefore, even those administrations that actually want to roll back the welfare state are often unwilling to describe their policies as doing this, wishing instead to appear committed to its continuation (Timmins, 1996). This sets up much of the ideological confusion that characterises social care policy for adults, as we will highlight.

The conflicting ideas surrounding the welfare state have had particular consequences for the organisation of adult social care. The dispersal of public funds was the responsibility of the welfare departments created out of the National Assistance Act 1948 (Means and Smith, 1998). Supporting people who needed state help to fund their care was therefore characterised as a public responsibility. Approximately 90% of such care was in fact directly provided by the public sector before the community care revolution in the 1980s (Gosling, in Ferguson and

Lavalette, 2014). The consumerist ideals that have characterised contemporary policy were far in the future.

There are three particular dualities that emerge through this brief history of the origins of the welfare state that we believe have never been satisfactorily resolved. The first of these, as we noted earlier, is the notion of the 'deserving' and 'undeserving' poor, from the implementation of the Poor Law Amendment Act 1834. This has continued to be a major theme of policy relating to benefits, and echoes of this sort of language can currently be heard in the rhetoric surrounding people on benefits. For example, in 1992 Peter Lilley, then Secretary of State at the Department for Social Security, gave a parody of the Lord High Executioner's 'little list' song from Gilbert and Sullivan's *The Mikado* to the Conservative Party Conference. This contained lines such as:

> 'There's young ladies who get pregnant just to jump the housing queue / And dads who won't support the kids / of ladies they have … kissed / And I haven't even mentioned all those sponging socialists / I've got them on my list / And there's none of them be missed / There's none of them be missed.'

More recently, at the time of writing this book (summer 2014) a UK television documentary, *Benefits Street*, has sparked widespread controversy and criticism. A headline such as the following has not been uncommon and, again, exemplifies the kind of rhetoric to which we refer:

> 'Get off the sofa and get a job' Council chief blasts Benefits Street welfare claimants (Sheldrick, 2014)

The second duality is the decision regarding whether services should be universally or selectively available. There are obvious financial restrictions which have to be taken into account: it is difficult to think of services and benefits being freely available for all. However, the choice of what is made universally available is highly significant, particularly in times of financial stringency. There is also a long-standing dilemma in that, although some universal benefits may appear to target people who do not necessarily need them, as was the case with Child Benefit until 2013, they are actually much cheaper to administer than means-tested benefits, which need to be calculated on an individual basis. Thus we see the continuing theme of needing to curtail public spending on benefits. Finally, there is a particular dilemma that has become more evident in recent years; the difficulty of meeting social welfare objectives – the support of disabled people, for example – using market mechanisms.

The development of social work

The formal origins of social work in Great Britain are customarily taken to date from the foundation of the Charity Organisation Society (COS) in 1869 (Payne, 2005). Although other elements are important – for example the work of the Poor Law Relieving Officers (Harris, 2008) – it is the rationale that underpinned the foundation of social work through the COS that is particularly important for our argument. This is magnified by the fact that the social work devised by the COS was a direct expression of the social policy of that organisation; consequently social work was formed as an occupation with specific beliefs about the nature of society and found its earliest form of professional identity in the enactment of this system of beliefs. The starting point of the COS was the conviction that the poverty of many in society was accompanied by a 'mass of chronic pauperism, beggary and crime' (Bosanquet, 1914: 5) and a very real concern about what the social consequences of this might be in terms of civil unrest. Hence, once again we see an element of regulation of the poor in the developments. The essential causes of poverty were seen as moral failings rather than economic problems. In the view of the COS two factors combined to create these problems, which the organisation made no attempt to deny. The first of these was their view that relief through the Poor Law was both inadequate and indiscriminate, which did nothing to alter people's circumstances. The second was the fact that, since the inadequacies of the Poor Law were well known, there had been a rapid and disorganised growth of charitable giving which made matters worse (Bosanquet, 1914).

For the COS, the development of social work was a means to address the problems that poverty caused by going to the root of what they considered to be the 'problem' (Rooff, 1969). It proposed a coordinated response to social need, based on an assessment of each individual/family which must therefore be detailed, professionally organised and accurate, as it would form the basis of subsequent intervention (Webb, 1971). Quite clearly, the roots of contemporary social work can be glimpsed here (Harris, 2008). It is particularly interesting that social work was developed and introduced as a core feature of the social policy of the COS – social work as a form of intervention was intended to bring about major social change. However, this was predicated on an acceptance of one of the most contentious elements of the COS – that people could be subdivided as being either 'deserving' or 'undeserving' of assistance. While this was entirely in keeping with the thinking that informed the Poor Law, this almost Manichean split has created much heartache for social work since.

The other key route of development for social work at around the same time was the Settlement movement founded by Canon Barnett (Barnett and Barnett, 1915). This was a different approach to social change, although it also stemmed from religious motives – particularly the sense that the well-to-do had a moral responsibility to better the circumstances of those who were less fortunate than themselves. Importantly, Barnett did not feel that poverty was the outcome of a flawed character, but was a consequence of social inequality:

Custom is perhaps as powerful as law in putting obstacles in the way of life's wayfarers. It is by custom that the poor are treated as belonging to a lower, and the rich to a higher, class: that employers expect servility as well as work for the wages they pay: that property is more highly regarded than a man's life: that competition is held in a sort of way sacred…. Many of our customs, which survive from feudalism, prevent the growth of *a sense of self-respect and of human dignity.* (Barnett and Barnett, 1915: 148–9; emphasis added)

We have highlighted the final part of the above extract as we see it is critical to an understanding of Barnett's worldview. It is important to note the considerable difference between this and the stigmatising effects of much of what had preceded it. Largely because he was deeply religious, he wanted to enable all people to be able to realise their full potential as human beings. He felt that people did not require the gifts of charity: rather, he felt that the only effective way to change their circumstances was through education and example. As a result, his approach was to establish 'settlements' in poor parts of cities – starting with London but soon spreading to other large cities such as Birmingham and Liverpool – where educated people could spend a portion of their time living with poor people and in improving their lot through education (Barnett and Barnett, 1915).

Barnett was sure that the example that such people could show would provide both a valuable service to poor communities, while also enabling the middle classes to understand more about the lives of poor people and the constraints that there were upon them. He saw this as a form of 'practicable socialism' (Barnett and Barnett, 1915) that would enable the creation of a better, more equal society. His vision differed in many critical ways from the work pioneered by the COS. In particular, he focused on the community rather than the individual: he was concerned to develop a much wider sense of social reform. However, despite his analysis of the inequities of 19th-century society, he was not concerned to change the system that produced these inequities – this was left for others (Webb, 1971). Nonetheless, his primary orientation was clearly a major progenitor of community work and the legacy of his thinking can be seen in the philosophy of many who would identify as part of the radical movement (it is implicit throughout Bailey and Brake, 1975, for example).

Our focus on the origins of social work is not to suggest that there have been no significant developments since then; rather, we wish to highlight the development of the two core approaches to social work that continue today – the individual as against the collective. Indeed, there has been an influential strand of thinking that has taken the collectivist response further. The development of radical social work (Bailey and Brake, 1975) argued both that structural, economic and political factors were responsible for the problems of society, and that changes to these elements were required as a result. (A good example of this thinking in relation to adult social care can be found in Ferguson and Lavalette, 2014.) Radical social work suggested that as an individualist focus had left the fabric of society essentially unchanged, social work should organise itself in such a way as to change the way in which society was structured and organised. Only then can some of the recurrent themes identified earlier in this chapter, which have bedevilled the development of welfare, be challenged. While never becoming a large-scale movement within social work (Payne, 2006), the radical position is very important analytically. In particular, it continues to remind us that there are alternative ways of understanding the causes of the problems that adult social care seeks to address.

Community care: care services dragged to market?

As we have previously indicated (see Chapter Two), the primary reason for the implementation of community care – its 'deep normative core' (Lewis and Glennerster, 1996) – was the capping of an out-of-control budget. However, what has been described as a 'near core objective' (Lewis and Glennerster, 1996) was the insertion of a market into social care. (Indeed, Meryl Aldridge [1996] used the phrase 'dragged to market' to encapsulate this period – we have borrowed it for the section heading.) This has been a remarkably successful process: it has been reported that the vast majority of care services are now provided by the private sector, in contrast to the previous situation where such services were more likely to be directly provided by the local authority, as noted earlier (Gray and Birrell, 2013). The vehicle for this shift was the requirement to ensure a flourishing independent sector (DH, 1989); it was hastened by the obligation that was placed on local authorities to spend at least 85% of the Special Transitional Grant in the independent sector (Lymbery, 2005). Successive governments have been rhetorically committed to the notion that the location of care providers was unimportant (even though the march towards privatisation gives the lie to this commitment): what has been regarded as more vital has been to open up the care industry to increased levels of choice and competition. It was argued that the enhancement of choice would enable people to 'shop around' for the service that would best meet their needs (Ferguson and Lavalette, 2014), thus instituting a consumerist vision that has been given greater scope with the development of personalisation (see below).

The ostensible purpose of the community care reforms was 'to promote the development of domiciliary, day and respite services to enable people to live in their own homes wherever feasible and sensible' (DH, 1989: 5). This was an aim with which few could disagree, particularly if they were aware both of the institutional bias of policy (Means et al., 2002) and the numerous flaws with the existing system (Audit Commission, 1986). Indeed, it was strongly stated in some of the key documents of the era:

> Promoting choice and independence underlies all the Government's proposals. (DH, 1989: 4)

The rationale for this reorganisation is the empowerment of users and carers. (DH and SSI, 1991: 7)

This helped to mobilise support from practitioners in health and social care behind the policy changes. It certainly enabled many in practice to be committed to the operationalisation of policy, possibly without a full recognition or understanding of what that policy entailed (Lymbery, 2005). The policy seemed to be in accordance with the highest principles of improving the welfare of people who needed care services. However, there were also writers who highlighted concerns about the contradictions in policy, noting its ideological underpinnings and the imperatives to save costs (Hudson, 1990; Levick, 1992). In reality, even if one believes that the primary purpose of community care was to improve the lives of people needing services by enabling them to preserve their independence (as can be seen in Chapter Two, this is not our view!), the pressures to save money and to impose markets on social care have vitiated any positive impact that the policy might have had. In addition, as we will explore further in Chapter Nine, the requirement to collaborate with private care agencies was a significant change in the social work role. The impact of the private sector changed the way that care managers made decisions about service provision. Consequently, the creation and growth of the market in health and social care radically changed work within health and social care agencies. The inconsistency in the quality of care agencies created numerous issues; a lot of care managers' time was taken up in dealing with the problems that arose from variability of service, such as carers failing to arrive. There was a lack of effective formal mechanisms to judge the standards of care provided by agencies thereby placing service users at risk (Postle, 1999). In addition, care management work took place in a climate where the very awareness of risk was heightened, in the context of a society characterised by notions of risk and danger (Beck, 1992). Much care management assessment therefore focused on the degree of risk in which a person is placed; even a cursory glance at the assessment forms used in practice highlights the extent to which considerations of risk are paramount. Indeed, the more limited risk of loss of independence still governs the 'eligibility criteria' for services (DH, 2010a). As funds have tightened, so this emphasis on risk as a governing criterion for eligibility has dominated assessment processes.

Indeed, it is the gradual transformation of social care into a marketplace that has been the strongest legacy of community care. It was originally trailed as a non-ideological policy (Ferguson and Lavalette, 2014) and it was stressed that the cost, flexibility and quality of services was more important than who provided them. Nonetheless, community care policy hinged on a belief that the benefits of flexibility and efficiency were supposedly particular to the independent sector and these benefits would be transferred to the provision of care. At the same time, because of the rigours that competition would provide, the independent sector would be able to ensure higher quality standards (Lymbery, 2014b). In reality, the performance of independent sector providers has been mixed, with some spectacular failings over recent years. The increased centralisation of providers, often in the hands of large, multinational companies, has been a major factor in this (see Scourfield, 2007a and 2012 for a trenchant analysis of this), alongside the reality that there are inadequate regulatory mechanisms to ensure the quality of such care (Lymbery, 2014b). Three well-publicised failings combine to make this point (see also *Community Care*, n.d.). The first of these is the abuse scandal at Winterbourne View (to which we referred in Chapter Two), a private 'hospital' run by a for-profit organisation, Castlebeck Homes (Flynn, 2012). This also highlighted the limitations of the Care Quality Commission, the inspection body with responsibility for ensuring the quality of residential and nursing homes. The second is the failure of the company Southern Cross, the largest provider of care homes in the country, and the consequences of its financial collapse (Scourfield, 2012). While very different, they both point to the inadequacies of regulation and the perverse incentives that the profit motive can create for care. The third is the developing industrial dispute in Doncaster between Care UK and staff employed to care for people with learning disabilities (Boffey, 2014).

In the case of Winterbourne View, the abuses that occurred there only came to light when a member of staff blew the whistle on poor practice (Flynn, 2012). This was ignored by both the home and the regulators, leading to an unofficial recording of practices at the home which was broadcast on *Panorama* in 2011. The appalling nature of what went on at the home created an instant scandal; numerous court cases were mounted as a result, several resulting in lengthy prison terms. There was also an official response to the events at the home, leading to a detailed governmental report (DH, 2012). As the report commented 'this case has revealed weaknesses in the system's ability to hold the leaders of care organisations to account. This is a gap in the care regulatory framework which the Government is committed to address' (DH, 2012: 8). The report went on to say that:

> The review has highlighted a widespread failure to design, commission and provide services which give people the support they need close to home, and which are in line with well established best practice. Equally, there was a failure to assess the quality of care or outcomes being delivered for the very high cost of places at Winterbourne View and other hospitals. (DH, 2012: 8)

The report goes on to express its concern that the residents of Winterbourne View were there at all, and castigated the 'failure to design, commission and provide services which give people the support they need close to home' (DH, 2012: 8). While the cost of care at Winterbourne View is noted – it was estimated that residents were accommodated there at an average cost of £3,500 per week (DH, 2012: 13) – the report focuses largely on the malfunctioning of internal management processes at the hospital and the parallel failures of external monitoring and oversight, both of which are undeniable. However, the very model of market-based care does not come in for any criticism, despite this also being a major source of concern.

This point is made even more starkly in relation to the collapse of Southern Cross in 2011. As it was the largest provider of residential care for older people, this had severe consequences for both the residents and the funding bodies. For Scourfield (2012) this highlighted the dangers of the marketisation of care services, as it placed the most vulnerable people at the mercy of large financial organisations. Certainly, the behaviour of the private equity firm that asset-stripped Southern Cross, rendering it unable to manage its level of debt, leaves little doubt that the profit motive had, in this instance, outweighed the ideals of care and service (Lymbery, 2014b). In the light of this, the debate in *Community Care* about the pros and cons of outsourcing (Buchan and Pile, 2010) raises a sardonic chuckle, as the protagonist in favour of outsourcing is the pre-collapse Chief Executive of Southern Cross!

The third issue is also reinforced by the prevalence of private equity firms in health and social care, and represents a developing scandal of a different order. At the time of writing (summer 2014), care workers are on strike in Doncaster because their employer, Care UK (owned by the private equity firm Bridgepoint), has downgraded their pay and conditions, leaving them with an income that, the workers argue, does not represent a living wage (Boffey, 2014). As a commentator has argued, this makes it clear that the values of the private company are incompatible with the values that should inform both health and social care (Hutton, 2014). To our mind, the dispute makes it clear that many private companies – particularly private equity firms – are engaged in a 'race to the bottom', eviscerating the pay and conditions of the workforce. Indeed, every scandal in the care sector has the oppression of the workforce at its heart (Williams, 2014). We believe that the morale of workers materially affects the quality of service that is provided: as a consequence, we should all be concerned about the meaning of such disputes.

None of these problems is at all assisted by the increased preference for systems of 'light-touch' regulation across health and social care, where the priority has been to reduce the regulatory burden rather than robustly ensure compliance with high-quality standards (Bevan, 2008). Indeed, in the third of the issues, the pay and conditions of staff are outside the terms of reference for the regulator. From the perspective of the agencies that fund the care of large numbers of those people seen as most vulnerable, this is where the financial imperatives that attended the introduction of community care are once again revealed: while more can be done to improve the quality of monitoring, without question, the overriding issue is that there is simply not enough money in the system. We contend that the underfunding of social care has long been a problem. Although this became more apparent with the advent of community care, and many of the other reported problems stem directly from this, there has never been a time – from the Poor Law onwards – when adult social care has been adequately resourced.

Two issues that had particular prominence in community care continue to be significant in relation to personalisation. The first is in the primacy of finances to the policy (Lewis and Glennerster, 1996); this required local authorities to prepare highly bureaucratised and proceduralised forms of working to ensure that they were able to manage the cash-limited budgets that were available. Importantly, this reduced staff's autonomy and ensured their greater regulation. In themselves, these ways of working constrained the effectiveness of policy; when combined with the second issue, the extension of the marketplace into care services, an incendiary cocktail was mixed. This has had ongoing ramifications, and there is no indication that personalisation has served to change the essential direction of adult social care. Indeed, because of the austerity measures of the Conservative-led coalition, resource constraints are even more of a problem. Collaboration with private care agencies has also represented a significant change in the social work role. In the context of community care, the care management and, specifically, assessment processes which developed were predominantly conceived of as managerial systems concerned with the cost-effective administration of resources (Lewis and Glennerster, 1996). At the same time the policy of promoting user choice and self-determination has been a theme of the community care reforms, potentially redefining the professional role in service delivery; this is a particular feature of personalisation. Yet choice for users has long been exposed as a myth in the context of social services provision (Schorr, 1992); 'choice', in practice, being strongly related to what is available and the ability to the individual to realise the choice that is made (Glendinning, 2008). In a variety of ways, therefore, the impact of the private sector has changed the way that social workers made decisions about service provision, a change that has persisted to the present day.

Personalisation: social citizenship or consumerism?

When we look at community care, we can see a clear tension between the traditional dynamics of the welfare state and the importation of market principles. In the case of personalisation, there has been an extension of the confusion, as the policy straddles uneasily the dimensions of social citizenship and consumerism. As we noted in Chapter Three, personalisation came about because of perceived failings of community care. Once again, there was a rhetorical commitment to issues of choice and control, virtually identical to the language that was used to describe community care. However, an alternative understanding of what has been attempted can be elaborated, which draws attention to a range of other issues. The purpose of this section is twofold: first, we seek to describe the way in the policy of personalisation can be described as being about the extension of social citizenship to disadvantaged people and groups, which is in line with the way in which the policy has been presented. Second, we outline a more critical perspective, arguing that the policy is primarily concerned with the further development of neoliberal, consumerist ideas into welfare.

It has been suggested that conceptions of citizenship and rights are central to personalisation. While we do not provide a detailed analysis of these ideas (for such an analysis see Taylor-Gooby, 2009), we do seek to identify the ways in which they have been argued to be consistent with the policy. Discussions of citizenship normally start with the work of Marshall (2006), who divided its components into three elements – civil, political and social. For Marshall, the status of citizenship could be conferred upon all those who are full members of a community; he regarded all the above three elements as vital to this condition, despite his acknowledgement that social citizenship is the most problematic – and the most important in relation to social welfare. For Harris (1999), Marshall's formulation was notably depoliticised as he suggested that the state should only have a general duty to provide services, stopping short of the conclusion that social rights should become enforceable as individual entitlements to services. However, as Rummery (2002) has observed, given the high levels of social inequality within society, it is impossible for many service users to exercise their rights as citizens without the support of welfare services that are constructed to facilitate their social participation. Consequently, it has been argued that the ideal of social citizenship requires the parallel adoption of a set of social rights and a more just distribution of resources (Plant, 1998). However, successive governments have not acted on the basis that people have entitlements that would enable them to achieve a full measure of social citizenship, since this would imply the necessary commitment of resources to support their rights (Plant, 1998). As a result there is a clear interrelationship between the ideals of citizenship and the adequacy of resources. The benefits of direct payments – a particular element of a drive to citizenship for people with disabilities – are severely minimised if the levels of resource available for individuals are inadequate in relation to their needs and wishes.

As noted above, the initial pressure to change the pattern of adult social care, which led to the introduction of direct payments, largely came from the user-led movement (Harris and Roulstone, 2011), which is underpinned by notions of citizenship (Beresford, 2007). (Of course, successive governments have translated this into the policy of personalisation, which is a top-down concept.) For example, Hasler (2004) argued that all services for disabled people should be constructed on the basis that they will enable people to fulfil both their rights and responsibilities as citizens. Oliver (1996) contended that, for many disabled people, society has not traditionally granted them this, consequently they have been limited in the social, political and civil rights they are able to exercise. Critically, Oliver (1996) argued that welfare services have contributed in large measure to this situation; his frustration with the slow and limited pace of change – particularly in relation to the social work profession – becomes increasingly apparent in his later writing (see Oliver, 2004). For such writers there seems little doubt that their vision of citizenship encompasses both rights and entitlements.

From the perspective of disabled people, social citizenship is therefore the organising logic underpinning personalisation. As a result the policy can be seen as entirely positive, because it appears to give people who have been effectively disenfranchised enhanced opportunities to play a full role in society. From this point of view, any criticism of personalisation can be taken as indicative of a desire to obstruct the capacity of service users to exercise their status as citizens (Roulstone and Morgan, 2009). However, the close connections between social citizenship, social rights and entitlements remain problematic in this context. As Plant (1998) has observed, cost constraints have always limited the ability of people to exercise their rights. At a time of significant cuts to local authority expenditure (Taylor-Gooby and Stoker, 2011) this is an obvious problem.

By contrast, we have to recognise the argument that policies underpinning personalisation are a direct manifestation of neoliberalism. For Gamble (2001) neoliberalism has become a 'common-sense' paradigm which permeates all policy areas: as a consequence of this, 'the state increasingly comes to endorse a politics of individual recognition over the politics of collective redistribution' (Webb, 2006: 38). As we have shown, disciplines of the marketplace have penetrated deep into the provision of public services, changing the essential ways in which they are perceived.

For Rose (1999), the application of neoliberal principles to welfare has signalled a gradual transition *away* from themes of citizenship; he argues that this is being replaced by ideas of consumerism. Here, the most significant way of understanding people is to conceive of them as capable of activating their rights in the marketplace; the role of public agencies is to support their ability to act in this way. Houston (2010) has characterised the idealised self-actualising individual envisaged as '*homo economicus*'. Rather than assuming that many people cannot manage and therefore need assistance to do so, the presumption has shifted such that it is now believed that people are competent to take control of every aspect of their lives. Rose (1999: 145) suggests that this has engendered a 'neo-social' perspective, where the imperative is no longer to conceptualise people as needing to be looked after but rather to ensure that their capacity is strengthened, enabling them to look after themselves. As a result, the focus of government has moved in order to assist people 'to understand and enact their lives in terms of choice' (Rose, 1999: 87), while simultaneously disparaging the value of public provision (Clarke, 2004a).

It can be argued that the policy of personalisation is entirely in line with such perceptions. Although it was originally trailed as an idea that could transcend the limitations of both paternalism and consumerism (Leadbeater, 2004), some of the core intellectual impetus for change clearly derives from individualistic starting points (Le Grand, 2007a), often framed in relation to each person's economic best interests (Houston, 2010). This problem has been acknowledged in some of the countries that make up the United Kingdom; for example, the Welsh Assembly has recognised that 'the label "personalisation" has become too closely associated with a market-led model of consumer choice', and hence prefers to use different language in describing the policy (Welsh Assembly, 2011). However, in England there is little sense in either official documents or local practice that collective solutions to people's problems will be prioritised, highlighting the reality that a collective approach represents a road not taken in relation to the development of social work.

Advocates for the enhancement of choice in public services have justified their approach by highlighting the limitations of available alternatives. Consequently, Le

Grand (2007a) suggests that choice and competition represent the most effective ways to reconcile the different requirements for high-quality public services. While he acknowledges that no effective system can entirely disregard elements of trust, targets and voice (Le Grand, 2007a: 36), he believes that there are three core reasons why a mechanism of choice and competition should be favoured:

- It fulfils the principles of maximising autonomy and responsiveness to users' needs.
- It provides incentives to providers.
- It is likely to be more equitable.

There are, however, a number of flaws in this conception in relation to the provision of social care. Far from being a one-off event entered into by a fully functioning, psychologically strong individual, many decisions that affect people's social care are required when that person is psychologically and/or physically frail, and where their capacity to exercise choice is liable to be limited (Lymbery, 2010). In addition, providers' incentives arguably have become less to improve quality than to cut costs (Knapp et al., 2001). Transaction costs also represent a considerable extra burden in systems defined by competition (Knapp et al., 2001) and there are various ways in which both purchasers and providers can interact that may create additional problems – the 'gaming' tendencies that Le Grand (2007a) suggests might affect performance management. With specific application to social care, there is little understanding that the choice that one person makes might tend to affect the range of options open for another. For example, if 30 users of a local authority day centre decide not to use that service it may well become unprofitable and have to close, denying the choice of another 30 users that the service should remain unchanged. In this context, the determining factor is not the *capacity* to make a choice, it is the ability to *realise* that choice (Clarke et al., 2008; Glendinning, 2008). In addition, if choice is conceptualised as a largely individualised issue, its public dimension – inherent in considerations of social care – is not fully considered, hence limiting its adequacy as a governing framework for the organisation of services (Stevens et al., 2011).

The claim that enhanced levels of choice can prove more equitable than alternative mechanisms for public service delivery is particularly contentious – certainly, the example cited above illustrates some of the potential problems in this respect. It is hard to avoid the conclusion that one of the core issues that Le Grand cites as problematic in relation to mechanisms of enhanced voice would also apply for choice:

> many individualistic voice mechanisms favoured the educated and articulate. The better off have louder voices: they also have better contacts and sharper elbows. (Le Grand, 2007a: 31–2)

It is clear that educated and articulate service users are also much more likely to be able to realise their choices than many others in receipt of social care. Although Le Grand argues that people in lower socioeconomic groupings are equally likely to express their choices, because he does not explicitly consider social care he fails to take account of the issues which might limit their ability both to exercise choice and to have their choices realised (Lymbery, 2010). To acknowledge this is not to take a paternalistic view of people in need of care and support: it is simply to recognise the impact that their frailties will have on the levels of choice they are able to make, or the possibilities of that choice being realised. Careful reading of the largely positive findings from the IBSEN study (Glendinning et al., 2008) give some support to this conclusion: older people in receipt of care services – who tend to be physically and/or cognitively frail – often did not desire the additional responsibilities that they felt would attend the personalisation process. In a number of ways, therefore, the introduction of greater levels of choice into social care may actually contribute to increased levels of inequality.

In arguing from this angle, the purposes of personalisation are clearly problematic. The appeal to citizenship – which is, as we have seen, strong at the rhetorical level of policy – can be seen as masking the *real* dynamics of policy (see Clarke, 2005): the neoliberal insertion of consumerism into welfare. As a result, the development of personalisation has been subject to strong criticism from writers who use a critique of neoliberalism as their starting point (Ferguson, 2007; Houston, 2010).

It is obvious from the tone and content of this book that we see personalisation as more aligned with the extension of neoliberalism and consumerism into social care than as a genuine attempt to secure a fuller measure of social citizenship for people with disabilities. However, it would be an error to disregard entirely the perspective that the policy was influenced by the service user movement: this was obviously the case (Glasby, 2014) – at least in part – and forces critics into a more guarded response to the policy overall. There remain concerns, however, about the essential nature of personalisation, and it is hard to avoid the conclusion that its impact is critically affected by the ideological confusion that has attended its introduction.

The critical issue here is the capacity for personalisation to be interpreted in two different ways – in relation to social citizenship or the spread of neoliberalism. As we have identified, each has its antecedents and consequent impact on the policy in reality. When combined with the financial pressures noted above, it is the adequacy of the resource base on which personalisation depends that represents the most significant problem, and which dictates the way in which it will be put into effect. The overall conclusion is clear: if resources are insufficient, it is hard to see how some of the more liberating elements of the policy can be brought into being.

Conclusion

Obviously, a key ideological dilemma here focuses on solutions that are individually oriented as opposed to those that are based on collective provision. This was the central division in social work in the 19th century; the development of radical social work has sharpened that even further. One of the particular problems with the way in which personalisation has been constructed rests on its individualism, which tends not to allow that more collective responses to need may be equally valid. As this chapter has outlined, there are several other points of ideological confusion that can be identified. Some of these are central to the whole of public policy as they play on the distinctions between the 'deserving' and 'undeserving' poor, which persist into contemporary life (see, for example, *The Guardian*, 2012). The essential problem with the idea that only the people who 'deserve' help should receive it is that, in the words of a commentator on the outcome of policy in the 19th century: 'the "unassisted" might be those who most needed help but least deserved it ... while those helped, the respectable and provident, ought least to have needed help' (Mowat, 1961: 37). However, it remains a consistent theme in British social policy and assists in explaining other elements of confusion that characterise policy.

While the sense of stigma that characterised the Poor Law no longer exists, there remain some uncomfortable reminders of the distinctions between rich and poor in relation to social care. For example, an older person reliant on state support is going to be unable to enter the highest quality residential homes, as the overriding concern remains to cut costs as opposed to maximising the quality of care for all. The fact that adult social care remains funded out of general taxation exemplifies this problem, as no major political party appears able to suggest that this should be increased, even if it would result in a general improvement in the services available for the more vulnerable members of society.

The extent to which services should be universally or selectively available has magnified this element. It has been a problem for the development of social care that it was never deemed to be free at the point of use – it has always (from the National Assistance Act 1948 onwards) attracted a charge from the user. When added to the insufficiency of the funds that support social care from the public purse, it means that there is a consistent argument about who should, and should not, receive financial support. This has been thrown into even sharper relief by the government's commitment to cutting public spending. Even so, it was somewhat of a shock to read that money was no object when it comes to the relief of flood victims in the winter of 2013/14, according to the Prime Minister, David Cameron (Wintour and Booth, 2014). This is diametrically opposed to the line adopted in relation to the entirety of welfare expenditure for the duration of the current administration's time in office.

This leads to the biggest area of ideological confusion – the clear contradiction in seeking to meet welfare goals through market mechanisms (Taylor-Gooby et al., 2004). As the response to the floods indicated, there are a number of issues that cannot be left to the market to resolve. We would suggest that the care of the most vulnerable in society is precisely one such issue. However, this is emphatically not the policy of the British government. Once this is properly comprehended, many other decisions are more readily understood. For example, the focus on choice and competition is about saving money as much as it is an expression of an individualistic approach to policy. The promotion of choice in public services is also a reflection of the preference for individual 'solutions' to problems over collective ones.

For social workers, one of the main areas of difficulty is that they have to practise in the context of these ideological battles. The long-standing conflict within social work between individual and collective solutions to problems is a clear indicator of this. There is no easy way to resolve this conundrum; while it could be suggested that a *rapprochement* between the two traditions should be attempted (Ferguson and Woodward, 2009; Lymbery, 2013), others would argue that there is a fundamental incompatibility between them (see, for example, Simpkin, 1983). We suggest that a social worker needs to find a balance between the two – to practise in a way that is informed by political considerations, with a full understanding of the ideological complexities and contradictions of the social work world, while striving to benefit the individuals with whom s/he works.

SIX

Deprofessionalisation

Introduction

When discussing the changes to the nature of social work with adults the term 'deprofessionalisation' is often used to describe what has happened (Hugman, 1998; Clark, 2005). The word is often used as if there is complete understanding of what is meant by the concept. It is often implicitly accompanied with reference to a past 'golden age' for social work, which – for adult care at least, the subject of this book – never existed (Lymbery, 2005). Nonetheless, it has immediate recognition for many within the social work world: it seems to be describing something that chimes with many people's experiences (Rogowski, 2010). This is ironic because, in many ways, social work now has more of the traditional professional trappings – notably the fact that 'social worker' became a protected title under the Care Standards Act 2000 – than has previously been the case.

However, for the concept to be meaningful in relation to the specifics of adult social care a number of questions have to be satisfactorily answered.

- Is social work a profession in general terms, and – if not – should it aspire to be one?
- Has social work ever achieved professional status in the specific context of adult social care?
- How did the detail of community care implementation affect this?
- Has the development of personalisation changed this in any meaningful way?

These represent important issues to be resolved if we are fully to understand the place of social work in the context of adult social care. From our perspective, this understanding is critical: if we are to argue that social work has an important place in the future worlds of adult social care we need to be clear about how the previous policy developments have affected it. As we will argue, there seems little doubt that these processes have curtailed the breadth and extent of social work involvement.

In this chapter we will start by discussing the nature of professions and the extent to which social work should be considered to belong to this group of occupations. We move to discuss the elements of deprofessionalisation, to clarify our understanding of what this process means for any profession where this happens. Having established the basic contours of our argument, we discuss the impact on social work of the two main policy developments in the past 20 years. First, we consider the process of community care, arguing that it had apparently contradictory implications for social workers: while the enactment of community care heralded the entry of many more social workers into the adult social care workforce, their role was very often dominated by bureaucratic and procedural considerations (Gorman and Postle, 2003). The recent development of policies around personalisation has been accompanied by some positive statements about the centrality of social work (see for example, ADASS et al., 2010), but – as we have explored in Chapter Three – the financial context within which local authorities are working at the time of writing militates against social workers' active engagement in the policy. Consequently, as we argue, it is possible to see the extended period from the full enactment of community care in 1993 to the present as a lengthy period of deprofessionalisation for social workers.

What is a profession?

'When I use a word,' Humpty Dumpty said in rather a scornful tone, 'it means just what I choose it to mean – neither more nor less.' 'The question is,' said Alice, 'whether you can make words mean so many different things.' *(Lewis Carroll, Through the Looking Glass, Chapter Six)*

The language used when discussing the nature of social work tends to assume that it can clearly and uncontroversially be regarded as a profession. In reality the thinking on this subject is more complex than such a simple assertion would indicate, for a number of reasons. For example, there is a strong element of feminist thought that views any profession as the exercise of masculinist principles, which contribute to the subjugation of women (Dominelli, 2002); consequently, the status of a profession should not be sought. In addition, there has always been a firm element of radical thought that rejected the very notion of professionalism in relation to social work, on the basis that this created an artificial separation between those who provided and those who received social work (Bailey and Brake, 1975; Illich, 1977). The purpose of this section is to open up some of these complex areas in an attempt to secure greater clarity about the nature of professions and the extent to which social work could be claimed as one.

It has been suggested (Evetts, 2006) that there has been a gradual progression in approaches to thinking about the nature of professions. First, the key argument was that a profession helped to ensure social stability: it was deemed as essential to ensure the robust health of society, such that lay people could trust a professional – for example, a lawyer or doctor – to carry out his (it was normally a man!) role to the best of his abilities. An example of the level of trust placed upon professionals was the requirement that a UK passport application must be countersigned by a professional (now replaced by someone working in or retired from 'a recognised profession' or being 'a person of good standing in their community'). As such, a profession was an inherently conservative institution, devoted to maintenance of social structures. The notion of trust was critical to thinking about the way in which professionals operated – they were trusted to carry out their duties without reference to their own best interests, purely in the assistance of those who needed their services. In this conception, professions were an unmitigated benefit for society and their existence was described in functionalist terms. Evetts (2006) has argued that this way of thinking led directly to the attempt to identify the characteristics of those occupations that could be termed 'professions'. In the history of social work, this contributed to considerable contention about whether it should properly be classed as a profession at all (Bisman, 2004). This has been defined as the 'trait' approach to professions, a classic example of which was expressed by Greenwood who maintained that a profession should have:

- systematic theory
- community sanction
- authority
- an ethical code
- a professional culture. (Greenwood, 1957, cited in Wilding, 1982)

The 'trait' approach starts from a position where professions are positively regarded: indeed, it reveals the elements that supposedly made a profession such a constructive force within society. While the 'trait' approach has been largely superseded in sociological debate (Evetts, 2006), it has been – and continues to be – influential in studies about the professional status of social work. For example, numerous writers have classified social work as a 'semi-profession', the argument being that it does not possess all the traits that are deemed to characterise a full profession (see, for example, Toren, 1972). Even in more contemporary writing there remain echoes of the trait approach (see, for example, Reid and Edwards, 2006). There is now a widespread recognition, however, that it is an inadequate and incomplete way of thinking about the professional status of social work (Weiss-Gal and Welbourne, 2008).

A number of elements contribute to this recognition. There is no clear differentiation between professions and other occupations, nor is it possible to define clearly which occupations would, or would not, be accepted as a profession (even though this is generally acknowledged in the cases of law and medicine, it is a matter of great uncertainty in relation to others – for example, teaching and social work). In addition, it has been argued that the attributes are more a reflection of professionals' claims than they are an objective statement (Wilding, 1982). In addition, it fails to accommodate the essentially moral character of social work, which highlights the vital nature of both the purposes and processes of the occupation (Bisman, 2004; Clark, 2006).

A range of more sophisticated critiques of professionalism have also been developed in recent years, and these significantly extend our understanding of the nature of professions. In addition, they also help in understanding the critical points from feminist and radical perspectives, noted earlier. One of the early examples of this can be found in the work of the sociologist Terry Johnson (1972), who suggested that a more fruitful way of analysing professions was through an examination of the way in which they had managed to secure a degree of control over their occupation. Using this analysis, what distinguished social work (which he does specifically discuss) from more established occupations was the limited level of power and control it had been able to exercise over the essence of its practice. This insight is particularly true in the UK (McDonald et al., 2003). By contrast, Johnson argued that what characterised a more successful profession – like medicine – was the extent to which its practitioners had been able to secure a greater measure of occupational control in relation to it. This was a key source for the anti-professional views voiced by the radical movement (Hugman, 1998) as well as the feminist critiques of professionalism (Dominelli, 2002).

Other theorists have modified and extended Johnson's thinking in the direction of what has been termed a 'market closure' (Evetts, 2006) or a 'power' approach to professions (Weiss-Gal and Welbourne, 2008). In these conceptions, the key element is the extent to which a given profession has been able to further its own self-interest through increasing the level of control over all aspects of its work. A particularly strong example of this can be found in the work of Larson (1977). She drew extensively on the early work of Freidson (1970), exploring the extent to which professions have been able to organise a market for their services and thereby enhance their collective status and prestige. (Interestingly, the growth of independent social work could be argued as a demonstration of Larson's point; see chapter ten for a brief discussion of this.) She termed this process of professionalisation the 'professional project', which she held to be characteristic of the way in which all professions operate. This perspective is close to the thinking of Abbott (1988), who was particularly interested in the jurisdictional disputes between different professions, a fruitful area for analysis in relation to health and social care. Unfortunately, the potential value of much of this work is undermined by the rather simplistic notion of George Bernard Shaw that 'all professions are conspiracies against the laity'. As a consequence there is relatively little sense that professions may have both a practical and a social utility.

Another alternative sense of how professionals work is generated in the influential paper by Jamous and Peloille (1970). The authors seek to understand the balance between the elements of professional work that can be defined as technical knowledge as against those that are more indeterminate in nature, deriving from the uncertainty that underpins much human interaction. Professional practice, they maintain, is dependent upon the maintenance of a balance between 'technicality' and 'indeterminacy'. Jamous and Peloille (1970) define the balance between them as the 'indeterminacy/technicality ratio', which they suggest typifies the operation of professional systems within occupations. For social work, the elements of technicality and indeterminacy are both clear. For example, the various managerialist attempts to establish tighter procedures (highlighted in Chapter Four) can clearly be seen as an attempt to increase the elements of technicality in social work practice, seeking to deliver an improved quality of practice but also having the effect of shifting the indeterminacy/technicality ratio. However, various writers have noted that the greater attention paid to procedural elements has detracted from the ability of social workers to explore depth and meaning in their interaction (Howe, 1996; Gorman and Postle, 2003); these are the elements that cannot so easily be measured and represent the indeterminacy of social work practice. By contrast, in relation to personalisation, it has been suggested that the development of the policy will enable social workers once again to explore the details of human relationships (Williams and Tyson, 2010), thereby shifting the balance in a different direction.

In the development of his theory of reflective practice, Schön (1991) draws on a similar distinction between the 'high ground' of abstract theory and the 'swampy lowlands' that characterise the decision-making environment for professionals. While he recognises that the 'high ground' is necessary to enable clear critical thinking about – for example – the theoretical basis of intervention, his focus is on the complex judgements that enable professionals actually to operate within the 'swampy lowlands' that typify practice. What characterises this, he suggests, is the fact that practice cannot be prescribed to fit any given circumstance. Although using different language, Schön (1991) is concerned with a similar subject to Jamous and Peloille – understanding how professionals perform in action. Both theoretical approaches stress the limitations of knowledge as a sufficient basis for practice, arguing that to be successful professionals require more than simply the ability to recognise and understand abstract theory.

Consequently, for social work – as with many other occupations – it is important to move beyond the simplicities of either the 'trait' or the 'power' approaches to professions. In addition, a profession must be able to address both the radical and feminist critiques of its operations. To accomplish this it is first important to understand how social workers act in practice: after all, social work can never be a passive occupation, where the practitioner applies a set of pre-determined actions to predictable circumstances. This is why the thinking of Jamous and Peloille (1970) and Schön (1991) have such purchase, as they focus on the indeterminate elements of professional practice. Indeed, the more experienced the practitioner the more s/he will be expected to work in situations of uncertainty and complexity (Lymbery, 2003). This not an optional extra: it represents the core of what a social worker should do, particularly in relation to adult social care. Of course, the way in which a professionally qualified social worker should relate to those people with whom s/he works is critical. It is our contention that social work needs to consider the potential – and actual – benefits that can derive from the performance of its sensitive, complex, inherently professional work (Foster and Wilding, 2000).

However, the professional status of social work has long been questioned – even as early as 1915 the American professor Abraham Flexner argued that social work did not merit the appellation of profession because it was an essentially 'intermediary occupation', possessing no defined repertoire of knowledge and skill (in Lewis, 1996). This is an ongoing debate, and it is arguably impossible to reconcile all the competing interpretations of what constitutes a profession. In our view, however, taking all of the foregoing arguments into account, social work *is* a profession: the primary reason for stating this is the fact that its practitioners engage in complex work, balancing the elements of technicality and indeterminacy in their practice. To that extent it meets the criteria outlined by Jamous and Peloille (1970). In addition, the notion that social workers operate in the 'swampy lowlands' (Schön, 1991) also has merit to us: we recognise that practitioners function in circumstances that are resistant to the application of prescribed theoretical interventions (Gorman and Postle, 2003). However, we are also aware that the status of a profession has often been used – particularly by professionals themselves! – as a barrier between professionals and others (Hugman, 1998; Dominelli, 2002), and believe that such a barrier is antithetical to effective social work practice (Healy and Meagher, 2004). Consequently, rather than reject the notion of professionalism, we believe that what is important is to reconstruct the profession of social work so that it can put itself at the service of those people who need its assistance (Lymbery, 2001), in the process engaging with both the feminist and radical critiques.

To this end, the later writing of Freidson (2001) is particularly useful. Here he significantly amends the perspectives that underpinned much of his earlier work, which was strongly critical of the essential nature of professions (Freidson, 1970). By contrast, he later argued for the possibility that a profession should be regarded as a viable and potentially important way of organising work, in relation to the dominant alternative visions of the market and bureaucracy, both of which, he felt, were less likely to provide a top-quality service – and both of which have been strong elements in the development of social work for adults, as we have previously noted. He accepted that professions should be analysed *both* in terms of the search for economic gain and monopoly control *and* in relation to their ability to provide a vital service to those people who require it. Central to this argument is the concept of 'trust' – the extent to which professionals can be relied upon to carry out their work to the benefit of those who need services (Freidson, 2001); this is a critical conception for social work, as we will argue.

As a consequence of this, Freidson argues for a restructuring of the concept of professions; he also indicates that the prospects for this have been rendered particularly complex by a number of related issues. He suggests that all professions 'have suffered some loss of public confidence and trust, and many have come under financial pressure to reduce the costs of their services to consumers and the state' (Freidson, 2001: 193). This is particularly true in the case of social work, which has been beset by a combination of public criticism and hostility (Munro, 2004), allied – in recent years at least – to governmental disdain. The erosion of trust – in institutions and professionals – has been highlighted as a key characteristic of contemporary British society, with particular reference to social work (Smith, 2001); indeed, as Munro has suggested, the quest for greater levels of public accountability is a root cause of this problem. In such circumstances, it is hard to rebuild the confidence that is needed for professionals to operate well with people (although Healy and Meagher, 2004, have started this process).

If we examine how our understanding of professions translates into practice in interprofessional environments, we see how many of these issues are played out. For example, numerous commentators highlight the impact of professional differences on the practice of all members of interprofessional teams (see, for example, King and Ross, 2003; Baxter and Brumfitt, 2008). By way of contrast, other writers have tried to identify what makes social workers unique in the interprofessional context (see, for example, Beresford et al., 2006). If we are able to begin the process of understanding the unique nature of the professional social worker's role within a multi-disciplinary environment we will also be able to make the case for the maintenance of this role.

Baxter and Brumfitt (2008) have argued that there are three ways of examining this problem, by looking at:

1. knowledge and skills
2. professional role and identity
3. power and status.

All of these factors potentially represent problematic areas for social workers as well as other professionals, and much literature highlights the difficulties that they can cause in the interprofessional setting. For example, in an integrated mental health team all of these issues potentially characterise divisions between psychiatrists and community psychiatric nurses. By contrast, a clear understanding of the potential of qualified social workers to contribute a unique perspective helps towards a defence of their location within adult social care. Where we would locate this is in relation to the context within which they operate. A skilled social worker is valued for her/his ability to balance different and potentially competing priorities – autonomy, risk and protection – while maintaining constructive relationships within the interprofessional work environment. At its best, skilled social work could be seen as the element that binds such a team together (Herod and Lymbery, 2002).

The deprofessionalisation thesis

As we noted in Chapter Four, the deprofessionalisation thesis contains a number of elements, several of which are discussed here. They include a reduction in professional control of the objectives of work, combined with a decrease in the discretion that professionals have in dealing with individual cases. In addition, the thesis suggests that workers may both be required to act in ways that are opposed to their professional perspective on a client's best interests, and to work in accordance with policies and objectives with which they disagree. Finally, professionals are increasingly likely to be replaced by workers without a recognised professional qualification (Clark, 2005). As the first edition of this book noted, there were clear indications of a deprofessionalising process at that time (Gorman and Postle, 2003), such as in reductionist recording systems and a faster throughput of work, giving less time for each individual. As we will argue, this has only accelerated in recent years.

It is important first to understand the various factors that have brought this into being. In particular we need to understand the nature of what has been defined as the 'bureau–professional compact' that has characterised social work in recent times (Harris, 1998; Lymbery, 2014d). Given the centrality of the local state to the development of social work in the United Kingdom (Johnson, 1972), it is important to understand the nature of this compact and how it emerged in relation to social work. In Chapter One, we drew on the analysis of Derber (1983) in identifying the two key forms of managerial control to which public services professionals are subject, 'ideological' and 'technical'. Writing in the early 1980s, Derber contended that many occupations – including social work, which he specifically discussed in his analysis – had ceded ideological control of their work to politicians and managers, while retaining substantial control of the technical means by which it is carried out. In essence, this is how the 'bureau–professional compact' (Harris, 1998) was established. Social workers accepted the limited scope of their practice in exchange for a sense of security that such work would continue to be needed, an interpretation which the experiences of social workers under community care aptly illustrates. This protection is now under threat; the element of control that is now most clearly evident in adult services is the decisions about the numbers of social workers that are required and the work that such qualified staff should undertake – both of which reflect a more direct intervention. Both of these are core elements of the deprofessionalisation thesis, noted above.

In this analysis, the fact that social work has developed in the UK as a state-mediated profession (Johnson, 1972) – quite unlike the situation elsewhere in the world (McDonald et al., 2003) – is critical; it has meant that the government has a direct impact upon the way in which social work is developed. Indeed, various forms of government policy have fostered a divergence between social work with children and families – where the presence of qualified staff is retained – and social work with adults, where this is more questionable. Consequently, despite the various statements about the centrality of social work to policy in adult social care (see, for example, ADASS et al., 2010), there are pressures that render this unlikely; the state-mediated nature of social work for adults has rendered this utterly impracticable. In addition, some have argued that the rise of the ideology of managerialism has created a fertile climate for the deprofessionalisation of social work in general terms (Rogowski, 2010; see also Chapter Four). As a result, the arguments that there has been a deprofessionalisation of social work in adult social care rest on both the state-mediated nature of social work and the government-created push for managerialist 'solutions' to perceived problems (Clarke, 1998). As we will examine in the following sections, it is the combination of the two factors that has been critical.

Community care: the start of the deprofessionalisation process

While the pace of professional development in relation to social work was relatively slow and patchy in the years leading up to the implementation of community care (Lymbery, 2005), it is a sad irony as far as the profession is concerned that, while the enactment of community care legislation increased the numbers of qualified social work staff working in this area of activity, the circumstances of their employment also contained the elements whereby their professional status could be undermined. The reason for this is the realisation that increased numbers of social workers were needed to control the costs of care – hence their work focused much more on gatekeeping and rationing than it did on exercising their full range of professional skills (McDonald et al., 2008).

Once community care was implemented, a variety of factors further eroded any belief in the professional status of social workers. These included a lack of confidence in public sector care, the development of welfare pluralism, a market in health and social care and the growth of managerialism. When combined, they provided fertile ground for the growth of anti-professionalism in general and anti-social work feelings in particular. These sentiments did not diminish with the election of a Labour government in 1997, despite hopes that there would be a shift in the prevalent ideology. Conflicts arose when decisions had to be taken about the quality of life of others that reflected the interpretation of social care as a commodity, with users of services configured as 'consumers' of welfare. (As we have seen in Chapter Five, that interpretation gathered pace with the implementation of personalisation.) From the perspective of care managers, who were usually professionally qualified as social workers, there was an expectation that they had some professional autonomy in their role and that they could operate as advocates for the user, thus acting in their best interests in securing the best care available (Brandon and Hawkes, 1998), both of which are in accordance of what they understood to be key elements of a professional role. Yet the reality was that the many changes experienced by those working in the welfare system minimised the consideration of issues of principle in favour of getting the job done to meet targets set by a management agenda. The failure to observe fundamental values such as mutuality (interpreted by Holman [1993] as the recognition of shared obligations stemming from a common notion of kinship, in which material reward is not the major force) appeared to skew the idea of 'community care' to mean an individual care compact that was strongly and openly influenced by managerial controls. This affected the work of social workers in community care and, for some commentators, led to a lack of recognition of the richness of human diversity (Hadley and Clough, 1996).

The downgrading of professional tasks and a focus on outcomes rather than the processes of care was a stressful and disheartening experience for many care managers, especially those who were fieldworkers before the move to care management and who became care managers working primarily with older people. This was amply illustrated in the first edition of this book (Gorman and Postle, 2003). For example, one care manager stated:

> 'The quality of the relationship with the client seems to have changed.... There's always been administration in social work.... However, the paperwork and the bureaucracy was, compared to now, minimal.... You had more time to see clients ...'

The opportunity to improvise, to use practice wisdom to the best advantage, was often, but not invariably, lost. There appeared to be three sets of reactions at play: accommodation, resistance and a response to day-to-day pressure that may not necessarily be in the best interests of the users of the service. Lipsky (1980), in *Street Level Bureaucracy*, recounted similar dilemmas of the individual in the public service. There was a rearguard action of social workers/care managers re-owning the attributes of social work, for example honing assessment skills and seeing new opportunities, such as a significant role in the commissioning of services (Gorman and Postle, 2003). The 'going the extra mile' was not necessarily viewed as something that was rewarded by employer organisations, who were seen by some as paying more attention to appearances rather than realities (Postle, 1999). The response of some care managers was consciously to play the system, or at least make the system work for them. They had to learn fast in a welfare world that included the private sector as a major player. These reactions ranged from over-exaggerating a service user's needs in order to get appropriate funding for care to being less than precise about the completion of workload monitoring audits, ignoring administrative demands and taking more time with clients than would meet with managerial approval. An example of the line taken by some managers, which some frontline staff were trying to counter, was one quoted by Gorman and Postle (2003) who said:

> 'There just isn't the time for them to be giving of themselves in the way that they were and while that may be very nice for the client, and it may be very nice for them in terms of job satisfaction, it's not very good for the fifty people who are still waiting for someone to step through their door.... I'm not putting down the counselling, but it's got to be seen as something apart from what we do ... we should actually be purchasing counselling skills, buying them in from a secondary provider.

For Lipsky (1980),criticism of the street-level bureaucrats who failed to deliver services to the community that were responsive and appropriate was explained by an analysis of the problems that social workers experienced in reconciling needs, resources and the ambiguous aims of the bureaucracy. He suggested that the exercise of professional discretion was problematic in a context where demand outstripped supply, recognising that the work orientations of public sector bureaucrats determined a great deal of actual public policy as experienced by the users of services. He commented on the desire of street-level bureaucrats to maintain their discretionary capacity and being interested in processing work consistent with their own preferences and those agency policies that were so salient as to be backed up with agency sanction. Street-level bureaucrats may also use existing regulations and administrative provisions to circumvent reforms which limit their discretion.

Clearly, therefore, Lipsky's analysis (1980) was highly relevant to social work in the context of community care. There are also other elements of his thinking that remain highly pertinent in the context of a discussion about professionalism and social work. For example, he contended that it was actually impossible to eliminate discretion within public services (see Evans and Harris, 2004, in relation to social work); indeed, Scourfield (2013) has suggested that the exercise of discretion in adult social care is further complicated by its 'dispersal' – the fact that there are numerous other professionals also with some responsibility for decision making. As a result, we can argue that the maintenance of professionalism is an inevitability, at least in part. Lipsky (1980) also pointed out a critical tension between professionals and their employers: while professionals tend to seek to enhance their discretion (the element of 'indeterminacy' identified above), employers will tend to seek to increase their control over employees, thereby increasing the element of 'technicality', also noted above.

As we have indicated, the development of social work under community care would suggest that this balance shifted in favour of managers during this period. However, Lipsky (1980) commented on the difficulty for managers in trying to ensure compliance in such circumstances. Indeed, he suggested that the search for greater accountability might actually reduce service quality, due to the capacity of workers to subvert any performance management mechanisms that are introduced. The potential for performance management to have perverse consequences was further amplified by de Bruin (2002). However, there was limited contemporary recognition of this, and it did not obstruct the managerialist attempt to control the actions of professionals (Clarkson, 2010).

In the conditions of indeterminacy that characterise the work of street-level bureaucrats, Lipsky (1980) argued that workers have three broad ways of seeking to respond to the problems that are created:

1. They can seek to practise in such a way as to limit the demands that are placed on their services.
2. They can amend their conceptions of the job so that they can manage their work more effectively by reducing or restricting their objectives, and hence reducing the dissonance between their ideal and the realities of practice.
3. They can modify their conceptions of people who require services to maximise the chance that they will be successful according to bureaucratic criteria.

There is plentiful evidence in community care of social workers seeking to adapt their work in accordance with the third of these possibilities (Gorman and Postle, 2003). Looking forward, Ellis (2007) has provided compelling evidence of social workers undertaking this process in relation to the implementation of direct payments (see also Clark et al., 2004).

Lipsky was particularly interested in the inevitable collision between the work practitioners carry out and the resources that they are able to deploy, which he suggested would always be inadequate to respond effectively to the level of need with which the street-level bureaucrat is confronted. In relation to community care, social workers inevitably experienced such constraints when attempting to respond to need. (Indeed, as we have suggested in Chapter Three, this balance is only becoming more problematic in relation to personalisation.) As Lipsky argued, in general terms:

> Street-level bureaucrats work with inadequate resources in circumstances where the demand will always increase to meet the supply of services. Thus they can never be free from the demands of significant constraints. (1980: 81)

In the context of community care, social workers necessarily operated in circumstances that required the exercise of considerable professional judgement, but also where resources were extremely limited. This situation created an intolerable 'existential problem' for social workers: the basis of this was simple: 'with every single client they could probably act flexibly and responsively. But if they do this with too many clients their capacity to respond flexibly would disappear' (Lipsky, 1980: 99). As a result they had to find ways of managing the contradictions with which they were confronted. For Lipsky (1980: 143), the more idealistic the worker the more these accommodations would be experienced as problematic, as indicated by the quote from the manager, above.

This is interesting in relation to other work on the motivations of staff (see, for example, Le Grand, 2003; Martin et al., 2004). For example, Le Grand has questioned the assumption that those who work within the welfare state are primarily enthused by a benevolent impetus – what he terms 'knightly' motivations. Instead, he claimed, this perception was overturned by a core tenet of the new public management, the view that the sector's staff are motivated more by self-interest than a concern for the welfare of those they serve. He translated this into a more critical perspective, putting forward the idea that 'knavish' motivations should be considered as more of a factor. He suggested that this frame of reference can also be extended to the users of public services; under the traditional conception of public services, he suggested that they were treated as 'pawns', which he argued was being replaced by a more powerful 'queenly' characterisation. (The statements of the disability movement in relation to social care would tend to support this analysis [see Harris and Roulstone, 2011].)

Martin et al. (2004) applied the thinking of Le Grand specifically to social work under community care. They highlighted the conflicts of social workers when confronted, on the one hand by rigid organisational and bureaucratic requirements and, on the other, by sets of burgeoning and apparently unlimited needs. When the inadequacy of funding was added to that mix their role became even more problematic. Martin et al. (2004) concluded by suggesting that this all created a lack of fit between the supposedly user-focused intentions of policy and the bureaucratic nature of the care management process that was created to put the policy into effect.

This encapsulates what we consider to be an accurate picture of the position of social workers under community care, which is consistent with the first edition of this book (Gorman and Postle, 2003). While social workers did retain elements of discretion about the way in which they carried out their tasks, there had been efforts by managers and organisations to constrain this. In line with the national guidance issued to govern the care management process (DH and SSI, 1991), each local authority constructed a forest of policies and procedures (Lewis and Glennerster, 1996) – one of us contributed to a relatively sizeable wood in Nottinghamshire! While this was not necessarily derived from malign intentions – the realities of community care were sufficiently complex that they needed careful explanation – the effect on professionals was stark. In our analysis, while the latter recognised the complexities of service user need, which required a maximisation of their ability to act creatively, they were hampered both by the detailed guidance and lack of resources needed to act with sufficient flexibility. Reflecting back on the elements of deprofessionalisation (Clark, 2005), many of them are plain to see. There was a reduction in the level of professional control exercised by social workers, and there were also concerted attempts to curtail their discretion. Having said that, the implementation of community care saw a substantial increase in the numbers of qualified social workers operating within adult social care (Lymbery, 2005), even if this was largely part of the financial management process (Lewis and Glennerster, 1996). However, there was no wholesale replacement of qualified staff with unqualified workers at this stage. The limitations of the resource base increasingly affected the practice of social workers, and arguably pushed them into both having to accept policies with which they disagreed and to act in ways that were incompatible with their perceptions of the interests of service users. As the interviews reported in the first edition indicated (Gorman and Postle, 2003), social workers retained a strong sense of ambivalence about the nature of their practice – but still retained a largely positive sense of their potential positively to affect people's lives. As one practitioner put it, social work:

'can be rewarding because we can buy services in, which is something we never had before, it is a wonderfully powerful thing … a couple of years ago I could not get anything. One can have influence on the way money is spent … there is a certain amount of autonomy in spending up to a limited amount without referring back.'

Personalisation: the deprofessionalisation process accelerates

Despite the changes wrought by community care, the deprofessionalisation process had not been completed, as we have indicated. Indeed, the bureau–professional compact appeared to be still in place: while practitioners were required to carry out tasks that did not always fit comfortably within their own conceptions of social work, there had been a marked growth in their numbers (Lymbery, 2014d). However, there were signs of problems within the system that had knock-on consequences for social workers. Of particular moment was the fact that social care budgets were increasingly proving inadequate in relation to increasing levels of need (Carvel, 2007; BBC, 2014a); as we have indicated, the inadequacy of budgets has long been recognised as a problem for street-level bureaucrats (Lipsky, 1980). In relation to the sense of deprofessionalisation experienced by social workers, this magnified the likelihood of their judgements being questioned and of service users losing out as a consequence. We believe that there are three main events occurring in the context of personalisation:

1. Social workers have been increasingly required to undertake the relatively few tasks – such as safeguarding – where a social work qualification is needed (DH, 2009; ADASS et al., 2010; SCIE, 2010a), and hence have effectively been withdrawn from large areas of practice that had hitherto been regarded as a social worker's domain. This weakens the bureau–professional compact as it further tightens ideological control of social work (as noted by Derber, 1983).
2. There is a widening gap between needs and resources in social care, which has forced social care departments to tighten their eligibility criteria. This has negated the focus on prevention and early intervention that should characterise personalisation, and has also enhanced the level of ideological control, further limiting any chance for social workers to be more widely engaged.
3. As discussed in Chapter Three, the inadequacy of resources has become a particular issue for all local authorities. As a consequence, they are having to think seriously of ways of save money (McNicoll, 2014). A number of approaches are being tried; one particular local authority has planned to outsource large elements of its provision, including replacing social workers with care assistants in adult assessment and care management teams (Donovan, 2014). Indeed, this happened to some degree in the case of community care, as managers were aware of the potential to save money by replacing qualified with unqualified staff (Postle, 1999). This is the point where the bureau–professional compact is being most obviously threatened: here, the 'ideological' control has been increased to such an extent that it is rendering it impossible for social workers to have any 'technical' control of their practice (Derber, 1983).

It is therefore the post-austerity period in England that is promoting the fullest possibilities of deprofessionalisation, fracturing the bureau–professional compact that had existed throughout community care (Lymbery, 2014d). Consequently, the efforts that are being expended to argue the case for continued social work involvement (Milne et al., 2014) seem to be largely irrelevant.

While Derber's thesis (1983) represents an incomplete analysis of how to interpret social work's contemporary position within adult services, we believe that the processes that he described of increasing levels of ideological control – characteristic of the community care era – are now being supplemented by ever-growing forms of technical control, under the banner of personalisation. The state-controlled nature of social work has, of course, created the conditions for this to occur (Lymbery, 2008). Despite the rhetoric of policy – and the attempts to construct a business case for social work (Davies, 2014) – the social work role in adult social care is under severe pressure as a result of the combination of financial pressures and a managerialist discourse that devalues professional activity (Healy, 2009; Lymbery, 2014d).

Conclusion

While it is being argued that there is both a moral and economic case for the involvement of social work in adult care (TCSW, 2012; Davies, 2014), the reality is that the difficult financial climate is having a chilling impact on the deployment of social workers in the context of personalisation (Brookes et al., 2013). Since local government is bearing the brunt of cuts within British society, local authorities are required to be creative about the ways in which they find savings to meet their reduced means (McNicoll, 2014). These materially affect adult social care, a major component of local authority budgets. While the sums involved in relation to social work support are relatively low, there is certainly evidence that at least some local authorities are shedding social work posts (Donovan, 2014), echoing concerns that were expressed several years ago (Lombard, 2011), but which also directly link to community care (Postle, 1999). The reduction in numbers of qualified staff is perhaps the starkest element of deprofessionalisation in adult social care.

However, as we have argued, there are other elements of this process. The notion of professional autonomy is bound up with a sense of accountability to the clients or users of services. This in turn relates to conceptions of professional values. England (1986) has articulated the emotional difficulties that can be faced by social workers when they feel that their professional values have been compromised by the welfare bureaucracy that employs them. He concluded that the organisation of social work poses problems of immense complexity and this situation is compounded by a lack of clarity about the social work task, so that neither the social worker nor the agency is clear about their role. Social work has never been differentiated in the public mind from the routine provision of social care services; indeed, the ways in which social services organisations have evolved have often been inimical to social work practice. Just as a codified and bureaucratic response to need dominated the construction of care management in this country, so too is such a construction dominant under the circumstances of personalisation. In both cases, the emphasis on a bounded needs-led service has masked the realities of resource limitations.

It is possible that such a gloomy prognostication might not come to pass in the stark manner that we have outlined. There is certainly potential to be found in the work to redefine the role of social work in the context of adult social care. In addition, there is also recognition from other professionals within multi-disciplinary teams that social workers have a distinct contribution to make. If the notion of social work that is proposed – that social workers should be involved in 'the effecting of adult social care when a relationship is required which goes beyond customer boundaries' (Chamberlain and Jenkinson, 2013) – were to be more widely adopted, it would clarify the circumstances when social workers should be involved. In addition, we would suggest that social workers could legitimately be involved in a broader range of activities that might contribute to the well-being of older people (Davies, 2014). This would also play on another aspect of their professional development. Similarly, it is possible that closer links between health and social care – an ambition of governments for many years – may also serve to protect professional's roles. However, it is hard to avoid the conclusion that decisions will be taken that are predominantly financially based, with consequent limits on the role of social workers.

SEVEN

Assessment and decision making

Introduction

Assessment has often been the central core of social work with adults (Richards, 2000) – although this has frequently been used explicitly for gatekeeping purposes. As we have previously noted, numerous policy documents often indicate that social workers should become more involved in advocacy and brokerage (HM Government, 2007; DH, 2008) and that, consequently, they would be required to perform fewer assessment tasks than has been the norm under community care. The assumption that staff will complete fewer assessments is also implied by the rhetoric validating self-assessment as the appropriate and favoured model (HM Government, 2007), as well as by the widespread adoption of formulaic resource allocation systems (RAS) that appear to obviate professional engagement in the task (Series and Clements, 2013). As, in times of reduced resources, assessment in community care was largely reduced to a gatekeeping exercise, it is not surprising that proposals for self-assessment would seem to be an unquestionably welcome development. On the surface, who would question that a person's own view of their needs would be better than a formulaic approach, solidified and codified into a bureaucratic procedure?

The more the link between assessment and gatekeeping has been asserted and translated into practice, the less understanding has been evinced about the core professional nature of assessment. Indeed, for many social work staff, 'an assessment' represents a form completed at the outset of work with someone, rather than an ongoing, iterative process. However, for personalisation to work effectively, there is a need to think beyond the apparent simplicity and reliability of self-assessment as a solution. In addition, we need to construct approaches to assessment that are more sophisticated than the rote application of resource allocation formulae. We consider that good-quality assessment is a core part of social work and, as such, it should have been essential for the effective implementation of community care and it will certainly need to be in relation to personalisation. As such, assessment is more than simply the gateway through which individuals must pass in order to secure services – the legally sanctioned process familiar within community care (Mandelstam, 2005) – it is also the main way in which people can be helped to articulate their needs, wishes and preferences, without which they are unlikely to secure services which are meaningful to them.

For us, the issue of assessment is critical; its resolution would be the single most compelling reason to retain social work as a core feature of personalisation. For this reason, we have given over a chapter in this text to discussing assessment, as we seek to illustrate both why it is central to social work and how it can fulfil an important function within personalisation. With this in mind, we start from a general consideration of the centrality of assessment in social work, including reflections on a range of different models of assessment. We discuss how assessment was intended to be a core element of community care, even though it became somewhat perverted by the focus on rationing and gatekeeping that came to characterise it. However, as segments from the first edition of this text indicate (Gorman and Postle, 2003), practitioners always recognised how important an informed and skilled assessment was in securing what people needed. Finally, we discuss the implications of self-assessment in more detail, highlighting those aspects of it that are less likely to be successful. We also consider the worrying impact of RAS on the professional roles of social workers.

Assessment in social work

Assessment is a critical element in the social work process, irrespective of the setting or service user group. It is impossible to act clearly and decisively unless there is a detailed understanding of the situation at hand. It is simply impossible to construct accurate care arrangements without clarity about what a service user wants and needs, her/his strengths, the capabilities of the family or other informal support and the views of other professionals where needed, alongside the availability of services and resources. This last point is critical: while it should not come to dominate the assessment process, understanding the limitations of these practical matters is essential, particularly in circumstances where there remain tight eligibility criteria (as noted in Chapter Three). Weighing up these elements often involves a delicate balancing act (Milner and O'Byrne, 2009). Nonetheless, good assessment should highlight not only eligibility for existing services but, importantly, as we will go on to discuss, other problems in the person's wider community or network which could appropriately be addressed (Smale et al., 1993).

Despite the fact assessment has always been a core part of social work, Milner and O'Byrne (2009) have suggested that it has been relatively neglected in social work literature. They argue that, where assessment does feature, it often appears to be an apparently logical, value-free, individualistic activity which is often presented reductively (Milner and O'Byrne, 2009). To borrow Payne's terminology (2006), this particularly privileges the individualist-reformist perspective. In our view, this does not capture the complexity of assessments, nor does it adequately encapsulate their essentially 'artistic' nature (England, 1986). Further, such individualistic approaches do nothing to highlight problems beyond the individual's immediate situation (Smale et al., 1993). In addition, such a conception denies the social dimension of assessment, which is critical when exploring the specific circumstances of all adults, perhaps particularly older people (Lymbery, 2005). If we are to adopt a broader conception of assessment, this potentially could help in moving beyond the individualist-reformist perspective and, crucially, help practitioners to get in touch with more therapeutic and collective orientations (Lymbery, 2005).

If such an undertaking – which we acknowledge as being ambitious! – is to prove successful, it has to be based on a different sort of relationship between social worker and service user (Lymbery, 2001), the absence of which has proved particularly trying for disabled people (Oliver, 2004; Harris and Roulstone, 2011). This relationship would focus on the specific sets of circumstance confronting the service user – including individual, family, community and social issues – and vary in accordance with what is uncovered about them (Healy, 2000). In adult services in particular – although the principle holds for every aspect of social work – there must be clarity about the nature of the social work role and how the assessment can ensure the maximal involvement and participation of the service user, a key requirement of personalisation.

The social worker's understanding of the assessment process is critical to this, and here we suggest that an understanding of each of the three general approaches to assessment identified by Smale et al. (1993) is central for a social worker. Smale et al. (1993) suggest that these are the 'questioning', 'procedural' and 'exchange' approaches, the key characteristics of which are as follows. In the 'questioning' approach, the model is based on the presumption of the professional expertise of the assessor. Consequently, s/he secures information from a service user based on a process of questions; the outcome of this is a course of action proposed by the assessor based on her/his interpretation of the service user's needs and wishes. In the 'procedural' approach, as the name would imply, the assessment is primarily governed by both the function of the agency and the resources that are available. In this approach, common in adult services due to centrality of eligibility criteria, the direction of the assessment is determined by the extent to which it is able to fit the service user to the eligibility criteria. The essential extra details about a person and their circumstances that enable an assessment to come alive are almost an irrelevance. By contrast, if the 'exchange' approach is used this starts from an entirely different set of assumptions. It is presumed that a service user and/or people in her/his network (allowing for the fact that a cognitive impairment may limit the person's own participation) is pre-eminently the expert in her/his situation, and has a range of strengths and experience on which to draw. The role of the assessor is to forge a more equitable relationship, which allows the service user, in partnership with the worker, to articulate and develop her/his understandings, both of the problem at hand and the most effective way of responding to it. It also presupposes that the assessor has a range of expertise on which to draw, which is placed at the disposal of the service user, thereby changing the essential relationship between the two (Healy and Meagher, 2004). Decisions about a potential course of action are, wherever possible (assuming there may be situations concerning risk/safeguarding which preclude this), the shared responsibility of the service user and the assessor – in this case a qualified social worker – taking into account the perspectives of family members and other interested parties.

The 'exchange' approach would be significantly more responsive to the concerns of service users, increasing their control over both the process and the outcome. It does not deny the skills and knowledge of the social worker; these skills are particularly evident in relation to relationship building and communication, while the knowledge of the social worker in relation both to the impact of changes in life circumstance – typical of all people who need the support of adult social care services – and the range of services that potentially can be made available are both critical (Smale et al., 2000). Necessarily, effective assessments that are carried out in accordance with the 'exchange' approach will tend to take longer; it is important to recognise, however, that they are much more likely to be robust as well as producing outcomes that are acceptable to service users (Lymbery, 2004).

Unfortunately, the assessment models, as devised by Smale et al. (1993), have, rather like the nature of assessment itself, lost something in translation over the years. For this reason, we will briefly digress to a little myth-busting, to clarify the essential importance of the exchange model which, alone of the three models, both prioritises the importance of hearing the service user's agenda and is potentially empowering. The following are some common misunderstandings about the assessment models which lead to confusion and can distract from the centrally important role of assessment as empowerment:

1. There is a choice between models. This may stem from the different meanings of 'model'. Smale et al. use 'model' to mean 'example', rather than 'ideal'. They make it clear the exchange model is the preferred one for the reasons given above.
2. 'Procedures' are synonymous with the 'procedural model'. Smale et al. were realistic and knew there would always be procedures to complete, although there is a strong sense that they hoped that reductionist procedures would not replace the tacit and complex process of assessment. The important issue here is not allowing procedures to determine how an assessment is conducted but, rather, to see completion of the procedures as secondary to the skilled process of assessment – a difficult task indeed when confronted by lengthy and complex forms.
3. There are circumstances in which the questioning model is appropriate. Beckett (2010), for example, advocates this in relation to areas of work such as fostering or adoption assessments. This seems to miss the point that Smale et al. did not negate the worker's use of their expertise; indeed, as we have shown above, that is all part of the 'exchange'. Hence, as in Beckett's example, in a fostering assessment, prospective carers are the experts in their lives and in what they think they can bring to children's lives, while the worker has knowledge and expertise in children's needs, legislation and policy, assessment of risk and a host of other areas.
4. The exchange model cannot be used with everyone. There may be concerns that someone with limited capacity, such as an older person with dementia or someone with severe learning impairment, cannot, as Beckett (2010) suggests,

contribute to the exchange. Similarly, both Beckett (2010) and Milner and O'Byrne (2009) suggest that an exchange model may not be feasible in situations of risk. This viewpoint does not take account of the potential for the worker to gain the person's own perspective of risk and, importantly, to gain the perspectives of others in the person's network. In work with older people, for example, it is crucial to understand whether they have taken risks all their lives and to ascertain how well those close to them are coping with any risk-taking behaviour. Again, the worker uses their own knowledge and expertise, including, importantly, knowledge of guidelines on mental capacity, in an exchange of information.

5. If the service user/people in their network have all the expertise, the social worker seems to have none. As points 3 and 4 demonstrate, this is far from the case. While the exchange model enables people to be experts in themselves and to have potential for thinking of ways to address their difficulties; there are many ways in which workers exercise expertise. We have indicated these above and they are most helpfully listed in Smale et al. (2000: 152–3).

6. Workers can move from one model to another. As Smale et al. (2000: 22) themselves stated, 'some dimensions of each exclude the application of the others' and they explicitly advise against a 'mix and match' approach.

If we examine the specific steps that make up an assessment (Milner and O'Byrne, 2009), we can see how the 'exchange' approach can be usefully applied. The first stage is that of *preparation*, whereby the practitioner seeks to secure clarity about what information needs to be discovered, where such information can be found and how it should be processed. This leads directly to the stage of *data collection*, which involves both the collection of 'data' through a variety of mechanisms, and its storage and retrieval. It is important to be aware that the collection of 'data' is a much broader and less clinical process than the term implies. Crucially, the worker needs to be aware that they do not see this stage in the assessment process as reverting to a procedural model but, instead, use their observation skills and, as succinctly outlined by Smale et al. (2000) use empathy. For example, most social workers, at some point in their career, have entered an older person's house and been almost overpowered by a strong smell of urine. Indeed, one of us recalls not choosing her seat carefully enough and needing to detour to the dry cleaners with her coat on the way back to the office! Rather than asking a direct question about incontinence (the likely source of the smell and certainly of the damp coat), the worker can tactfully explore this issue, thus gleaning the 'data' they need while also ensuring they convey empathy to the person/those with them about what may very well be a difficult/embarrassing problem. In addition, this stage also pays attention to how the reliability of 'data' can be checked and where there are key gaps in the 'data'. It is also critical to ensure that this 'data' is stored and retrieved appropriately, and that its reliability is checked and what gaps there are in the 'data' are fully ascertained. In line with the 'exchange' model, all of these stages need to involve the service user: it should never be forgotten that s/he is the focus of intervention and should be engaged at every stage. Importantly, workers need to ensure that they have not compartmentalised their learning and fully employ their communication skills in their work at this stage, as in any direct work with people (Koprowska, 2007).

For Milner and O'Byrne (2009) the third stage is *weighing the data*, which entails the process of making judgements about the person's situation, and involves the critical process of identifying any themes and patterns that might exist in the data. This is a necessary precursor to the fourth stage, *analysing the data*. The key part of this stage is the development of hypotheses that might help to explain what is happening. This is also the point where advanced levels of theoretical understanding are clearly important, with the professional deploying the extra layers of skill and knowledge at her/his command. This is not to suggest that s/he should control the assessment; rather, these levels of skill and knowledge need to be placed at the disposal of the service user (Healy and Meagher, 2004). This is consistent with the 'exchange' of expertise outlined by Smale et al. (1993). Any conclusions that are drawn at this stage are necessarily tentative, and must be checked out with all the key participants, above all, as far as possible, with the service user. This leads to the final part of the process, *utilising the analysis*. This refers to the establishment of a plan to address the issues raised through the entire assessment process. As with all of the other stages, it is essential that feedback is sought about the proposed plan from the person/people in their network so that it can be amended before being put in place, if necessary. This approach to assessment can easily be used in conjunction with the exchange model, thus avoiding the risk that the use of professional judgement becomes the exercise of power, thereby, as discussed in Chapter Six, being disempowering. This would not fit with our understanding of the central relationship between social workers and service users. We believe that the social worker needs to demonstrate a high level of skill in relation to the assessment role, but that the way in which the role is carried out is equally vital to its effectiveness.

Assessment in community care

If everything we have said here identifies a core role for assessment within the context of social work generally, it also holds good for community care. Although the copious guidance on community care had a lack of detail about many aspects of the overall process of intervention (see Clements and Thompson, 2011), this was not the case in relation to assessment. While a care management cycle of seven stages was introduced to explain the process, assessment was clearly defined as the key element. Evidence for this is in the official guidance (DH and SSI, 1991): while 22 pages were devoted to guidance concerning the two stages of assessment, only 28 pages were allocated for all of the other five stages (Payne, 1995). Reference back to the 'deep normative core' (Lewis and Glennerster, 1996) of community care helps to explain why this was the case: since a key requirement of the legislation was the need to control costs, it followed that one of the key purposes of assessment was the question of whether an individual was 'eligible' to receive care services (Gorman and Postle, 2003). It is important to note that the notion of 'eligibility' was central to community care, even before the Gloucestershire judgement and the subsequent publication of the *Fair Access to Care Services* eligibility criteria (DH, 2002).

As a result, assessment became heavily dominated by procedural requirements, where the single action that dominated most assessments was the decision about where the person fitted within local authority's eligibility criteria (Lymbery, 2005). While, according to S.47 of the National Health Service and Community Care Act 1990, there was a statutory obligation for the authority to assess all people who appeared to be in need of community care services, because of the limitations of resources there was no parallel obligation to provide a service. As we have previously indicated in Chapter Two, this created the need for stringent eligibility criteria. Consequently, whether a person met the local authority's eligibility criteria or not was largely decided by the assessor, who was – in most cases – a qualified social worker. S/he had to grapple with numerous ambiguities and tensions in practical circumstances, in order to reach an informed decision. It is important here to remember the obvious point – there are more or less infinite levels of complexity within each individual's set of circumstances. As such, it is useful to reflect upon some dilemmas of decision making that confronted social workers in community care, as these indicate the levels of complexity and depth that could appear in even the most apparently straightforward cases. In the following section we have therefore given some case examples for readers to consider, perhaps thinking about parallels in their own work.

Susie's use of a day centre which best suits her needs

The first of these is whether a social worker should have sought to offer care services that match a service user's preference or services that meet her basic needs. For example, in the situation of Susie, who had learning disabilities, she wanted to go to the Cedars day-care because she could swim there and swimming helped her to relax and keep mobile. However, since the nearest day-care centre to where she lived was less expensive than the one where she could swim, the social worker was told by a senior manager to offer this cheaper facility, even though it did not have a swimming pool. As we have indicated, it was always likely that financial priorities would affect any decisions that were taken and so, despite the more expensive day centre being appropriate for Susie's needs, and hence fitting within the overt purpose of community care she could not go there.

Mrs Jones' distress at the state of her house

The second issue concerns whether a social worker was justified in inflating a service user's care needs to ensure that she fell within the eligibility criteria. This problem remains current of course, particularly given the financial parameters within which local authorities are operating (see Chapter Three). To illustrate this we can explore the circumstances of Mrs Jones, who was 84 and lived alone; she had occasional dizzy spells and rheumatoid arthritis. She became very upset because her net curtains needed washing and she needed some help with the housework. She had maintained high standards all her life and was so upset that the state of her house was deteriorating. The local authority said that it did not provide such services. Her neighbours thought that she was 'going a bit strange' and getting depressed and worked up about the state of her house. Under the eligibility criteria she did not fit into the 'substantial' category that the local authority would meet – the only way to secure services for her, which are clearly needed in order to prevent further decline. In many cases, social workers will have considered over-emphasising the list of her 'needs', thereby enacting an example of 'deviant social work' (Carey and Foster, 2011). This would have been acting within the parameters of the preventative strategies originally intended in community care policies and would be consistent with research findings (Clark et al., 1998). Such an action, however, is directly contrary to the intentions of the policy that established eligibility criteria as a rationing mechanism (DH, 2002).

Poor-quality meals-on-wheels

Another example is evident through the commissioning process. In the absence of effective regulatory mechanisms, what is a social worker to do in relation to continued commissions of a service about which there are concerns over quality, even though there have been no official complaints? For example, a social worker became aware of a number of reports from various sources that many of the meals provided by a catering company purchased by adult social care were not really meeting the needs of minority ethnic elders, but there had been no official complaints. These reports had also specified that on occasions meals containing meat had been provided for vegetarian clients and that apples were ordered for people with no teeth! It would have been hard to withdraw the service without potentially attracting a complaint from the provider, which would be difficult to counter without the existence of hard evidence. The best way to resolve the problem would be to persuade those who had made verbal complaints to commit them to written form. This is easier said than done, however – particularly if the complainants are older people in receipt of the meals (Ware et al., 2003).

Jim's difficulties with his alcohol use

In the final example, we explore the question of whether a social worker should keep cases open when the operation of care management systems prioritises their closure as soon as the initial intervention has been completed. This is particularly the case where a service user has ongoing concerns (Lymbery and Morley, 2012). For example, we can consider the case of Jim, an older service user, who had alcohol problems. In normal circumstances he managed quite well, but on occasion he went out at night to the local pub, got drunk and could not find his way back home, sleeping rough in the local park. He was not considered a complex case but he did present the occasional risk to himself and others. In relation to eligibility criteria, he would not be considered as a sufficiently high priority for services, even though he had periodic lapses where his level of need was much more intense. With winter approaching, his social worker was increasingly concerned for his safety if he slept out in cold weather and, additionally, was worried that Jim could easily be a target for anti-social behaviour.

The above dilemmas related to decisions that social workers have to make on a regular basis; indeed, the continued existence of eligibility criteria means that they remain relevant as we move from community care to personalisation. In fact, it could be suggested that all of them are particularly relevant to the core tenets of personalisation – choice, prevention and early intervention. If social workers were to adopt a procedurally dominated approach to assessment in every case the outcomes could easily have been against the best interests of the service users. For example, Mrs Jones' distress at the state of her house is likely to worsen without some support. In a more responsive model of assessment, a number of additional factors have to be taken into account. The main elements for consideration in decision making in this context can be isolated as interpretations of the following:

- risk and frailty;
- the rights of users and carers;
- need in a climate of rationed resources;
- the duties and powers of local authorities in relation to eligibility criteria;
- the extent of continued professional support, that is, the social work role;
- the wider role of communities and community involvement;
- ways of working 'upstream' to address potential problems/problems in their early stages, rather than solely 'downstream' in crises (Smale et al., 2000);
- the potential for strengthening the voices of service users themselves (Postle and Beresford, 2007).

While the role of the social worker is circumscribed by management, there remains an element of decision making that relates to professional discretion and the personal values that the practitioner brings to the decision-making process (Gorman et al., 1996; Evans, 2013). However, the procedurally dictated approaches to assessment promoted by community care militate against professionals' ability to exercise their discretion; we do not see this as likely to change significantly under personalisation.

If social workers are to prove able to hold on to their professional identity, a number of issues need to be identified. For example, the personal orientation of the social workers seeking a satisfactory resolution in each of the above examples is critical (Stevenson and Parsloe, 1993). A variety of forces could affect decision-making outcomes, including the practitioner's family background and early socialisation, their education, the influences of religion, politics and ideology, as well as the continuing changing values of society. It could be argued that under community care agencies have constrained and even eroded professional values, replacing them with technical and procedural decision-making practice; indeed, this is one of the hallmarks of managerialism. However it may also be the case that the 'community care revolution' exposed some of the processes involved in decisions about eligibility that had remained largely unexamined and unchallenged because of the power of authority vested in the professional 'to make the right decisions'. The examples we have given could have afforded an opportunity for social workers to humanise systems that were often bewildering to people on the receiving end; an equivalent possibility is that social workers could have acted to follow rules that were the opposite of humanising. It might have been impossible for those making decisions about who gets what service to be 'neutral', but equally it could have been possible to make appropriate decisions based on ethical principles (see Chapters Eight and Nine).

Although the possibilities for a more inclusive form of assessment and decision making clearly did exist under community care, we argue that practice became increasingly reductionist, due to the spiralling pressures on social workers in particular and the system in general. While we do not wholeheartedly embrace notions, commonly part of official rhetoric when the shift towards personalisation was first mooted, that community care 'failed', there are, perhaps inevitably, elements of 'failure' built into a system that had cash savings at its heart. In many ways, the policy achieved what was intended: effective management of the out-of-control Social Security budget, and the insulation of government from the effects of cost cutting. However, the impact of community care from the perspective of assessment and decision making was often not in the best interests of services users – as such it arguably did not meet the principled goals enshrined in the original policy, notably the greater empowerment of users and carers. In all of the examples above, it is possible to see how actions could be taken that would be more focused on the protection of the organisation and its budget than the interests of the service user, even if elements of preventative work, such as for Mrs Jones, might have been more beneficial all round in the long run (Clark et al., 1998). In practice, it is quite probable that these agency-focused 'solutions' would have been the outcome. The next section will explore the extent to which the new system of personalisation has made it more likely that the interests of users and carers have been given priority.

Assessment compared and contrasted with self-assessment

In our view, there is a continuity from community care to personalisation, as far as assessment and decision making is concerned. Many of the issues we have raised in the previous section would still apply. In addition, there are a number of concerns that are specific to personalisation. For example, we believe that alongside the assessment process being both undervalued and misunderstood in social work generally, the particular emphasis on self-assessment in personalisation downplays the potential role of social workers' professional assessment. Two problems derive from this emphasis. The first concerns the assumption that all service users have both sufficient insight into their circumstances and adequate knowledge about feasible ways of addressing their difficulties to be able to assess accurately. While this is doubtless true for many adults needing social care, there are limits on many people's capacity to undertake full self-assessment if they have significant cognitive impairment, either through dementia, severe learning disability or acute mental ill-health. As we have argued, the numbers of people with dementia is increasing and will inevitably increase significantly in years to come as our population ages. The second problem lies in recognition of possible conflicts of interest between users and carers, although these groups of people are conjoined as 'experts and care partners', respectively (HM Government, 2007: 4). It is accepted that there will be circumstances in which the perspectives of user and carer may be in conflict; such as concerning a partner's need for a break from their caring/supporting role and what might be the best way of facilitating this, and that some external bodies, potentially social workers, may need to be involved in resolving such conflict. However, given the focus on self-assessment and the absence of skilful social work assessment, how will such conflicts be identified, never mind resolved?

We have noted that the change to personalisation was predicated upon the presumed 'failure' of community care. It was suggested that placing the service user at the centre of the process would resolve the concerns that were being expressed. As has been outlined in numerous sources, the development of personalisation has been problematic on many counts (Clements, 2008; Lymbery, 2010; Needham, 2011; Spicker, 2013), but for this chapter it is the way in which assessment has developed that concerns us. There are two particular manifestations of this that present a range of problems – the introduction of self-assessment and the development of RAS.

The notion of self-assessment was highlighted as part of the early development of personalisation (Clements, 2008). It was argued that servicer users were the best judges of their requirements in relation to social care, and that they therefore should become central to the process of personalisation (HM Government, 2007). Clearly, from everything we have said earlier in this chapter about the exchange model of assessment (Smale et al., 1993), this is a view that we would, as far as possible, endorse. However, it was quickly recognised that simply constructing processes whereby people assessed their own needs ran the risk of contravening the legislative requirement for local authorities to carry out assessments (Clements and Thompson, 2011). Consequently, the language changed to reflect the legal position more accurately, with authorities creating discourses around 'supported assessment' or 'supported self-assessment'.

If we look back at the history of personalisation, discussed in Chapter Three, we see that its origins began with direct payments, a policy generated by pressure from disabled people themselves. An example of a group of disability activists was the Hampshire Coalition of Disabled People, who put pressure on their local authority to devise a direct payment scheme (Self-Operated Care Scheme [SOCS]). This scheme was a forerunner to direct payments, and was operated by the Hampshire Centre for Independent Living (HCIL). It clearly demonstrated that disabled people were easily capable of assessing their own needs (see Beresford and Carr,

2012). However, there are three factors that need to be taken into account. First, the responsibility for assessments in social care rests, under law, with the local authority (Clements and Thompson, 2011), and cannot therefore be delegated to service users directly. Second, since circumstances are very different once the rationing role of assessment is factored in to the equation, particularly in a financial climate that is severely restricted (Brookes et al., 2013), the role of an assessment is often to judge the extent to which an individual should receive a service – a judgement that is exercised in relation to government guidance about eligibility criteria (DH, 2010a). It would clearly be impossible for any given service user to accommodate this. Finally, as we explained in looking at the exchange model of assessment (Smale et al., 1993), while people may well be experts in assessing their own needs and having a very good idea of how these can be met, the social worker can bring her/his expertise to the situation in many ways (Smale et al., 2000). This would, of course, include the need to explain financial constraints and also, importantly, rights of redress and channels for action (McDonald, 1997; Postle and Beresford, 2007).

Perhaps the most difficult problem to beset the principles of self-assessment is, as we outlined at the start of this section, a recognition of the cognitive problems experienced by many people who would be defined as eligible for social care assistance. As has been pointed out earlier (see Chapter Five), these will not be the people most able to act as self-actualising consumers. Of course, this could be used as an argument that qualified social workers should remain actively involved in the assessment process. However, as we have previously noted, there have long been suggestions that social workers should not be engaged in assessment activity, but put their talents to other uses such as advocacy and brokerage (ODI, 2008). As a consequence, qualified social workers have often not been involved even in complex cases, for example where there may be a significant level of cognitive impairment, serious safeguarding issues that are not recognised as such by the service user or direct conflict of interest between users and carers (Lymbery and Morley, 2012). As we have previously argued (Lymbery and Postle, 2010) and the earlier part of this chapter details, good assessment is the foundation of appropriate social care: it is therefore vital that it be as accurate and as sensitive a process as possible. Of course there are problems for local authorities in seeking to achieve this, given the resource constraints currently experienced within local government. However, there remains a legislative responsibility for them to ensure that their services are appropriate in relation to need – limitations of resources cannot determine what each individual receives (Clements and Thompson, 2011).

The second level of problem refers to the increasing numbers of local authorities that are using variants of an RAS to determine eligibility. Here, assessments are carried out through completion of prescribed pro-formas, where 'the multiple choice nature of the questionnaires currently in use is a response to the perceived need to produce a set of standardised answers to generate points for the purposes of resource allocation' (Clements and Thompson, 2011: 77). Unfortunately, this repeats the sorts of concern expressed by social workers under community care

(Postle, 1999). However, there is a striking key difference: such approaches appear no longer to require skilled social work involvement to complete, although this was not the intention when the policy was first conceived. Without such an involvement the legislative basis of social care appears to be compromised. Because there is no longer any requirement that a skilled social care professional should be engaged in assessments, it has been defined as a process through which need is fully commodified, in line with other neoliberal manoeuvres (Series and Clements, 2013).

This would matter less if the outcomes of the RAS were accurate, and reflected a sophisticated perception of the service user's circumstances. Concerns with its bureaucratic nature in the process of implementation have been expressed for several years (Boxall et al., 2009); these seem to be hardening (Duffy, 2014b). In addition, there are considerable discrepancies between the indicative budget as defined by the RAS and the actual allocation (Series and Clements, 2013), doubtless affected by the savings that local authorities are currently having to make (Duffy, 2013). As a consequence, there are concerns that the principles of personalisation are being sacrificed, and – for many people at least – the new watchword is abandonment (Duffy, 2014b). That such a critique comes from someone who was closely associated with early moves towards personalisation renders it particularly worrying.

If we start from the premise that many people eligible for care services require the assistance of a skilled assessment both to define what they need and to enable them to argue for a preferred outcome, there are two key things that will make a difference to the current lamentable state of affairs. First, the financing of adult social care seriously needs to be increased to adequate levels. It is worth remembering that, even in times of relative plenty, it was argued that substantial investment was needed just to bring about modest improvements in the quality of care (Wanless, 2006). Since the formation of the Conservative/Liberal Democrat coalition government in 2010, the two areas of service that represent over 50% of the cuts that the government is making fall in two areas – local government and benefits (Duffy, 2013). As a consequence, the weight of the cuts falls particularly on people in poverty, disabled people and those in receipt of social care (Duffy, 2013). This, of course, gives the lie to the Chancellor of the Exchequer, George Osborne's, words which we quoted earlier that 'We are all in this together'! Given that, in the Prime Minister David Cameron's words, 'we are a wealthy country and we have taken good care of our public finances' (Wintour and Booth, 2014), and there is apparently both reason and resources to increase the allocation, it is surprising that such arguments appear to have little traction. Possibly this is because the core public belief remains that local government – through which most care budgets are organised – is wasteful and bureaucratic.

Second, we need to ensure that there are professional social workers able to lead the most vulnerable people through the challenging labyrinth of social care assessment and provision. For the reasons discussed earlier in this chapter, this is a complex task and the advantages of social work involvement need to be loudly promoted. While there is a range of potential areas for social work involvement (Milne et al., 2014), full engagement at the point of assessment is particularly vital as it is from this point that the rest of the options flow. In addition, it is important not just to see this in economic terms – there are also vital moral, legal and professional considerations to take into account (Milne et al., 2014). Fundamentally, it can also be a false economy to ignore the importance of professional assessment because there is always a risk that, if someone's needs are not adequately met, they will, sooner or later, return for further help (Postle, 1999).

It is perhaps the moral argument that holds most force for us. From the mindset of two long-time social workers, academics and writers, it is frankly astonishing that the paucity of resources for the people who may be the most vulnerable and disadvantaged in society is not popularly regarded as a national scandal. Whenever failings do emerge – as in the case of Winterbourne View or in another Panorama exposé *Behind Closed Doors: Elderly Care Exposed* – they tend to be treated as the regrettable by-product of poor regulation and management rather than as inevitable outcomes of the funding choices that have been made. In fact, at the time of writing this book, in June 2014, we are hearing more details of yet another care home scandal, this time at Orchid View in West Sussex (BBC, 2014b). One relative, speaking when this scandal first hit the headlines, described such care homes as treating residents as 'cash machines' for the companies who run them and this epitomises the point we make here (BBC, 2014b). In addition, there is rarely any discussion of the malign consequences of the wholesale privatisation of adult care services (Scourfield, 2007a: 2012), even though this manifestly contributes to the problem. Indeed, the Orchid View home was operated by Southern Cross, whose financial problems created a major problem in the care industry in 2011; it has been suggested – by more temperate commentators than us! – that the financial strategy of the organisation created the conditions for death at Orchid View (Gentleman, 2014).

Conclusion

There are a number of propositions that arise out of what we have discussed here. For example, we agree that service users should, wherever possible, have the opportunity to assess their own needs and that professionals should be facilitating this. Indeed, there is some evidence to suggest that models of 'co-production' might improve services and outcomes (Needham and Carr, 2009). However, we also argue that more consideration should be given to the added value that social work assessment could provide, particularly the reality that such assessment may be needed to identify, and then work to resolve, problems. Reductionist, procedural (Smale et al., 2000) approaches to assessment that have prevailed in community care have obviated consideration of the valid notion that assessment should be based on the exchange of expertise between the service user (and her/his network) as an expert in her/his own life and a professional social worker, with the latter acting directly on behalf of the former. This would also ensure that the elitist critique of professions and professionals – which appears to underpin much of the government's thinking – has no purchase.

In addition, there is an interesting observation from research (Gorman, 1999) that users of services may be unaware of the significance of who their social worker is and how s/he represents their case when resources are allocated. There is a view expressed by social workers that users don't realise how important it is for them who is tasked with representing their interests. Social workers have also expressed concern about the internal battles that they had to engage in to get services for people they worked with; indeed, a 'pushy' social worker may be successful in accessing more services. Underlying this view is the prime role of the social worker as an advocate for the service user – a position we explore further in Chapter Eight. Clearly, there is a conflict between the advocacy role and the essential task of a social worker in adult social care – the gatekeeper of resources. However, advocacy has long been a role traditionally accepted as part of social work theory, training and practice (Brandon and Brandon, 2002).

In carrying out assessment tasks, therefore, social workers should not see themselves as neutrally seeking to find some 'objective' truth about a service user's life and needs. Rather they should construct themselves as morally engaged (Clark, 2006), seeking to respond to that individual's unique set of circumstances in such a way that the service user both feels valued by the intervention and that it is successful in securing vital and much-needed resources. However, this pitches each practitioner into the zero-sum paradox of contemporary adult social care. Given that the resource base is inadequate, successful arguments that one person should be allocated adequate budgets to meet need may often imply that others will be unable to secure the resources that would be equally important in their specific case. Such a dilemma is complex to resolve, but central to the experience of any given social worker in adult social care. As a result, it feeds directly into the following chapter, which considers the importance of social work values, and how essential it is for a practitioner to operate in the full awareness and understanding of them.

EIGHT

Reasserting the importance of social work values

Introduction

In seeking to make the argument that social work should be more central to personalisation we are aware that there are numerous hurdles to overcome. As we have noted in previous chapters, circumstances have not been supportive of such a move. We have traced the gradual deprofessionalisation of the social work task in adult social care back to the days of community care, with its emphasis on rationing resources. In addition, we have charted how the financial basis of adult social care has become increasingly constrained, with clear temptations to replace social workers with less costly unqualified practitioners (a process which can also be traced back to community care: Postle, 1999). What arguments, then, can we make to justify our call for an enhanced role for social workers in the policy of personalisation?

The starting point for this is to reflect on the *Code of Ethics for Social Workers* (BASW, 2012), as this contains a number of directives that are pertinent for social work and personalisation, particularly in the context of austerity. These need to be read in conjunction with the Health Care Professions Council (HCPC) documents that focus on standards of conduct of registered professionals (HCPC, 2007) and the standards of proficiency that social workers are required to exhibit (HCPC, 2012), alongside The College of Social Work's *Professional Capabilities Framework* (TCSW, 2013). There are three core ethical principles that social workers need to uphold, each of which is applicable to the context of personalisation, albeit in different ways. In this chapter we will examine two of these: the third – along with a set of ethical practice principles – will feature strongly in Chapter Nine. The first of the core ethical principles is the idea of 'human rights', which contains five elements:

- Upholding and promoting human dignity and well-being.
- Respecting the right to self-determination.
- Promoting the right to participation.
- Treating each person as a whole.
- Identifying and developing strengths. (BASW, 2012: 8)

These injunctions coincide neatly with the ethos of personalisation, as well as conveying the sense that social workers need to work to engage with service users in different ways in order to secure the changes that are desired (Lymbery, 2001; Healy and Meagher, 2004; Postle and Beresford, 2007), further highlighting the need for flexibility in their practice. They also are central to some visions of the way in which social work should construct its entire approach (Ife, 2012). While some of the concepts – for example advocacy and empowerment – can be used simply to ensure that people are enabled to secure an appropriate share of resources, there is also an underpinning element of social justice that attaches to them. While empowerment is not a zero-sum game, as we will argue, there is little doubt that its effective introduction does change the political balance between service users and the welfare system. As such, for empowerment to be effective it has to be about both human rights *and* social justice.

The second set of ideals comes together around the notion of social justice. These are arguably more contentious, as they cast a social worker into a different, potentially more confrontational, role in relation to society in general. This is encapsulated in the following statement:

> Social workers have a responsibility to promote social justice, in relation to society generally, and in relation to the people with whom they work. (BASW, 2012: 9)

Once more, this principle has five elements, which are:

- Challenging discrimination
- Recognising diversity
- Distributing resources
- Challenging unjust policies and practices
- Working in solidarity (BASW, 2012: 9)

As we will discuss further in the second part of the chapter, it is the fourth and fifth of these aspects that represent the most difficult challenge for social workers. This is particularly accentuated by the experiences of many service users that the forms of intervention that are open to them have been both paternalistic and patronising (Postle and Beresford, 2007). Consequently, forms of participatory democracy need to be established, to ensure that people feel included within the political processes that shape their lives (Blaug, 2002). It is noteworthy that, despite the rhetoric that apparently champions greater service user involvement in social care, there has been no recognition of the role that social workers can play in supporting this development (Postle and Beresford, 2007).

It is also worth noting that the principles of human rights and social justice are a core part of the international definition of social work:

> Social work is a practice-based profession and an academic discipline that promotes social change and development, social cohesion, and the empowerment and liberation of people. *Principles of social justice,*

> human rights, collective responsibility and respect for diversities are central to
> social work ... (IFSW, 2014; emphasis added)

While it is never easy to ensure that an international definition has direct applicability to each country, the final sentence is clear and unambiguous. Consequently, there are obligations placed on social workers to ensure that human rights and social justice become central to their practice.

This chapter is organised into three distinct parts. In the first, we focus on the importance of the 'relationship' to social work, arguing that this is the basis for all successful interventions in people's lives. In the second section we make the connection between this and the various elements of the ethical commitment to human rights. In the final section we explore the difficult terrain of social justice, particularly those elements that are less comfortable for governments and employers. We suggest that it is in this area where the true character of social work can be found.

The nature of the relationship

It seems to us that it is neither possible to uphold an individual's human rights nor to promote social justice on their behalf in the context of adult social care without the establishment of a productive relationship between social workers and service users. However, we do not advocate a return to forms of social work that are not politically engaged, as was often the case when relationship-based social work was promoted several decades ago (Cooper, 2010). Indeed, as the British Association of Social Workers (BASW) *Code of Ethics* makes clear, social workers need to focus on issues of social justice, which automatically pulls social work into a more political dimension. At the same time, we recognise that there needs to be a form of practice that focuses directly on the people who require intervention, and their immediate needs. This implies finding a way to bring two competing visions of social work – relationship-based and radical respectively – together into a unified whole (Lymbery, 2013).

The significance of the relationship to social work has been argued for many decades (Biestek, 1961). However, more recently some in the social work profession have advocated a renewed focus on the relationship, alongside other elements of the role (see, for example, Jones, 2014). In addition, in recent years the service user movement has recognised that the relationship is vital in enabling people to achieve their fullest potential; given what we have argued through this book, this is a perspective that carries particular weight. When the service user-oriented literature is scrutinised this becomes clear: the nature of the relationship that social workers are able to develop is generally cited as highly significant (Doel, 2010). The following quotation makes this absolutely clear:

> Service users stress that they want workers who truly listen to them,
> who treat them with equality and respect, who value and understand

diversity, who show empathy and warmth towards them, are reliable, well-informed and understand the barriers that face them, and work with them to challenge such barriers. *They consistently talk about the key human qualities they value in social workers as well as their skills.* (Beresford, 2008: 86; emphasis added)

The highlighted sentence at the end of the quotation is particularly noteworthy. If a social worker is able to act in accordance with these requirements then s/he will establish a secure base to ensure that the principles of human rights and social justice are evident in practice. It is important to be reminded that the practice of social work is therefore much more than the competent delivery of a set of standardised policies and procedures (Clark, 2006). Indeed, as Bisman (2004: 115) has put it, 'without values and morality, what good is the knowledge attained and the skills used by social workers?' In advocating a return to relationship-*based* practice, it is important to draw a distinction between this and relationship-*focused* social work (Doel, 2010); we are not suggesting that the relationship itself should be the focus of change, rather that it is through the quality of the relationship that change can be achieved. This represents the core of a social worker's professional capabilities and not simply an optional extra.

As we have noted in previous chapters, this implies a different form of professional relationship than the one that has traditionally existed. We suggest that a social worker needs to establish a connection with a service user that is based on a sense of common humanity (Gosling and Martin, 2012) and which is substantially different from the focus on separation and difference that is more typical of traditional professions (O'Leary et al., 2012). This would be the main way in which the inequalities of power that exist between social workers and service users can be addressed. At the same time, it would contribute to a general sense that any perceived irrelevance of social workers to the lives of people with disabilities could change (Harris and Roulstone, 2011).

The next section highlights a number of specific issues that have become recognised as social work values, but which derive particularly from the human rights perspective. Among these we focus particularly on advocacy and empowerment.

Human rights: advocacy and empowerment

There is little doubt that the values associated with human rights remain significant to social workers in adult care, and that many of them also specifically relate to the equalising of power relations. As we noted earlier, the BASW *Code of Ethics* (BASW, 2012), contained five elements, which closely resemble the traditional characteristics of social work (see, for example, Biestek, 1961). Consequently, in principle, they should readily be adopted by social workers. However, some of the details that relate to how social workers should carry these out are a little more problematic. For example, if we examine element three, 'Promoting the right to participation', the specific detail is as follows:

> Social workers should promote the full involvement and participation of people using their services in ways that enable them to be empowered in all aspects of decisions and actions affecting their lives. (BASW, 2012: 8)

While this appears clear, the notion of empowerment that underpins it is not at all straightforward, as we explore below (see also Postle and Beresford, 2007).

The five elements listed at the start of this chapter (BASW, 2012: 18) are also very similar to those that are often framed as the core fundamentals of personalisation. However, their ideological sources are very different; if we consider empowerment, for example, we can see that it has its roots in the activist movement, but is now also promoted as a key plank in the marketisation of social welfare (Askheim, 2003), as we outlined in Chapter Four. This implies that a substantial rethinking of the essential meaning of the term has taken place. A similar history can be seen in relation to advocacy. In both cases, it is clear that some of the original oppositional content of the concepts has been leached out leaving, as with assessment, a simulacrum of the original.

To expand on this a little, we first have to acknowledge that the precise meaning of advocacy is more complex than is often understood. There are a number of different forms of advocacy (Brandon and Brandon, 2002), yet the differences between them are not often fully recognised and understood. Consequently, for many, the role of advocate has substantive meaning while for others it has become more of a myth. As the term is currently understood, there are two main forms of advocacy. The first of these stems from a legalistic position, which thinks of advocacy as speaking out in support of something. For example, in the US judicial system an advocate is required to do this in court. The second refers to the practice of supporting someone to make their voice heard, which has much more currency within the social care world. If we think about the second of these interpretations, it can be deployed in two different ways. The first of these relates to enabling an individual or groups to get their fair share of existing resources: this might be referred to as a conservative/individualistic vision and seems to be the interpretation that most fits with the official vision of personalisation. The second betrays a more politicised conception, as it refers to the process of supporting people to argue for their rights – which may well involve arguing for what does not currently exist. It is therefore important to understand what the different perceptions are of 'advocacy' when it is used, as they fundamentally change its meaning.

If we expand on the final point above, standing up for service users' rights may involve conflict with a range of other professionals as well as with wider social systems or even with one's own employer, as the following quotes from the first edition of this text make clear (Gorman and Postle, 2003):

'The skill is working with people, it's advocating on their behalf, it's advocating to get them benefits or whatever that they deserve.'

However, there is a reverse side to this sort of action as another respondent indicated:

'The state has never liked us as advocates, like most of us I have had my share of run-ins with Social Security and Housing.'

As we can see, advocacy may make social workers unpopular with other professionals or even their own employers, and they may be seen as irritants within the world of social care. However, effectively carrying out an advocacy role is a core part of what a social worker is required to do (Postle, 2007). Brandon and Brandon (2002) have concluded that a key ingredient of the advocacy process lies in the accomplishment of tasks, defined by the service user. The fact that these tasks are constructed by any given service user is critical to an understanding of the fullest potential of advocacy in relation to human rights. It implies that the process should not be limited to the more conservative aspects of the task, as the above quotations make clear. It can – and arguably should – involve the social worker in conflicts with other parts of the system, whether welfare benefits, health or housing.

The need to be responsive to the needs of others in general, which is at the heart of advocacy, is tied up with the art of helping (Shakespeare, 2000). Emotional labour, responsiveness to other human beings in the context of work, is an interesting concept when applied to the role of the social worker in adult social care, where the procedural requirements of the role often force the worker to behave in a regulated and often unreflecting and even insensitive way. The circumscription of the role through the use of administrative forms and procedures and the application of imposed eligibility criteria, coupled with the lack of importance given to the development of personal relationships, have all affected the emotional labour of the social worker. It has reduced the effectiveness of the worker's connection to the service user, relegating the social worker to being the person who defines need via a prescribed, procedural assessment process (Gorman, 2000). However, it remains vital to protect and sustain this emotional labour, as it is crucial to the goal of assisting people to attain the fullest measure of control over their lives.

Helping people to achieve control over their lives has often been termed 'empowerment'; while acknowledging that it is a term which has been reduced to jargon through over-use and lack of clarity, Croft and Beresford explain that:

For service users, empowerment means challenging their disempowerment, having more control over their lives, being able to influence others and bring about change. (2000: 116)

People who have experienced paternalistic, patronising and clearly disempowering social work provision (Oliver, 1996: Shakespeare, 2000) leave their readers in no doubt that this serves only to reinforce notions of dependency. As Shakespeare has observed:

> The institutionalisation of helping … often fails those who have a right to expect their needs to be met. Alongside the well-known failures of residential care (inflexible routine, lack of choice, dependence on others, lack of privacy) have to be set the failures of empowerment and participation which are clear from evaluations of community care. The current climate for many service users – older people, people with HIV/AIDS, disabled people and people with learning difficulties or mental health problems – is of minimal services and maximal dependency. (2000: 57)

It is important to acknowledge that empowerment is a complex and contested term which, somewhat deceptively, is often used in a non-problematised way, as if its meaning was uncontested and it was an unquestionably positive concept. As Servian (1996) suggests, there is a danger that we all assume we know what empowerment means. In reality, as his research demonstrated, there is little agreement about this. Further, empowerment can be paradoxical in that, in some situations, one person may feel empowered at the expense of another's perceived disempowerment (Servian, 1996). An example of this paradox can be found in Clark and Spafford's work about the extension of the direct payments scheme to older people. They found that, when carers used the scheme as a way to obtain more choice over their caring arrangements (such as by buying respite care), this resulted in a potential reduction in choice for the people for whom they cared (Clark and Spafford, 2001). As in examples given by Servian, this could be seen as empowering carers but at the possible risk of disempowering the people for whom they care. Of course, the reverse outcome can easily be seen if a service user's wishes prevail over those of the carer: in such a case it would be the carer who was disempowered. Under conditions of austerity, the likelihood of such conflicts appears to be increased because the scope for funding imaginative, creative and individual ways to address problems such as a carer's need for respite breaks has been severely curtailed.

Empowerment can then easily be oversimplified, thus rendering the concept empty and meaningless. It can also be used in false notions of 'partnership', disregarding the importance of power imbalances, or taken to mean a process of adaptation to and acceptance of powerlessness (Ferguson and Woodward, 2009). Indeed, the term 'partnership' can also be deployed as another of the 'warmly persuasive' (Williams, 1975) words we noted earlier in Chapter One. It is another term which has appeared both positive and uncomplicated, and – as such – has found its way into much policy guidance. However, in reality there are numerous problems with the concept, particularly in relation to the relationship between social workers and service users. Whereas the term implies notions of equality and power balance, these are often not present in the relationships between social workers and service users (Gosling and Martin, 2012). Indeed, where social workers are involved in the protection of vulnerable people or in statutorily defined work it is hard to construct a sense of equality. We would also add that the inequality inherent in a social worker's role as rationer of restricted resources also militates against notions of partnership (Gorman and Postle, 2003).

There is a risk of becoming so bogged down in debates about the difficulty of defining empowerment that its meaning and importance for service users, highlighted at the start of this chapter, become lost. To summarise, the context in which we are using 'empowerment' involves a shift in the locus of control and monopoly of expertise from professionals to people using services, a position that we have consistently advocated throughout this book. Such a shift needs to happen in ways which challenge inequality, oppression and discrimination in all their multiple forms (Gosling and Martin, 2012). Drawing on Foucault's work, the understanding of empowerment underpinning the discussion throughout this chapter embodies the notion of power as relational and capable of generating resistance, not something fixed which can be given to or shared with another (Foucault, 1984).

It is in trying to grasp Foucault's understandings of power/resistance (never easy, we accept!) that the scale of the misunderstandings about empowerment becomes more evident. All too often we have been marking students' work and read that empowerment is something that can be done for others by one's actions: 'I empowered Mrs Smith by arranging meals-on-wheels', for example. In addition, because social workers are supposed to act in empowering ways, there is a tendency to describe any action as empowering, even when this seems unlikely! By contrast, some students/professionals may have a problem with the concept of empowerment, as they could equate the empowerment of a service user with the disempowerment of a professional. This is what we referred to in Chapter Seven when outlining misunderstandings about the assessment models (point 5 refers: p.107). This understanding seems to assume that power is a finite quality, where the ability of one person to assume a greater level of power automatically leads to the reduction in the power of another. It is important to challenge this zero-sum notion: in reality, enabling service users to exercise more power over their lives is a legitimate goal for all social work, and power should not be perceived as a finite attribute. Enhancing the power of service users does not necessarily mean that social workers have less. It is also important to recognise that, as an ethical principle, social workers should not be seeking power for its own sake. The primary purpose of the power that social workers have vested in them is to improve the lot of service users, many of whom have the least amount of power within society. It is also important to grasp the concept that 'power' is not an automatically negative attribute; there are positive ways in which power can be used – the refusal to accept that there are 'good' ways to exercise power as well as 'bad' (Gosling and Martin, 2012) would be a critical flaw for social workers.

Of course, it is also important to consider power in connection to the relationship between a social worker and her/his employing organisation. Too often, for reasons that we outlined in Chapter Four, social workers have not been sufficiently empowered by their own managers and employers to feel confident in acting in genuinely empowering ways with service users. Indeed, when he presented the models in a public lecture in 1992, Gerry Smale posed a crucial question, 'Can we expect workers to empower others if they do not feel empowered themselves?' (Social Work Studies, University of Southampton, 2003). In order to accomplish empowerment, practitioners need to feel both valued and supported. They should have solid reasons for acting in particular ways, and need to be able to justify any action taken. It remains important to ensure that there is proper managerial support for any action that is proposed; in this context it is vital to recognise that, because many social work managers share the same professional background as their workers, they are likely (hopefully!) to be convinced by arguments that reflect social work values and ethics (Lymbery, 2004). In addition, workers need to ensure that they are offered, and use, good quality supervision, as this can help to ensure that judgements remain sharp (Hawkins and Shohet, 2006).

Social justice: a radical vision

A commitment to the principles of social justice is a core element of the vision of personalisation that was first adopted by service users (Duffy, 2010). As we have previously indicated, the conception of personalisation – originating in direct payments schemes – that was adopted by groups of service users and disabled people was democratic; however, its implementation has been much more in accordance with consumerist approaches. There is a clear dichotomy between these two approaches as Beresford (2012: 25) points out:

> the managerialist/consumerist approach ... has its origins in the market-led politics of the New Right, and the democratic or emancipatory approach advanced by the disabled people's and service users' movements and their supporters ... is grounded in a commitment to collective self-advocacy ...

As a result, implementing some of the tenets of social work's *Code of Ethics* (BASW, 2012) that relate to social justice is distinctly tricky, particularly when the more consumerist, marketised vision of personalisation is considered. The first two points, 'challenging discrimination' and 'recognising diversity' are relatively unproblematic as each of them has been a core element of social work's value base for a long time (Beckett and Maynard, 2012). As such, these elements can readily be incorporated into a social worker's repertoire: the challenges that are implied may be problematic, but do not address the issue of the adequacy of resources which is, as we have indicated throughout, the key problem confronting the implementation of personalisation. In this context, the third point, 'distributing resources', assumes an inevitably awkward character.

It is the two final points, 'challenging unjust practices' and 'working in solidarity' that are particularly significant in that they require social workers to adopt positions that would unquestionably be challenging, particularly in times of austerity. For example, in the words of the fourth element, challenging unjust practices entails the following actions:

> Social workers have a duty to bring to the attention of their employers, policy makers, politicians and the general public situations where resources are inadequate or where distribution of resources, policies and practice are oppressive, unfair, harmful or illegal. (BASW, 2012: 9)

We will go on to explore the implications of this a little later in the chapter. At the same time, we will explore the ramifications of the requirement for social workers to act in solidarity with others:

> Social workers, individually, collectively and with others have a duty to challenge social conditions that contribute to social exclusion, stigmatisation or subjugation, and work towards an inclusive society. (BASW, 2012: 9)

These points remind us of the radical side of social work's history, where attention was paid to collective and collaborative issues, rather than the individual response to need associated with recent and current practice. There is a long history of social work's engagement with such issues, even going back to the early work of the Settlement movement in the late 19th century (Barnett and Barnett, 1915). Although this was not a radical movement in the terms that we would currently understand it, it was a reaction against the individualistic approach of the early social work pioneers of the Charity Organisation Society (Jordan, 1984). A similar interpretation can be placed on the response of Barbara Wootton (1959) to the individualistic notions then current in writings about social work (see, for example, Younghusband, 1955) and later the Barclay Report (1982), which argued for more emphasis on community-based work which could address wider problems than just those of individuals.

However, it was not until some years after the earlier texts mentioned that this thinking coalesced into what has become known as radical social work. The first British text on this theme was published in the mid 1970s (Bailey and Brake, 1975); it paved the way for a succession of writings that lead into the present day (see, for example, Ferguson and Woodward, 2009). While this movement has not succeeded in changing the way in which practice is perceived, it seems that these two elements of the *Code of Ethics* are heavily influenced by radical thinking. As such, it is important to be clear about some of the main elements of radical thought. A summary of what the radical movement believes can be extracted from the Case Con Manifesto which argued for the need for social workers to change society in order to tackle the fundamental causes of people's problems, rather than working in individualistic ways:

1. The problems faced by service users and consequently social workers derive from the capitalist structure of society and the place of welfare within it: effective practice must stem from an understanding of how the welfare state has developed, and the pressures to which it is subject.
2. The principle of universal entitlement to welfare services has been gradually eroded in the post-war period, and responsibility for responding to social problems has transferred from the state to families.
3. One of the functions of social work has been to divert attention from the real causes of poverty, which are primarily economic in their origin.
4. Social work cannot, in itself, resolve the basic inadequacies and inequalities of society. (adapted from the Case Con Manifesto, 1975)

The third of these points is particularly important, in that it argues that social work has obscured the primary causes of poverty; however, the actions suggested by the wording of elements 4 and 5 of the *Code of Ethics* are focused on highlighting the economic basis of the problems encountered by many service users.

In many ways, a lot of the arguments presented in the mid 1970s have even greater force today. The austerity programme of the Conservative/Liberal Democrat coalition government has hugely increased pressures on welfare services, given the way in which the government has focused on local government and the benefits budget to bear the brunt of its cuts (Duffy, 2013). Because of this, and despite the 'there is no alternative' rhetoric of the government, it is important for all social workers to recognise that the way in which public finances are organised is not inevitable, but the outcome of political choices (Lymbery, 2014c). Given a growing awareness of the persistence of high levels of social inequality (Dorling, 2011) alongside a recognition that more equitable societies perform better than those that are unequal (Wilkinson and Pickett, 2009), it is vital for social workers to concentrate their efforts on the elements of the ethical base that focuses on social justice. Since the austerity process most affects the very people at whom the policy of personalisation is directed this is particularly important. It is important that there is a grassroots social work pressure group, the Social Work Action Network (SWAN), whose mission is to highlight the inequities that exist within society, and which affect both those who use services and the social workers employed to respond to them:

> SWAN is a network of social work practitioners, academics, students and social welfare service users united in their concern that social work activity is being undermined by managerialism and marketisation, by the stigmatisation of service users and by welfare cuts and restrictions. (SWAN, n.d.)

It is vital that social workers recover the will to think and act politically in relation to the world as they experience it. In addition, acting in this way is clearly in accordance with the original impetus from the disability/service user movement, whose members have long argued for greater service user involvement (Glasby and Littlechild, 2009; Beresford, 2012; Glasby, 2014; Lymbery, 2014a). Certainly, the policy of personalisation would not exist were it not for the original action (such as that referred to in Chapter Seven) of these people in receipt of, or eligible for, care services; even though their original ideas have subsequently been co-opted – and arguably corrupted – by the official variant (Roulstone and Morgan, 2009). If we accept that the original service user-based values of the policy are worth defending, the ethical code for social workers ought to be invaluable in providing the support and guidance that will enable people to make the policy a reality (Beresford, 2008). This is particularly important given the contention about the way in which the original elements of personalisation became translated into the official policy. Indeed, the following statement – made in relation to the service user movement more generally – has clear applicability to personalisation:

> it seems evident that what started off as a politicised endeavour by service users who expressly intended to address imbalances in power relations was appropriated and transmuted by the neo-liberal agenda, which essentially *eliminated any reference to power* … (Bezzina, 2014: 48; emphasis added)

The final point is critical; the absence of considerations of power from the implementation of personalisation typifies the superficiality of the official variation of user involvement and its solidification in policy. If we accept, therefore, both that personalisation has become transformed into a policy that is far from the original democratic vision and that the issue of inadequate funding for the policy has become critical, the value position of social workers becomes vital. They are involved in implementing a policy where conflicts over resources are central to its progress. Of course, to act in accordance with the elements of the *Code of Ethics* requires a detailed knowledge of many things, including the resource base for social care and the extent to which it has altered. For example, one of these elements requires social workers to 'ensure that resources at their disposal are distributed fairly, according to need' (BASW, 2012: 9); this cannot be achieved without an understanding about the overall size of the budget. In addition, the *Code of Ethics* also states that social workers should bring inadequacies in the overall budget to the attention of those who can influence matters. Since the primary reason for a resource shortfall relates to government decisions, it seems clear that adhesion to the ethical framework that should guide a social worker will inevitably bring her/him into confrontation with the state.

It goes without saying that such conflicts need to be handled with great care. Many years ago community development workers agonised over the problems that being both 'in and against the state' (LEWRG, 1980) created for them. Given that social work in Britain remains a state-mediated occupation (McDonald et al., 2003) and that the vast majority of social workers in adult social care are employed within local government, this is a key problem once again. We cannot pretend that it is easy to act in accordance with all of the requirements of the *Code of Ethics*, but we have to stress that it is vital to do so. An example of how this might operate is appropriate here, to illustrate both the complexity of the problem and possible ways of resolving it. Readers may want to consider what actions they would take in working with Jacob.

Jacob

Jacob is a 25-year-old black British male. Until one year ago, he lived with his family in a Midlands city. Jacob has a moderate learning disability and Autistic Spectrum Disorder. He has had long-term contact with social services: his care was transferred from children's to adults' services through the 'transitions' process. As a teenager, Jacob became involved with what his mother termed a 'gang' and in the following years was involved in a number of offences. Those working currently with Jacob feel that he was coerced into such activities by his peers, who saw him as an 'easy target' who could be manipulated into compliance. Early this year Jacob assaulted his sister and presented behaviours that indicated a significant deterioration in his mental health. How does a social worker comply with the social justice elements of the *Code of Ethics* in relation to Jacob? (adapted from Lymbery and Morley, 2012)

Our discussion here is limited to the linked issues of the adequacy of resources and social exclusion (for a fuller working out of the practice issues of this case see Lymbery and Morley, 2012). On the first point, the problem of resources is evident here: not only does Jacob have learning disabilities and is located on the Autistic Spectrum, it is highly likely that he has undiagnosed mental health issues. In addition, the problem of social exclusion is also evident: while he may demonstrate improved behaviour patterns when separated from his peers, he has indicated that he has a preference to live in the area with which he is familiar, even though this has also been the location of his more problematic actions.

The starting point for any social worker responding to Jacob's issues has to be professional: what is the most effective way of responding to his complex set of needs? Consideration of resources is secondary at this stage: the first priority is to ensure that Jacob has access to the services that are needed. In this case, there is a range of issues deriving from the wide range of difficulties with which he has to deal. While engaging a response to these from a variety of sources is vital, it will probably be relatively straightforward due to the fact that Jacob has a number of diagnosable conditions. For example, the fact that Jacob is located on the Autistic Spectrum will automatically pull in the expertise of the health service. For this chapter, however, the issue of resources is critical, and the most problematic issue in relation to resources relates to the time of a social worker seeking to put all the aspects of a support plan together. It is by no means certain that a social worker would be allocated to the case (Lymbery and Morley, 2012), despite its complexity. The most intractable area of resource allocation may well therefore be the smallest. The best way of ensuring that social worker time is devoted to this case rests on the professional argument for its necessity – and by arguing that the resource implications that would accompany failure would be much more serious.

Issues relating to 'social exclusion, stigmatisation or subjugation' (BASW, 2012: 9) are highly complex to work out in this case. At one level, if Jacob has the capacity (Johns, 2010) to make decisions about where he lives, it would be relatively straightforward to act in ways that appear to foster his social inclusion. However, the strong suspicion that he had been coerced into offending behaviour by his peers makes it a more complex task to tackle issues of stigmatisation or subjugation. Any decision that is taken about where Jacob lives has to balance the three imperatives – social exclusion, stigmatisation or subjugation – which exist in an uneasy balance and which could readily be in conflict with each other. In addition, there are clear dimensions of risk and safeguarding – of Jacob and others – to be considered. Again, the ongoing role of a supportive social worker is critical to enable Jacob to come to a decision that balances these potentially incompatible principles.

In this case, the additional element of resource that is required is time rather than money: a qualified social worker is more likely to be able to hold the various aspects of Jacob's situation in balance and facilitate an outcome that is acceptable to all parties in general, and Jacob in particular. In other circumstances, the resources that may be needed are more likely to be financial. The same principles hold, however: the first requirement is for the practitioner to make a sound case for a principled course of action, and then be able to support this by reasoned argument. In many such instances, it is the quality of professional engagement that will make the difference between adequate and less acceptable outcomes.

Conclusion

While there are many other ways of configuring a chapter focusing on values, we find the BASW *Code of Ethics* useful for two specific reasons. First, the *Code* is binding on social workers operating in England, and hence has an authoritative status. Second, the *Code* enables us to highlight issues about aspects of social workers' practice that are often downplayed or ignored. It is important that practitioners are enabled to think about their work in context: if the unpalatable reality is a context of austerity, it is vital that social workers recognise the ethical imperatives that might help them to counteract this.

There is little doubt that this could bring social workers into conflict with the organisation within which they work, and also with the wider political context in which the organisation is located (Postle, 2007). It is significant to have strategies to manage these conflicts; they should certainly not be seen as unusual in any way. The first part of such a strategy is to ensure that the work carried out is of the highest quality. Our own experience would suggest that, for example, an assessment that is carried out in a professional manner, following the exchange model outlined in Chapter Seven, and which contains a series of recommendations that are fully supported by the available evidence, is much more likely to achieve support than one which is more shoddily put together or which relies solely on following a procedural model and restricting information to that which fits a prescribed form. In this respect, the quality of a social worker's practice is a critical element. For example, which of these assessments is likely to result in a more suitable and, importantly, more sustainable provision of support for Kim (Table 8.1)?

Table 8.1 Assessing Kim

How professionals see Kim	How family and friends see Kim
'He shows a moderate developmental delay at two years eight months with skills falling a little further behind due to a developmental plateau'	'He has such a great laugh and a lot of energy'
'He is showing a marked developmental regression'	'He tries so hard all the time. He never gives up'
'He has autistic tendencies'	'He communicates so beautifully'

Source: Slightly adapted from Brandon and Hawkes (1998: 23, citing Murray and Penman, 1996).

There are also numerous other areas where social workers can work to ensure that they are able to manage value conflicts (see Postle, 2007). For the purposes of this book, the critical element is to aim to operationalise the more democratic principles of personalisation as a challenge to the managerialist/consumerist version (Beresford, 2012). This necessarily sees social workers as the allies of service users, supporting them to challenge the restrictive forces on their lives and to enhance their capacity-building (Beresford and Croft, 2004; Postle and Beresford, 2007). Once again, if social workers are successful in changing the nature of debate so that the democratic elements of personalisation are in the foreground, they are much more likely to be able to secure support for their position from their managers. It would be hard for managers/budget holders to turn down any approach that is framed within the rhetoric of personalisation, even if that rhetoric has not fully been put into effect (West, 2013). We believe that some organisations are seeking to shift such responsibilities onto social workers; they will need to be extremely cautious about such an action, however, as it may leave them open to a legal challenge which could be extremely costly for them to resolve (Preston-Shoot, 2000).

In the following chapter we will provide examples to justify our position. We will particularly focus on issues relating to 'professional integrity', the third of the principles in the *Code of Ethics* (BASW, 2012). Using a number of case studies, we will endeavour to explore the dimensions of good social work practice, with a particular focus on the ethical obligations of a social worker.

NINE

Issues for practice

Introduction

The purpose of this chapter is to translate the learning from previous chapters into social work practice, with a particular focus on the dimensions of ethical practice. It is clear from what we have written that we regard social work as a 'practical-moral' activity (Parton, 2000), where the meaning of relatively abstract concepts becomes apparent through their translation into action. We intend what we have written to have both an impact on practice and – equally important, perhaps – on the way in which practice is conceptualised. For us, therefore, the test of an appropriate social work theory is the extent to which it can affect practice. A similar point can be applied in relation to values and ethics: the extent to which they can be given practical form is the acid test of their applicability and appropriateness.

Building on this, we wish to focus on the translation of a social worker's ethical obligations into practice. As a result, the first section of the chapter concentrates on the professional requirements of a social worker. We approach this using the ethical practice principles that have been drafted to complement the broad statement of values, which were discussed in Chapter Eight. Following this, we discuss how these ethical requirements can operate in practice, by focusing on a variety of case examples. In particular, we want to emphasise that following the *Code of Ethics* inevitably brings the social worker into the political arena.

Being a professional

In translating the broad parameters of the ethical requirements of social work into practice, it is necessary for all social workers to learn how to act 'professionally'. The British Association of Social Workers (BASW) *Code of Ethics* identifies a number of elements that constitute what is termed 'professional integrity', which combine with the subsequent 'ethical practice principles' to indicate in general terms how a social worker should act:

1. Upholding the values and reputation of the profession
2. Being trustworthy
3. Maintaining professional boundaries
4. Making considered professional judgements
5. Being professionally accountable (BASW, 2012: 10)

The obvious first point to make is that this presents the idea that social work is a profession without any recognition of the controversy that has attended this formulation (see Chapter Six for a fuller discussion); what is held to be crucial is to ensure that social workers act in ways that are consistent with their professional status. As we have argued elsewhere in the book (also see Chapter Six), there have been deprofessionalising influences that have made substantial inroads into social work's ability to claim professional territory in adult social care. However, we believe that there needs to be a reconsideration of social work's orientation and role. This would enable practitioners to use their skills in ways which serve people better than at present. Inevitably, if social workers are to take on a role as a promoter of social justice, this will involve then coming into conflict with their employers at certain times: it is also likely that it will involve an uncomfortable relationship with the forces of the state, as some government policies have a differential impact on disabled people (Duffy, 2013).

What accompanies this acknowledgement of professional status is the expectation of a particular pattern of behaviour, where each social worker is expected to take full responsibility for the actions that s/he carries out. This is encapsulated in the expansion of what being professionally accountable means:

> Social workers should be prepared to account for and justify their judgements and actions to people who use services, to employers and the general public. (BASW, 2012: 10)

Of course, this can be deeply problematic when a social worker is not enabled to act in ways that promote people's human rights, or to enhance social justice. However, the *Code of Ethics* emphasises that social workers have a duty to act in accordance with their professional values and principles, and that employers also have a responsibility to ensure that social workers are provided with the opportunity to do this (BASW, 2012). To emphasis this, 17 ethical practice principles are then listed – all of them starting in the same way: 'social workers should ...'. (There is an interesting level of consistency between this and the regulator's *Standards of Conduct, Performance and Ethics* document, which expresses itself in relation to the idea that a professional 'must' [HCPC, 2007].) However, as a result of this command there is a real danger that the requirements appear as little more than pious injunctions; it is important to put some flesh on the bones so that social workers are enabled to, for example, use 'authority in accordance with human rights principles' (practice principle 6: BASW, 2012: 13). Indeed, some of the actions to which they refer have proved awkward in other fields. For example, while principle 8 refers to the need for social workers to be prepared to blow the whistle on bad practice, experience indicates the problems that tend to occur for whistleblowers in reality (Francis, 2013), highlighting that additional organisational and managerial support needs to be made available to ensure that whistleblowers are not punished for identifying weaknesses (Calcraft, 2007). At the same time, many of the other BASW principles would be recognised as relatively unproblematic aspects of good practice.

An exacting problem for a social worker is to integrate all of these principles into a form of good practice, particularly given the contentious nature of some of them. For instance, it is complex to give practical expression to the abstract themes of human rights and social justice, particularly given that much social policy that affects adult social care appears antithetical to both. As we explore later in the chapter in case study 4, the bedroom tax appears as one such example. There are many things that act against the ability to turn abstract thought into concrete actions. For example, as we indicated in the previous chapter, the notion of empowering people (practice principle 7) becomes complex when seeking to turn it into action, due to the lack of clarity about what the term actually means. In addition, the encouragement to use authority in a way that is compatible with human rights is difficult to put into practice, especially given the difficulties that many social workers often have with the exercise of authority. By contrast, other principles are relatively straightforward both to understand and to implement – for example, practice principle 11 emphasises the need for social workers to maintain clear and accurate records (BASW, 2012: 14). This ought to be a routine element of a social worker's actions and therefore should apply in all cases. There are also many other general injunctions that apply to all of a social worker's practice (practice principles 12–17); as such they should present no particular difficulty in relation to the routines that social workers need to develop.

The following case studies provide a chance to consider the enactment of many of the more complex practice principles. They have been drawn from a variety of types of practice within the overall framework of adult social care. Not all of the examples showcase the same set of principles in equal measure. What we are seeking to illustrate is that, in particular sets of circumstance, different practice principles are particularly relevant. Readers could consider what they believe to be the best course of action, keeping in mind the BASW principles, to be taken in each case.

Case study 1: Leanne Somers

Leanne is a 21-year-old white British woman. She lives and attends college in a Midlands city. She copes very well socially and this can mean that people do not pick up on the level of her learning disability. Until recently, she lived in a council-owned flat with her partner, Sarah; however, this relationship has recently broken down. She describes her family as "nasty", having experienced physical, emotional, financial and sexual abuse from various family members since childhood. In the past she has been placed in mainstream direct access homeless accommodation, where her cognitive impairment has magnified her vulnerability to abuse and bullying. There are also reports of homophobic bullying and vandalism when she lived with Sarah, and a neighbour had reportedly been sexually coercive with Leanne in return for money. At times of crisis, Leanne has increased her alcohol consumption and cannabis use significantly, resulting in increased paranoia and self-harming behaviour. As a result she has been excluded from many services, on the basis of her volatility and occasional reliance on drugs and alcohol. On occasions she has phoned her social worker in the middle of the day, completely drunk and utterly unaware of where she is. Currently she is living in an adult placement scheme; she is positive about this, and the relationship she has developed with her carer, but sees it as a temporary measure and wishes once again to live independently – preferably in the same locality that she inhabited with Sarah. She has become increasingly insistent with this carer that she has the right to live independently and wishes to do this immediately, stating that she will "just go down housing aid and get a flat". (Adapted from Lymbery and Morley, 2012)

Underpinning this case is the issue of capacity and consent, which has become a consistent theme in much adult social care since the passage of the Mental Capacity Act 2005 (Manthorpe et al., 2008). It is arguably more complex in this case than in others, due to the complexity of Leanne's situation, and her ability to apparently cope well socially. This might have the effect of ensuring that her decision making is not subjected to scrutiny, and that her options for living are not fully explored. It is, for example, relatively easy to enable Leanne to live independently, but this could be at a serious risk to her safety and well-being (Lymbery and Morley, 2012). For example, in accomplishing this she would remain acutely vulnerable, both to her immediate family and elements in the wider community, judging from past experiences. A social worker would have to act in accordance with ethical principle 6 – 'using authority in accordance with human rights principles' (BASW, 2012: 13) – in order to reach an outcome that would be best for Leanne. This requires a fine balance between the issues of risk and protection.

There is an important issue of judgement that needs to be addressed here: does Leanne have the capacity to make a decision on where she should live? This is vital because a proper enactment of the Mental Capacity Act 2005 means that an individual who has capacity should not be barred from making unwise decisions (Manthorpe et al., 2008); it is probable that it would be decided that Leanne would have capacity in this respect. Given this, the key element here is the process of guiding Leanne to make decisions which are in her best interests. It would be a denial of the intentions of personalisation, we believe, if somebody such as Leanne were to be left alone to take the consequences of her decisions on the basis that this would be in accordance with the principle of independence. We need to acknowledge that there remains considerable scope for her to be exploited; as a consequence, her maladaptive 'coping' mechanisms (drink, drugs, self-harm) are liable to become even more difficult (Lymbery and Morley, 2012).

Consequently, Leanne urgently needs the benefit of an experienced, knowledgeable social worker to enable her to come to productive decisions. She needs to be persuaded to undertake actions that are in accordance with her best interests; such persuasion is particularly difficult because she is inclined, as she herself puts it, to "fly off the handle" when possibilities are outlined that she cannot immediately support. With time, and the opportunity to consider her options, she is much more likely to make wise decisions. Without time, skill and patience she is unlikely to be able to come to such a positive position. There is no question that the ability to live independently is critical: however, given the circumstances, she needs support to ensure that she can exercise her independence safely and securely.

In addition, Leanne's carer needs support and assistance given the volatility of Leanne's behaviour. If the relationship between Leanne and her carer were to break down the chances of reaching an agreed way forward will be substantially reduced. The opportunities for Leanne to enjoy her independence productively are likely to be enhanced if this can be managed in such a way that it can build upon positive recent experiences, so that it does not revert to previous exploitative scenarios. In the cases of both Leanne and her carer, the relationship-building skills of the social worker will be paramount; as well as reflecting what we consider to be the essence of social work (see Chapter Eight), this also is regarded as a key ethical practice principle: 'Social workers should communicate effectively and work in partnership with individuals, families, groups, communities and other agencies' (BASW, 2012: 12). The capacity of a social worker to accomplish this should have a major bearing on the ability of Leanne to live in a good way independently. In particular any person or organisation who works with Leanne in the future will need to become familiar with the ways in which homophobic bullying is carried out, along with its impact. If this is managed well, accompanied by tight organisational policies, she may be better prepared to combat it.

Case study 2: Thad Bell

> Thad Bell is an 80-year-old man of African-Caribbean origin who lives alone and has no immediate family living in this country. He has recently been discharged from hospital following a fall at his home. He is becoming increasingly physically frail due to arthritis, and has been diagnosed with Alzheimer's disease, leading to increasing problems with his cognitive awareness: however, he does not want to go into residential care. He can still manage some household tasks but has particular difficulty in lifting and carrying; he also needs prompting to carry out many elements of household management. He also needs help with his cleaning and laundry and gets very distressed when his living accommodation is not as clean as he would like it to be. His friend, who visits daily, reports that Mr Bell is getting increasingly depressed because he "needs help in the house". He also suggests that Thad has a very limited social life.

In many ways, Thad Bell's circumstances are quite familiar to a social worker. A majority of people who come to the attention of adult social care services are old, and a significant number of these have dementia (McDonald, 2010). In fact, the population of people with dementia is forecast to increase rapidly towards the middle of this century (Alzheimer's Society, 2007), meaning that the circumstances of people like Thad Bell will become even more common. Given this, it is particularly important that the individuality and personhood of Thad is retained (Kitwood and Bredin, 1992). Our thinking in this respect has been heavily influenced by alternative ways of conceptualising dementia, deriving largely from the work of Tom Kitwood. Kitwood focused particularly on the subjective experience of people with dementia, and argued that the dominant bio-medical paradigm for understanding dementia led to damaging processes of depersonalisation. Consequently, he suggested that the focus of dementia care needed to contribute towards the maintenance of an individual's 'personhood' (Kitwood, 1993).

While Kitwood's work has been criticised from a number of standpoints – for example, that it has little empirical basis (Adams and Bartlett, 2003), and that it underestimates and hence misrepresents the impact of dementia on care-givers (Davis, 2004) – it represents an important challenge for social workers, as it changes the ways of thinking about the needs of people with dementia. It also chimes with social work's ethical commitments; for example, it is particularly important in the case of people with dementia to develop effective professional relationships (BASW, 2012: 12), which naturally take time to develop – and this time is necessarily extended due to the cognitive impairments of people with dementia. However, as the moving accounts of Maura McIntyre (2003) indicate, the beneficial impact of this is considerable; consequently, this should be a starting point for both social workers and carers.

However, it has been strongly argued that the current organisational arrangements that govern social work in England do not allow for this amount of time to be devoted to relationship building (Tanner, 2013), meaning that it is a problem that cannot easily be resolved by any given social worker. In addition, it is also suggested that more work is required to ensure that people with dementia are given the opportunity to recapture elements of their citizenship that have been stripped from them (Bartlett and O'Connor, 2007). In both of these respects, the ethical requirement that social workers seek to defend the human rights of individuals (practice principle 8: BASW, 2012: 14) becomes critical.

Turning specifically to Thad Bell's circumstances, his dementia is the element that emerges as the key issue – it is also the one that is likely to prioritise his needs in relation to eligibility criteria. However, his social isolation is another key factor, particularly since it affects how he responds to his dementia (Cattan et al., 2005). In the future, it will be necessary to spread understanding about dementia, in order to make life a little more 'dementia-friendly' (Dementia Friends, 2014). In addition, Thad's race and ethnicity are also material: while there is no indication of any issue of racism or other ill-treatment, the fact remains that as an older man of African-Caribbean origin he may not be ideally served by many of the care options that are open to him. Indeed, there is strong evidence of the under-use of services by people with dementia from minority ethnic groups (Daker-White et al., 2002) and that assumptions are made concerning care-giving in minority ethnic communities (Ahmad and Atkin, 1996); it is possible to draw two key inferences from this. The first is that people from minority ethnic groups are unaware of the services that exist. The second is that they don't use them because they are not felt to be culturally appropriate. Given that it has been identified that social activities which target specific groups of people (Cattan et al., 2005) can be particularly important in relation to people with dementia, there is a clear need to explore what might be available for people of Thad's background. In this respect, Thad's race and ethnicity can be seen as by no means incidental factors. At the least a social worker needs to be mindful of the first two ethical principles under the general heading of social justice, 'challenging discrimination' and 'recognising diversity' (BASW, 2012: 9), as these are issues that are of particular import for people from minority ethnic communities such as Thad Bell. As a result of all of this, there are manifest community development issues in relation to the needs of people with dementia from minority ethnic groups (Beresford et al., 2011).

In relation to the ethical practice principles that should govern a social worker's practice, there are a number that come to the foreground of thinking. For example, as with all areas of activity, social workers need to be able to develop professional relationships with all service users with whom they have contact (practice principle 1: BASW, 2012: 12). It is from that base that all other elements of practice stem. In the case of Thad Bell, there are other principles which also come to mind. For example, any attempt to provide appropriate levels of service will be based on an accurate assessment of the levels of risk in Thad's circumstances, which will then need to be appropriately and sensitively managed (practice principle 2: BASW, 2012: 12). In this case there do not appear to be factors that would impinge on other people, which at least makes the judgement of risk more straightforward. The fact that he has been diagnosed with dementia is potentially problematic, as he may lack the capacity to make informed judgements about his requirements. However, it must not be assumed that simply because he has dementia he lacks the capacity to make decisions about his welfare and care needs: as noted earlier, if there is any question about this there needs to be a formal process through which the extent to which he has capacity can be confirmed.

Case study 3: Martha Lindford

Mrs Martha Lindford is a widow, aged 81. Mrs Lindford is in poor health, with diabetes and angina; she moved to a warden-aided flat in recognition of the problems she was experiencing in maintaining her independence in the family home. She is blind and both of her legs have been amputated. After being in hospital, following a stroke, she had gone to stay in a residential home, for a period of time that she assumed was for her convalescence. Assuming she would remain there, Martha's family had cleared her flat and sold all her possessions without her agreement. She was desperately unhappy in the residential home, was losing weight and saying she wanted to return home. Mrs Lindford's son and daughter – who are both married with families of their own – had recently stormed out of a review meeting, having refused to consider her return home and telling her, "If you were a dog we'd have put you down!"

This case is a good example of the conflicts that can emerge between a service user and family members, to which we alluded in Chapter Seven. It is important to think through the ramifications of what has happened in order to make the ethical judgements that surround the case absolutely clear. The first point is that the primary responsibility of the social worker is to Martha Lindford; this may seem to be an obvious point, but it is not at all uncommon for social workers to be affected by the loudly expressed views of family or carers. In this case, there is clearly much rancour within the family, and Martha's children have acted in ways that are neither consistent with her wishes nor in her best interests. At the same time, it has to be acknowledged that Martha has many problems that do make it difficult for her to live independently.

There are numerous ethical practice principles that apply particularly to this case. The starting point is the notion of 'empowering people' (practice principle 7: BASW, 2012: 13). There seems little doubt that actions have been taken that, in effect, have fundamentally *disempowered* Martha. It seems likely that assumptions have been made that she will remain in the care home, despite the fact that she has no wish to do so: certainly the actions of her children seem to bear this interpretation out. Indeed, it is possible that they did not consider what her desires were at all, and that their expressed anger reflects this.

However, it would be unwise to draw firm conclusions from how they have acted; what is significant is the fact that they have expressed remarkably cruel and hurtful things to Mrs Lindford, such that it can be presumed that they do not have her best interests at heart. In the light of this, the need to construct discussions about the case so that they do not secure access to potentially damaging material is critical. From this point of view one ethical practice principle is particularly important: the need to maintain confidentiality (principle 10: BASW, 2012: 14). There is a real danger that Martha Lindford's relatives could use any information they acquire for their own ends, in opposition to Martha's interests. The issue of confidentiality is important for all cases, but assumes a particular priority where there is such a fundamental conflict between the service user and family members.

In the face of concerted family opposition, and despite considerable concerns about Martha's ability to cope, a social worker would want to work with her to assess whether a return home would be feasible. The first point is to consider whether or not she has retained tenancy rights for her flat: assuming that she has, a return there could be viable. In such circumstances a social worker could take Martha back to the warden-aided complex and ensure that the warden and any friends from the centre were able to greet her. Mrs Lindford would need a lot of time to look at her flat and to think through the range of options that were open to her. There would need to be careful thought about what support Martha would need if she was to return, and the extent to which this could feasibly be managed. The assessment and management of risk (practice principle 2: BASW, 2012: 12) is absolutely central to the case. Mrs Lindford would need to understand what the risks and potential consequences were of returning home and be able to take an informed decision about these. A social worker would be carefully acting in accordance with Martha's wishes, ensuring simultaneously that she was adequately protected and that she was able to assume the responsibility for any risks that she might be running (practice principle 3: BASW, 2012: 12). There would also need to be detailed consideration about how to secure replacements for the items sold by Martha's children.

As a result, the social work task here is one of considerable sensitivity, dealing with the painful emotional responses and reactions generated by Mrs Lindford's children's apparent callousness, alongside the immensely complex process of enabling somebody with multiple disabilities to live independently. It has to be acknowledged that it may not be possible to secure outcomes that are the most desired for Martha in this case, given the problems to be overcome. To recognise this is not to suggest that the attempt to enable her to live independently should not be undertaken; rather, it is a call for a pragmatic response if this proves not to be possible. This is likely to prove emotionally challenging for the social worker, particularly if s/he has invested heavily in seeking to support Martha to return to independent living. Another aspect of sensitivity that a social worker requires is when there is a clear divergence between the interests of the service user and her family, which has already meant that it is unlikely that common ground can be found to link them. Difficult as it is, however, it would not necessarily be in Martha's best interests to cut off all contact with her family. All of this complex work places particular stress on the social worker's ability to forge a productive working relationship with Mrs Lindford and all those who would need to be involved in providing her care (practice principle 1: BASW, 2012: 12), and time is needed to accomplish this, alongside high levels of empathy and skill. In many disrupted families mediation may well be an effective way of resolving past problems and dilemmas (Postle and Ford, 2000); however, in this case the problems may well be more profound than mediation could aspire to resolve.

Case study 4: Charlie Melton

Charlie Melton is a 52-year-old man who lives on his own in a Housing Association two-bedroomed flat. He is divorced, and his former wife lives several hours' train journey away. He has two adult children, with whom his relationship is good. He has two significant health problems, which constrain his life in a number of ways, and which mean he is unable to work. He was diagnosed at the age of 30 with Multiple Sclerosis (MS). Initially this was the more common form of Relapsing-Remitting MS; after about 15 years it turned into Secondary Progressive MS, which means that there is no period of remission or recovery following a worsening of his symptoms. He also has emphysema, which relates to his former 60-a-day smoking habit (he no longer smokes). As a result, he has to use a wheelchair for any significant movement; his most recent grade on the Expanded Disability Status Score (EDSS) was 7.0. His flat was adapted a few years ago in relation to this. Due to his emphysema being in the later stages, he receives oxygen treatment through a large tank. Charlie is a proud and independent man, who has resisted official offers of assistance for many years. However, he has recently referred himself for support; among the many problems that he is experiencing are financial ones – he has been assessed as having a spare room and has consequently lost 14% of his housing benefit. He is also experiencing increasing support needs due to his MS – he is struggling to remain continent, for example.

There are a number of issues that indicate the need for social work support in the case of Charlie. In particular, the fact that he has finally referred himself is significant. It is interesting that it appears to have been the problems associated with the change in his financial circumstances that have prompted the referral. This is a particularly problematic area in a time of government-led assaults on the circumstances of people who claim benefits; it manifestly does not help that local government – the route through which many disabled people access care services and support – has been cut more than any other area of government expenditure (Duffy, 2013). It is worth noting two elements in BASW's *Code of Ethics*, as they appear to direct a social worker's actions. First, in relation to the principle of social justice, it is specified that:

> Social workers have a duty to bring to the attention of their employers, policy makers, politicians and the general public situations where resources are inadequate or where distribution of resources, policies and practice are oppressive, unfair, harmful or illegal. (BASW, 2012: 9)

Further, when the *Code of Ethics* discusses the translation of this general point into a practice principle, the following statement is made:

> Social workers should be prepared to challenge discriminatory, ineffective and unjust policies, procedures and practice. (practice principle 8: BASW, 2012: 14)

It is hard to avoid the conclusion that the bedroom tax (as it has popularly become known) discriminates against disabled people like Charlie, who have rooms that are calculated as more than he 'needs'. His argument is that he needs the additional room to store his wheelchair and oxygen tank as these are essential for his ability to remain independent. However, under the rules of the bedroom tax, these are not calculated as sufficient grounds to waive the penalty of 14% of his housing benefit. In fact, at the time of writing (summer 2014), many local authorities have used up the funds they had which were for people whose circumstances make it very difficult for them to move to a smaller property. This includes, for example, couples where one person has needs related to disability (Butler, 2013). As the policy is clearly discriminatory and unjust, social workers should therefore be prepared to challenge it. Even the government's own *Equality Impact Assessment* (DWP, 2012) has estimated that it is likely to have a disproportionate effect on disabled people. It is clear that the terms of the legislation would apply to Charlie:

the Government does **not** accept that the *Gorry* judgment also provides for an extra bedroom with respect to disabled adults – for example where the claimant is one of a couple who is unable to share a bedroom or where an extra room is required for equipment connected with their disability.... It therefore has no plans to introduce new housing benefit regulations that provide for an extra bedroom with respect to disabled adults. (Disability Rights UK, 2014a; emphasis in original)

These include the precise circumstances that affect Charlie.

It is important, from Charlie's perspective, that any challenge that is made to the Department of Work and Pensions (DWP) judgement seeks specifically to amend his particular circumstances. Consequently, we do not suggest that it would be directly helpful to Charlie if a social worker were to 'mount the barricades' and seek to change the policy through any form of direct action. However, it is important that a social worker does understand the possible ways in which the policy can be managed, and be prepared to contemplate action that is outside her/his employment (Postle et al., 2005). In this circumstance, Charlie urgently needs to be supported to seek appropriate legal advice about his rights, and what avenues are open to him for redress (Disability Rights UK, 2014b). Given the specific wording of the element of the Welfare Reform Act 2012 that applies to his case, it is unlikely that any appeal would be possible. However, there is a chance for him to be guided to claim for a Discretionary Housing Payment due to his particular circumstances. Indeed, an additional sum was allocated to local authorities for the administration of the bedroom tax precisely for the needs of people such as Charlie:

> we have announced that an extra £30 million per year will be added to the scheme, £25 million of which is intended to be used specifically to assist those disabled claimants who are in properties where a significant adaptation has been made to cater for their individual needs. This should help avoid someone who lives in a property that has been significantly adapted at public expense having to move to a smaller property where those adaptations would have to be made again and possibly removed from the original property. (DWP, 2012: 13)

However, this would not be a long-term solution to Charlie's problem, but would potentially provide some time-limited financial assistance. Finding a permanent answer to his problem that does not require him to move is manifestly more difficult. It is vital for social workers to recognise that specialist legal advice and guidance is essential in such cases – in other words to recognise the limits of their own expertise.

Securing a practical gain might also be helpful in enabling a social worker to address the physical health issues, which will occupy a huge space in Charlie's life in forthcoming years. It will be important for Charlie to be clear about the potential development of both Secondary Progressive MS and emphysema, as both conditions tend to be misunderstood. In relation to Secondary Progressive MS for example, many people are relatively unfamiliar with this stage in the condition. People are widely familiar with the more common form of the disease, Relapsing-Remitting MS, but are unaware that a large proportion of people who have this develop Secondary Progressive MS approximately 15 years after their initial diagnosis. The critical difference between the two forms of MS is that, as the name indicates, with Secondary Progressive MS the symptoms become progressive with no period of remission. Even so, there is no certainty about the rate of progression. However, the EDSS is the accepted measure for MS, and a score of 7.0 indicates a severe level of disability. At the same time, emphysema is not a progressive condition in itself, and the treatment is primarily oriented around both preventing a further deterioration of lung function and maximising the operation of the remaining lung tissue. The extent to which Charlie has access to specialised medical and nursing support is critical – and it is vital to ensure that information is appropriately shared among all members of Charlie's treatment team, many of whom will be health-based (practice principle 5: BASW, 2012: 13). At the same time, this has to be managed while upholding the maintenance of confidentiality (practice principle 10: BASW, 2012: 14), which is often made more difficult when other agencies are involved.

Given the extent of Charlie's disability, it is quite possible that he needs additional support with the activities of daily living – particularly shopping and cleaning – thereby potentially drawing other agencies into his life. However, there is no indication at this stage that he requires assistance with any aspect of personal care. Again, there is no certainty that he is willing to accept such services, but given that both his conditions are physically debilitating it would be something of a surprise if he had no needs in these areas. In some cases they can represent the difference between a successful and unsuccessful independent life. While the selection of a care agency to manage such issues is the responsibility of Charlie, the social worker has a key role to fulfil in two main ways. First, s/he has to present his needs in such a way as to ensure that he is placed within the band of needs that the local authority would undertake to meet. Second, the basis on which the care agency will be contracted to assist with his care will be addressed through the assessment, which therefore needs to be as detailed and thorough as is feasible, on the basis that the better the assessment the more likely it is that appropriate services will be supported (Lymbery, 2004).

Conclusion

It is far from straightforward for a social worker to accomplish ethically informed practice, but the above case studies provide some guidance about how this could be achieved in a variety of different circumstances. In addition, they focus on the exercise of specific ethical practice principles in different sets of circumstances. It is our view that the principles that should inform such practice are what delineate the work of a social worker as opposed to any other professional.

If we accept that a key role for a social worker is to be able to empower service users, we also have to recognise the importance of the words that are used to expand upon the notion of ethical practice principle 7 – 'empowering people':

> Social workers should promote and contribute to the development of positive policies, procedures and practices which are anti-oppressive and empowering. They should respect people's beliefs, values, culture, goals, needs, preferences, relationships and affiliations. Social workers should recognise their own prejudices to ensure they do not discriminate against any person or group. They should ensure that services are offered and delivered in a culturally appropriate manner. They should challenge and seek to address any actions of colleagues who demonstrate negative discrimination or prejudice. (BASW, 2012: 13)

Once again the dominant construction is that 'social workers *should*' act in particular ways. However, the preceding examples should convey a better sense of what social workers need to do in order to give life to the otherwise sterile words. If we were to summarise the elements of learning about what is needed to put these axioms into effect we would focus on the following:

- Learn from people using services what empowerment means for them rather than imposing understandings which may be meaningless or wrong.
- Work with the reality of empowerment, not the rhetoric.
- Be alert to ways of working which exacerbate people's dependency and militate against empowerment.
- Demoralised and disempowered staff are unlikely to be able to empower others.

In the context of this book, the final point perhaps needs to be particularly emphasised. We believe that social workers can help people to deal with some of the most complex and challenging tasks, but the demoralised and fragmented social work profession is hardly well placed to take up this challenge. It is this position that governments and employers can challenge, along with the social work profession itself. Social work has often been poor at convincing others that it has a unique contribution to offer to the world of adult social care: if this does not change, it will be hard to avoid a future when the only role played by social workers are those unwanted by other professions (Jones, 2014).

TEN

Conclusion

It is clear from our analysis in this book that, as far as social care is concerned at least, there has been little learning from the past. It seems that the policy of personalisation is following a similar trajectory to that of community care, launched with such a fanfare in 1993. Certainly, the importance that financial restrictions have assumed in the policy is a direct point of comparison. If this is the case, we can look forward to a period (perhaps 15 years hence) when personalisation is deemed to have failed. And, if the current position is any guide, the reasons for the presumed failure will focus on the staff who were required to implement it, not the economic problems that characterise the context within which it is being introduced. We concur with what Hart (2014: 114) has written in relation to personalisation, and we also recognise that this holds as far as community care was concerned:

> we [social workers] were always being set up for a fall. The problem was, and still is, that the rhetoric over-promised and has under-delivered, and that leads to disillusionment ...

Hart (2014) goes on to argue that there are insufficient resources to achieve the outcomes that are promised. This has been a consistent theme in this book; as with community care, we argue that the policy of personalisation has become distorted, leading to profound and worrying implications for social work.

Were we dispassionate commentators we could simply shrug resignedly and mutter *plus ça change*, while expressing no view about how things could be made better. However, this would neither be in the interests of service users nor helpful to the profession of social work, which we are proud to have been part of for a combined total of almost 60 years. As a result, we will do our best to be positive about the future as far as social work in adult social care is concerned.

As we have indicated throughout the book, we believe that the involvement of a skilled and experienced social worker will be critical in order to enable many people to take full advantage of the opportunities of personalisation. In addition, we have no doubt that these opportunities do exist. However, it is also apparent that the major obstacle to such a development rests in the underfunding of local government. Consequently our first point is to suggest – in the strongest possible terms! – that the funding settlement for adult social care should be revisited. It is clear from a number of different sources that the financial arrangements for the delivery of health and social care are no longer appropriate – if, indeed, they have ever been (Carr-West, 2012; Ham et al., 2012; Duffy, 2013; LGA, 2014). It seems to us to be entirely vacuous to suggest that the gaps in the funding system can be patched up by efficiency savings. It is also morally offensive to suggest that the problems of the financial world should be 'resolved' in large measure by pressure on the most vulnerable people in society.

Having made this obvious point, we have to think through the most effective ways to organise social work. To us, three suggestions present themselves:

1. Investment in the development of social work largely within the local authority.
2. Investment in the creation of quasi-independent social work practices.
3. Further creation of integrated teams between health and social care.

Since each of these ideas potentially takes social work in a different direction, it is worth examining them in turn. It should be emphasised, however, that policy should not fixate on any single 'solution', to the exclusion of all others.

If we look first at the option of investment to develop social work further within the context of the local authority, this has the clear benefit of working to support the profession within an environment where it has been located for several decades. Many of the functions of adult social care – for example, decisions about eligibility, safeguarding – are retained by a local authority under the terms of the Care Act 2014 and there remains a presumption that social care will continue to be separately funded. Consequently, the local authority needs to be strengthened to enable it to address the manifold problems that will remain. However, this also presents a potentially insuperable difficulty: it also would perpetuate the various problems that have characterised the separation of social care from health care over the decades. Many of these stem from the problematic idea that the responsibilities of health and social care can easily be distinguished and divided (Lymbery, 2006). This has created numerous problems of joint working; indeed, in the early years of this century the Labour government strongly emphasised the merits of partnership, and appeared to suggest that its existence would resolve many of the apparently intractable problems that beset welfare (Glendinning et al., 2002). However, the numerous exhortations to improve levels of collaboration tended to ignore the structural problems that had caused conflict between social care and other agencies, notably health (Lewis, 2001; Lymbery, 2006). To focus solely on improving social work within the context of the local authority runs the risk of cementing the problems that caused the upsurge in popularity of concepts such as collaboration and partnership.

In addition, there is a danger of missing the essential point, which is that the problems of social care cannot be resolved without looking at the connections between health and social care:

> Unprecedented funding pressures affecting health and social care mean that incremental changes to current models of care will not be sufficient to address these and other challenges. A much bolder approach is needed, involving a major shift in where care is delivered

and how patients and service users relate to health and social care professionals. (Ham et al., 2012: vii)

If we consider the development of independent social work, this central problem remains. The expansion of independent social work practices was first mooted in relation to child care; a working group was set up chaired by Julian Le Grand to explore the idea more fully. The overarching basis for the development of independent social work practices was the thought that social workers might be enabled to act with more freedom and creativity if freed from the deadening effects of local authority control. Le Grand's initial report (2007b) highlighted the potential for evaluative research to test out the validity and viability of the model, as it was at this point pitched at a relatively abstract, conceptual level. Consequently a research group was set up in 2010, reporting in 2012 (Stanley et al., 2012). Although the establishment of this group pre-dated the advent of the coalition government in 2010, the notion of social work practices was promoted very hard by the reforming Secretary of State for Education, Michael Gove (Schraer, 2014). Although the findings of this research were equivocal, they appeared to fit with the privatising bent of the then Education Secretary and received substantial publicity, which emphasised the positive elements of the work. However, it is important to be mindful of the cautious approach of the research team in relation to broadening this sort of development:

> This evaluation of a government-funded pilot found limited evidence to support arguments for relocating public services for children in out-of-home care in the independent or private sector. While most of the pilots appeared to offer a service that children and families found accessible and personalized, there seems no reason other than resource shortfalls why public welfare services should not be organized into small accessible teams where staff are informed about one another's cases, where supervision is of a high standard and where children and families receive a personalized service that makes them feel 'known' and valued. (Stanley et al., 2013: 38)

The ultimate conclusion of Stanley et al's research was that although independent social work teams contained numerous positive elements, it did not recommend a full transfer of powers away from the local authority. Indeed, it suggested that the public sector:

> is also more likely to offer continuity of knowledge, skills and care and, in this respect, it may be better placed to respond to the uncertainty that characterizes the needs of children in out-of-home care. (Stanley et al., 2013: 39)

This context is vital in terms of a lens through which we can analyse the parallel issue of independent social work practices for adults. Whatever the configuration of social workers – and there are some apparent advantages to the Social Work Practices with Adults (SWPwA) model (Manthorpe et al., 2014) – the core problem about funding remains unanswered. However, it is important first to recognise that many advantages of the model were evident:

> For most participants in this study – social workers, other practitioners, SWPwA managers and commissioners alike – SWPwAs offered the potential for job satisfaction, autonomy and in some cases greater opportunities for team working than they had experienced working for the local authority. (Manthorpe et al., 2014: 7)

This is a clear statement that participants experienced advantages in comparison to their normal life within the local authority, and is reminiscent of findings from the child care pilot projects (Stanley et al., 2012). But, it is important to note that many of the successes of the pilot projects appear to be as much due to the fact of being the focus of attention as any advantages of the model itself:

> One important message from this Evaluation is that how much practitioners and managers welcomed *positive* interest in adult social work assessment and care planning. (Manthorpe et al., 2014: 7; emphasis in original)

This is highly significant in itself – much prominence in recent years has been given to the failings of social work: these pilot projects promoted a more positive impression of social work practice and hence the profession of social work as a whole. As the evaluators recognise, such an outcome is equally possible for social workers based in the public sector, as noted in relation to the child care pilots above. In addition, in line with our approach through the book, we regard the provision of social care as a public utility that *ought* to be organised by the public sector. That this principle is widely accepted within the health service, but not extended to social care, is frankly a mystery to us (Barker, 2014). We have a particular concern that placing social work services in independent locations might have the unintended consequence of ripening them for privatisation (Cardy, 2010).

We also need to consider the potential for greater integration between health and social care. As we have noted earlier in the book, the separation between health and social care is a historical accident and does not reflect anything immutable about the work of either (Wistow, 2012). However, simple protestations about the need to bring them together have tended to founder on the uncomfortable reality of the funding differences between them, which emphasises the fact that they were designed to be separate rather than integrated (Wistow, 2012). As yet, no government has had the courage to argue that social care should be free at the point of use, as is the case for health care. The Care Act 2014 does not differ from this position. Indeed, its dilution of the principles of the Dilnot Report (Dilnot, 2011) indicates that there is little official pressure to change this; for example, the capping of lifetime care costs at £72,000 is welcome but the figure is substantially higher than Dilnot (2011) first proposed, simultaneously costing the exchequer less money to implement while ensuring that people with the misfortune to need considerable social care have to contribute a large amount to this.

However, there is a strengthening recognition that a full integration between health and social care is needed to address the severe and interdependent problems with which both are faced (Ham et al., 2012; Wistow, 2012; Barker, 2014). A quotation from one of the above reports makes the case abundantly clear:

> Unprecedented funding pressures affecting health and social care mean that incremental changes to current models of care will not be sufficient to address these and other challenges. A much bolder approach is needed, involving a major shift in where care is delivered and how patients and service users relate to health and social care professionals. (Ham et al., 2012: vii)

For Wistow (2012) the fact that organisational separation was based on the skills of providers rather than the needs of service users was critical. Barker has identified a number of factors that highlight the separate identities of each, and which make integration difficult:

- Lack of alignment of entitlements to health and social care
- Lack of alignment in funding streams
- Lack of alignment in organisations (Barker, 2014: 2–3)

Clearly, it is suggested, these issues need to be ironed out before integration can be properly successful. In addition, there needs to be recognition of the funding crisis in health and social care and a commitment to resolving it. In this respect, the conclusions from the King's Fund report are similar to those of Wanless (2006):

> as the numbers of older people increase, if standards and entitlements are to be maintained or improved in health and social care, more revenue will be needed. In addition, the extra pressures from rising health costs will need to be met. (Barker, 2014: x)

It is apparent from all of the above sources that influential figures are united in believing both that greater integration between health and social care is needed, and that this needs to be accompanied by a substantial injection of cash.

In recognising and supporting this we do not deny the real professional barriers to full integration, which have often been a stumbling block in the past (Lymbery, 2006). Social workers have often struggled to carve out a separately identifiable professional space alongside doctors and other health professionals. As indicated earlier in the book (Chapter Five), for integration to work professionally there needs to be full recognition of the contributions of multiple occupations. It is obvious that this is vital in relation to the provision of appropriate health and social care services.

In arguing that the integration of health and social care should be prioritised, this is not to suggest that improvements are unnecessary or irrelevant in other areas. Certainly, there will continue to be the need to focus on the provision of social work within the local authority, particularly in relation to the statutory roles that social workers will continue to undertake under the Care Act 2014. In addition, we are far from opposed to the provision of independent social work practices for adults, although we recognise that the positive evidence in their favour could equally have been found in well-supported projects within the local authority. As the evaluation report into them suggests (Manthorpe et al., 2014), the positive focus on the social work role that characterised many of the pilot projects was most welcome.

In order to work effectively in any organisational configuration, of course, the quality of education of all professionals needs to be assured. Given the nature of this book, we focus on the particular implications for social work education. As far as social work with adults is concerned, there have been several years of challenge, leading to continued uncertainty about the definition of the social work role with adults and the educational processes needed to prepare staff for future changes (Lymbery, 2009). Not many years ago, it seemed that the generic basis of social work education was assured (SWRB, 2009 and 2010). However, despite the positive nature of these reports they left unanswered a number of critical points, particularly around practice placements and financial resources (Lymbery, 2011). In addition, there remained a groundswell of opinion that was highly critical of the quality of social work education.

In this respect, perhaps the most notorious critical vision – within the social work academy at least! – is the review undertaken by Martin Narey (2014). On the basis of a somewhat anecdotal approach to evidence collection, Narey is highly critical about the failure of social work courses to prepare staff adequately to work with children and families, the focus of his report. Consequently, he suggests that social work education should be radically reshaped: for the purposes of this book, the suggestion that there should be a high level of specialisation in social work education is particularly troubling, as this would further marginalise the role of social work with adults.

It is interesting that another report into social work education was commissioned at a similar time, and also reported in the early months of 2014 (Croisdale-Appleby, 2014). There were of course comparisons made about the merits and demerits of the two reports (see, for example, Cleary, 2014), which tended to emphasise the greater degree of thoroughness and rigour that characterised Croisdale-Appleby's document. It has also been suggested that both reports emphasise the limitations of the earlier proposals by the Social Work Reform Board (SWRB) (McKitterick, 2014). One of the distinctive elements of the Croisdale-Appleby report (2014) is his acknowledgement that the scale of funding for some elements of social work education needed to be significantly increased, reflecting critical observations that had been made about the SWRB's proposals (Lymbery, 2011). One of these areas was the funding for practice learning, where Croisdale-Appleby recommended an increase to improve the experiences of students on placement. Only a matter of weeks later this was substantially cut, at a stroke demonstrating the limited support for social work education at official levels, and putting some third sector placement providers at imminent risk of closure (Turner, 2014).

We believe that there needs to be a continued focus on three specific, linked areas in social work education, all of which are vital to adult social care. As we have argued throughout this book, we suggest that it is vital to maintain social work as a core professional discipline within this field of practice. First, because service users particularly value the relational aspects of work, often downplayed in policy (Beresford et al., 2006), this should continue to be a feature of all social work education. It is vital that social workers are able to link these relational skills with a radical, politicised perspective (Lymbery, 2013). Second, social workers need to focus on developing alliances with service users and their organisations (Postle and Beresford, 2007); consequently, the active engagement of users and carers in the education of social workers must remain core. This also argues for the connection between the relational and political realities of the role. Third, social work needs to remember its collective heritage and move away from a preoccupation with individual cases (Harris, 2008). One key way in which this could be achieved in social work for adults would be a focus on health inequalities (McLeod and Bywaters, 2000), which have manifold implications for social care alongside health care. Again, this has serious consequences for how social work is taught.

It is clear that financial pressures have distorted the two main policies – community care and personalisation – to emerge in relation to adult social care in the past 25 years. In addition, the way in which these policies have had to be developed has twisted the nature of social work practice. Hence we see the 'distortion' of the book's title as referring both to the nature of policy and the conception of social work that has accompanied both community care and personalisation.

The final point that we wish to make is to reassert the moral case that the most vulnerable people in society should be provided with the highest level of support. For us, this implies the continued active involvement of social workers, performing a vital role in helping people adjust to the most difficult sets of circumstance. Naturally, this requires a substantial investment of resources, in order to employ and remunerate these practitioners. As we are indeed a wealthy country, a continued process whereby severely limited resources are all that is made available to people in need is nothing short of an outrage.

Bibliography

Abbott, A. (1988) *The System of Professions*, Chicago, University of Chicago Press.

Adams, T. and Bartlett, R. (2003) 'Constructing dementia', in T. Adams and J. Manthorpe (eds) *Dementia Care*, London, Arnold.

ADASS, DH, SFC, BASW and SCA (Association of Directors of Adult Social Services, Department of Health, Skills for Care, British Association of Social Workers and the Social Care Association) (2010) *The Future of Social Work in Adult Social Services*, London, ADASS/DH/SFC/BASW/SCA.

Adcroft, A. and Willis, R. (2005) 'The (un)intended outcome of public sector performance measurement', *International Journal of Public Sector Management*, 18 (5): 386–400.

Ahmad, W.I.U. and Atkin, K. (1996) *Race and Community Care*, Buckingham, Open University Press.

Aldridge, M. (1996) 'Dragged to market: being a profession in the postmodern world', *British Journal of Social Work*, 26 (2): 177–94.

Alzheimer's Society (2007) *Dementia UK*, London, Alzheimer's Society.

Alzheimer's Society (2014) *Dementia UK: Second Edition*, London, Alzheimer's Society.

Askheim, A. (2003) 'Empowerment as guidance for professional social work: an act of balancing on a slack rope', *European Journal of Social Work*, 6 (3): 229–40.

Audit Commission (1986) *Making a Reality of Community Care*, London, HMSO.

Bailey, R. and Brake, M. (eds) (1975) *Radical Social Work*, London, Edward Arnold.

Banks, S. (2008) 'Critical commentary: social work ethics', *British Journal of Social Work*, 38 (6): 1238–49.

Barclay Report (1982) *Social Workers: Their Role and Tasks*, London, Bedford Square Press and the National Institute for Social Work.

Barker, K. (2014) *A New Settlement for Health and Social Care: Final Report*, London, The King's Fund.

Barnes, M. (1999) 'Users as citizens: collective action and the local governance of welfare', *Social Policy and Administration*, 33 (1): 77–90.

Barnett, Canon S.A. and Barnett, Mrs S.A. (1915) *Practicable Socialism*, London, Longman Green & Co.

Bartlett, R. and O'Connor, D. (2007) 'From personhood to citizenship: broadening the lens for dementia practice and research', *Journal of Aging Studies*, 21 (2): 107–18.

Barton, R. (1966) *Institutional Neurosis*, Bristol, Wright and Sons.

BASW (British Association of Social Workers) (2012) *The Code of Ethics for Social Workers: Statement of Principles*, Birmingham, BASW.

Bauld, L., Chesterman, J., Davies, B., Judge, K. and Mangalore, R. (2000) *Caring for Older People: An Assessment of Community Care in the 1990s*, Aldershot, Ashgate.

Bauman, Z. (1992) *Intimations of Postmodernity*, London, Routledge.

Baxter, S.K. and Brumfitt, S.M. (2008) 'Professional differences in interprofessional working', *Journal of Interprofessional Care*, 22 (3): 239–51.

BBC (British Broadcasting Corporation) (2014a) 'Cuts forcing English councils to limit social care', *BBC News Health*, 14 September.

BBC (2014b) 'Orchid View care home scandal review "not enough"', *BBC News Sussex*, 9 June.

Beck, U. (1992) *Risk Society: Towards a New Modernity*, London, Sage.

Beckett, C. (2010) *Assessment and Intervention in Social Work: Preparing for practice*, London, Sage.

Beckett, C. and Maynard, A. (2012) *Values and Ethics in Social Work*, 2nd edn, London, Sage.

Beresford, P. (2007) *The Changing Roles and Tasks of Social Work from Service Users' Perspectives: A Literature-informed Discussion Paper*, London, Shaping Our Lives National User Network.

Beresford, P. (2008) 'Service user values for social work and social care', in A. Barnard, N. Horner and J. Wild (eds) *The Value Base of Social Work and Social Care: An Active Learning Handbook*, Basingstoke, Palgrave Macmillan.

Beresford, P. (2011) 'Radical social work and service users: a crucial connection', in M. Lavalette (ed.) *Radical Social Work Today: Social Work at the Crossroads*, Bristol, Policy Press.

Beresford, P. (2012) 'The theory and philosophy behind user involvement', in P. Beresford and S. Carr (eds) *Social Care, Service Users and User Involvement*, London, Jessica Kingsley.

Beresford, P. (2014) 'Advancing the positives of personalisation/person-centred support: a multi-perspective view', in C. Needham and J. Glasby (eds) *Debates in Personalisation*, Bristol, Policy Press.

Beresford, P. and Carr, S. (eds) (2012) *Social Care, Service Users and User Involvement*, London, Jessica Kingsley.

Beresford, P. and Croft, S. (2004) 'Service users and practitioners reunited: the key component for social work reform', *British Journal of Social Work*, 34 (1): 53–68.

Beresford, P., Adshead, L. and Croft, S. (2006) *Palliative Care, Social Work and Service Users: Making Life Possible*, London, Jessica Kingsley.

Beresford, P., Fleming, J., Glynn, M., Bewley, C., Croft, S., Branfield, F. and Postle, K. (2011) *Supporting People: Towards a Person-centred Approach*, Bristol, Policy Press.

Berger, P. and Luckman, T. (1966) *The Social Construction of Reality: A Treatise in the Sociology of Knowledge*, London, Penguin.

Bevan, G. (2008) 'Changing paradigms of governance and regulation of quality of healthcare in England', *Health, Risk & Society*, 10 (1): 85–101.

Beveridge, W. (1942) *Report of the Inter-Departmental Committee on Social Insurance and Allied Services*, London, HMSO.

Bezzina, A. (2014) *Service User Involvement in Social Work: Emergent Dynamics in the Maltese Context*, unpublished PhD thesis, School of Sociology and Social Policy, University of Nottingham, Nottingham.

Biestek, F. (1961) *The Casework Relationship*, London, George Allen & Unwin.

Bisman, C. (2004) 'Social work values: the moral core of the profession', *British Journal of Social Work,* 34 (1): 105–23.

Blaug, R. (1995) 'Distortion of the face to face: communicative reason and social work practice', *British Journal of Social Work,* 25 (4): 423–39.

Blaug, R. (2002) 'Engineering democracy', *Political Studies,* 50 (1): 102–15.

Bloy, M. (2002) 'The 1601 Elizabethan Poor Law', *The Victorian Web,* www.victorianweb.org/history/poorlaw/elizpl.html

Boffey, D. (2014) 'The care workers left behind as private equity targets the NHS', *The Observer,* 9 August.

Bornat, J. (1997) 'Representations of community', in J. Bornat, J. Johnson, C. Pereira, D. Pilgrim and F. Williams (eds) *Community Care: A Reader,* 2nd edn, Basingstoke, Macmillan.

Bosanquet, H. (1914) *Social Work in London,* London, John Murray.

Boxall, K., Dowson, S. and Beresford, P. (2009) 'Selling individual budgets, choice and control: local and global influences on UK social care policy for people with learning difficulties', *Policy and Politics,* 37 (4): 499–515.

Boyne, G.A. (2002) 'Theme: Local government: concepts and indicators of local authority performance: an evaluation of the statutory frameworks in England and Wales', *Public Money and Management,* 22 (2): 17–24.

Brandon, D. and Brandon, T. (2002) *Advocacy in Social Work,* Birmingham, Venture Press.

Brandon, D. and Hawkes, A. (1998) *Speaking Truth to Power: Care Planning with Disabled People,* Birmingham, Venture Press.

Brindle, D. (2014) 'What are the most important changes to the Care Act?' *The Guardian,* 5 June.

Brookes, N., Callaghan, L., Netten, A. and Fox, D. (2014) 'Personalisation and innovation in a cold financial climate', *British Journal of Social Work,* published online 5 June, doi: 10.1093/bjsw/bct104.

Buchan, J. and Pile, H. (2010) 'Outsourcing adult care: for and against', *Community Care,* 23 July.

Butler, I. and Drakeford, M. (2005) *Scandal, Social Policy and Welfare,* 2nd edn, Bristol, Policy Press.

Butler, P. (2013) 'Bedroom tax: one-third of disabled applicants refused emergency grants', *The Guardian,* 18 December.

Calcraft, R. (2007) 'Blowing the whistle on abuse of adults with learning disabilities', *Journal of Adult Protection,* 9 (2): 15–29.

Cameron, A., Lart, R., Bostock, L. and Coomber, C. (2012) *Factors that Promote and Hinder Joint and Integrated Working between Health and Social Care Services,* Research Briefing 41, London, Social Care Institute for Excellence.

Camilleri, P. (1996) *(Re)Constructing Social Work,* Aldershot, Avebury.

Cardy, S. (2010) '"Care Matters" and the privatization of looked after children's services in England and Wales: developing a critique of independent "social work practices"', *Critical Social Policy,* 30 (3): 430–42.

Carey, M. (2003) 'Anatomy of a care manager', *Work, Employment and Society*, 17 (1): 121–35.

Carey, M. and Foster, V. (2011) 'Introducing "deviant" social work: contextualising the limits of radical social work whilst understanding (fragmented) resistance within the social work labour process', *British Journal of Social Work*, 41 (3): 576–93.

Carr-West, J. (2012) *Plugging the Gap: The Social Care Challenge*, London, RSA.

Carvel, J. (2007) 'Councils turn backs on care for older people', *The Guardian*, 22 November.

Case Con Manifesto (1975) in R. Bailey and M. Brake (eds) *Radical Social Work*, London, Edward Arnold.

Cattan, M., White, M., Bond, J. and Learmouth, A. (2005) 'Preventing social isolation and loneliness among older people: a systematic review of health promotion interventions', *Ageing and Society*, 25 (2): 41–67.

Cattell, R. (2014) 'The Care Act receives royal assent: what does this mean for adult social work?' *The Guardian*, 19 May.

Challis, D. and Davies, B. (1986) *Case Management in Community Care*, Aldershot, Gower.

Challis, D. and Hugman, R. (1993) 'Editorial: Community care, social work and social care', *British Journal of Social Work*, 32 (4): 319–28.

Challis, D., Darton, R., Johnson, L., Stone, M. and Traske, D. (1995) *Care Management and Health Care of Older People*, Aldershot, Arena.

Chamberlain, J. and Jenkinson, A. (2013) 'New definition proposed for statutory adult social work', *Community Care*, 27 August.

Clark, C. (2005) 'The deprofessionalisation thesis, accountability and professional character', *Social Work and Society*, 3 (2).

Clark, C. (2006) 'Moral character in social work', *British Journal of Social Work*, 36 (1): 75–89. Clark, H. and Spafford, J. (2001) *Piloting Choice and Control for Older People: An Evaluation*, York, Joseph Rowntree Foundation.

Clark, H., Dyer, S. and Horwood, J. (1998) *'That Bit of Help': The High Value of Low Level Preventative Services for Older People*, Bristol, Policy Press/Community Care.

Clark, H., Gough, H. and Macfarlane, A. (2004) *'It Pays Dividends': Direct Payments and Older People*, Bristol, Policy Press and Joseph Rowntree Foundation.

Clark, L. (2007) 'Comedians and social care', *Community Care*, 31 October.

Clarke, J. (1998) 'Managerialisation and social welfare', in J. Carter (ed.) *Postmodernity and the Fragmentation of Welfare*, London, Routledge.

Clarke, J. (2004a) *Changing Welfare, Changing States*, London, Sage.

Clarke, J. (2004b) 'Dissolving the public realm? The logics and limits of neo-liberalism', *Journal of Social Policy*, 33 (1): 27–48.

Clarke, J. (2005) 'New Labour's citizens: activated, empowered, responsibilized, abandoned?' *Critical Social Policy*, 25 (4): 447–63.

Clarke, J. and Newman, J. (1997) *The Managerial State*, London, Sage.

Clarke, J., Smith, N. and Vidler, E. (2005) 'Consumerism and the reform of public services: inequalities and instabilities', in M. Powell, L. Bauld and K. Clarke (eds) *Social Policy Review 17*, Bristol, Policy Press.

Clarke, J., Newman, J. and Westmarland, L. (2008) 'The antagonisms of choice: New Labour and the reform of public services', *Social Policy and Society*, 7 (2): 245–53.

Clarkson, P. (2010) 'Performance measurement in adult social care: looking backwards and forwards', *British Journal of Social Work,* 40 (1): 170–87.

Cleary, T. (2014) 'Weighing up the evidence: a review of the Narey and Croisdale-Appleby reports on social work education', *Community Care*, 15 July.

Clements, L. (2008) 'Individual budgets and irrational exuberance', *Community Care Law Reports* 11 (Sept.): 413–30.

Clements, L. (2011a) 'Social care law developments: a sideways look at personalisation and tightening eligibility criteria', *Elder Law*, 1: 47–52.

Clements, L. (2011b) 'Disability, dignity and the cri de coeur', *European Human Rights Law Review* 6: 675–85.

Clements, L. and Thompson, P. (2011) *Community Care and the Law* (5th edn), London, Legal Action Group.

Community Care (2011.) 'The state of adult social care', *Community Care*, www.communitycare.co.uk/the-state-of-adult-social-care/

Cooper, A. (2010) 'What future? Organisational forms, relationship-based social work practice and the changing world order', in G. Ruch, D. Turney and A. Ward eds *Relationship-Based Social Work: Getting to the Heart of Practice*, London, Jessica Kingsley.

Croft, S. and Beresford, P. (2000) "Empowerment" in *Blackwell Encyclopaedia of Social Work* (Ed, Davies, M.) Oxford, Blackwell.

Croisdale-Appleby, D. (2014) *Revisioning Social Work Education: An Independent Review*, London, Department of Health.

Crowther, M.A. (1981) *The Workhouse System 1834–1929: The History of an English Social Institution*, London, Batsford.

CSCI (Commission for Social Care Inspection) (2008) *Cutting the Cake Fairly: CSCI Review of Eligibility Criteria for Adult Social Care*, London, Commission for Social Care Inspection.

Cutler, T., Waine, B. and Brehony, K. (2007) 'A new epoch of individualization? Problems with the "personalization" of public sector services', *Public Administration*, 85 (3): 847–55.

Daker-White, G., Beattie, A.M., Gilliard, J. and Means R. (2002) 'Minority ethnic groups in dementia care: a review of service needs, service provision and models of good practice', *Aging & Mental Health*, 6 (2): 101–8.

Dant, T. and Gearing, B. (1990) 'Key workers for elderly people in the community: case managers and care coordinators', *Journal of Social Policy* 19 (3): 331–60.

Davies, O. (2014) 'The moral and economic case for adult social work', *Community Care*, 18 March.

Davis, D.H.J. (2004) 'Dementia: sociological and philosophical constructions', *Social Science & Medicine*, 58 (2): 369–78.

de Bruin, H. (2002) *Managing Performance in the Public Sector*, London, Routledge.

Dementia Friends (2014) www.dementiafriends.org.uk/

Derber, C. (1983) 'Managing professionals: Ideological proletarianization and postindustrial labor', *Theory and Society*, 12(3): 309–41.

DH (Department of Health) (1989) *Caring for People: Community Care in the Next Decade and Beyond* Cm 849, London, HMSO.

DH (1998) *Modernising Social Services: Promoting Independence, Improving Protection, Raising Standards*, Cm 4149, London, HMSO.

DH (2000a) *The NHS Plan: The Government's Response to the Royal Commission on Long Term Care*, London, Department of Health.

DH (2000b) *A Quality Strategy for Social Care*, London, HMSO.

DH (2002) *Fair Access to Care Services: Guidance on Eligibility Criteria for Adult Social Care*, LAC(2002)13, London, Department of Health.

DH (2005) *Independence, Well-Being and Choice*, London, The Stationery Office.

DH (2006) *Our Health, Our Care, Our Say: A New Direction for Community Services*, Cm 6737, London, HMSO.

DH (2008) *Transforming Social Care*, LAC (DH) (2008) 1, London, Department of Health.

DH (2009) *Working to Put People First: The Strategy for the Adult Social Care Workforce in England*, London, Department of Health.

DH (2010a) *Prioritising Need in the Context of* Putting People First: *A Whole System Approach to Eligibility for Social Care, Guidance on Eligibility Criteria for Adult Social Care, England 2010*, London, Department of Health.

DH (2010b) *A Vision for Adult Social Care: Capable Communities and Active Citizens*, London: Department of Health.

DH (2012) *Transforming Care: A National Response to Winterbourne View Hospital*, London, Department of Health.

DH (2013a) *Adult Social Care Choice Framework*, London, Department of Health.

DH (2013b) *The Adult Social Care Outcomes Framework 2014/15*, London, Department of Health.

DH and SSI (Department of Health and Social Services Inspectorate) (1991) *Care Management and Assessment – Practitioners' Guide*, London, HMSO.

Digby, A. (1978) *Pauper Palaces*, London, Routledge & Kegan Paul.

Dilnot, A. (2011) *Fairer Care Funding: The Report of the Commission on Funding of Care and Support*, London, Commission on Care and Support.

Disability Rights UK (2014a) *The Bedroom Tax*, www.disabilityrightsuk.org/bedroom-tax, Accessed 25th November 2014.

Disability Rights UK (2014b) *Appeals and mandatory reconsideration*, www.disabilityrightsuk.org/appeals-and-mandatory-reconsideration, Accessed 25th November 2014.

Dissenbacher, H. (1989) 'Neglect, abuse and the taking of life in old people's homes', *Ageing and Society*, 9 (1): 67–71.

Doel, M. (2010) 'Service-user perspectives on relationships', in G. Ruch, D. Turney and A. Ward (eds) *Relationship-based Social Work: Getting to the Heart of Practice*, London, Jessica Kingsley.

Dominelli, L. (2002) *Feminist Social Work Theory and Practice*, Basingstoke, Palgrave.

Donovan, T. (2014) 'Council to farm out social care services to deal with government cuts', *Community Care*, 10 March.

Dorling, D. (2011) *Injustice: Why Social Inequality Persists*, Bristol, Policy Press.

du Gay, P. (2003) 'The tyranny of the epochal: change, epochalism and organizational reform', *Organization*, 10 (4): 663–84.

Duffy, S. (2010) 'The citizenship theory of social justice: exploring the meaning of personalisation for social workers', *Journal of Social Work Practice*, 24 (3): 253–67.

Duffy, S. (2011) *A Fair Society and the Limits of Personalisation*, Discussion Paper, Sheffield, Centre for Welfare Reform.

Duffy, S. (2012) *Is Personalisation Dead?* Sheffield, Centre for Welfare Reform.

Duffy, S. (2013) *A Fair Society? How the Cuts Target Disabled People*, Sheffield, Centre for Welfare Reform.

Duffy, S. (2014a) 'Personalisation was supposed to empower vulnerable citizens. It failed', *The Guardian*, 30 January.

Duffy, S. (2014b) 'After personalisation', in C. Needham and J. Glasby (eds) *Debates in Personalisation*, Bristol, Policy Press.

Duffy, S., Waters, S. and Glasby, J. (2010) 'Personalisation and adult social care: future options for the reform of public services', *Policy and Politics*, 38 (4): 493–508.

Dustin, D. (2006) 'Skills and knowledge needed to practise as a care manager: continuity and change', *Journal of Social Work*, 6 (3): 293–313.

DWP (Department for Work and Pensions) (2012) *Housing Benefit: Size Criteria for People Renting in the Social Rented Sector: Equality Impact Assessment*, London, Department for Work and Pensions.

Elliott, L. (2010) 'Alistair Darling: we will cut deeper than Margaret Thatcher', *The Guardian*, 26 March.

Ellis, K. (2007) 'Direct Payments and social work practice: The significance of "street-level bureaucracy" in determining eligibility', *British Journal of Social Work*, 37(3): 405–22.

England, H. (1986) *Social Work as Art*, London, Allen & Unwin.

Eraut, M. (1994) *Developing Professional Knowledge and Competence*, London, The Falmer Press.

Evans, T. (2013) 'Organisational rules and discretion in adult social work', *British Journal of Social Work*, 43 (4): 739–58.

Evans, T. and Harris, J. (2004) 'Street-level bureaucracy, social work and the (exaggerated) death of discretion', *British Journal of Social Work*, 34 (6): 871–95.

Evetts, J. (2006) 'Introduction: trust and professionalism: challenges and occupational changes', *Current Sociology*, 54 (4): 515–31.

Ferguson, I. (2007) 'Increasing user choice or privatizing risk? The antinomies of personalization', *British Journal of Social Work*, 37 (3): 387–403.

Ferguson, I. (2012a) 'Personalisation, social justice and social work: a reply to Simon Duffy', *Journal of Social Work Practice*, 26 (1): 55–73.

Ferguson, I. (2012b) 'From modernisation to big socitey [sic]: continuity and change in social work in the United Kingdom', *Cuadernos de Trabajo Social*, 25 (1): 19–31.

Ferguson, I. and Lavalette, M. (2014) *Adult Social Care*, Bristol, Policy Press.

Ferguson, I. and Woodward, R. (2009) *Radical Social Work in Practice: Making a Difference*, Bristol, Policy Press.

Flynn, M. (2012) *Winterbourne View: A Serious Case Review*, South Gloucestershire Safeguarding Adults Board.

Foster, J. (2010) 'Thinking on the front line: how creativity can improve self-directed support', *Journal of Social Work Practice*, 24 (3): 283–99.

Foster P. and Wilding P. (2000) 'Whither welfare professionalism?' *Social Policy and Administration*, 34 (2): 143–59.

Foucault, M. (1984) 'Truth and power' (from: *Power/Knowledge*), in P. Rabinow (ed.) *The Foucault Reader: An Introduction to Foucault's Thought*, London, Penguin.

Fox, N. (1995) 'Postmodern perspectives on care: the vigil and the gift', *Critical Social Policy,* 15 (4): 107–25.

Francis, R. (2013) *Report of the Mid Staffordshire NHS Foundation Trust Public Inquiry: Executive Summary*, HC 947, London, HMSO.

Freidson, E. (1970) *Professional Dominance: The Social Structure of Medical Care*, New York, Atherton Press.

Freidson, E. (2001) *Professionalism: The Third Logic*, Cambridge, Polity Press.

Gamble, A. (2001) 'Neo-liberalism', *Capital and Class*, 25 (3): 127–34.

Gaster, L. (1995) *Quality in Public Services: Managers' Choices,* Buckingham, Open University Press.

Gentleman, A. (2014) 'Financial strategy of Southern Cross homes blamed for old people's deaths', *The Guardian*, 9 June.

Giddens, A. (1991) *Modernity and Self-Identity. Self and Society in the Late Modern Age,* Cambridge, Polity Press.

Giddens, A. (1994) *Beyond Left and Right: The Future of Radical Politics,* Cambridge, Polity Press.

Glasby, J. (2014) 'The controversies of choice and control: why some people might be hostile to English social care reforms', *British Journal of Social Work*, 44 (2): 252–66.

Glasby, J. and Littlechild, R. (2004) *The Health and Social Care Divide: The Experiences of Older People*, 2nd edn, Bristol, Policy Press.

Glasby, J. and Littlechild, R. (2009) *Direct Payments and Personal Budgets: Putting Personalisation into Practice*, 2nd edn, Bristol, Policy Press.

Glendinning, C. (2008) 'Increasing choice and control for older and disabled people: a critical review of new developments in England', *Social Policy and Administration* 42 (5): 451–69.

Glendinning, C., Powell, M. and Rummery, K. (eds) (2002) *Partnerships, New Labour and the Governance of Welfare*, Bristol, Policy Press.

Glendinning, C., Challis, D., Fernandez, J.-L., Jacobs, S., Jones, K., Knapp, M. et al. (2008) *Evaluation of the Individual Budgets Pilot Programme: Final Report*, York, Social Policy Research Unit, University of York.

Goffman, E. (1961) *Asylums*, Harmondsworth, Penguin.

Goodship, J., Gummerson, N., Jacks, K., Lathlean, J. and Cope, S. (2004) 'Modernising regulation or regulating modernisation? The public, private and voluntary interface in adult social care', *Public Policy and Administration*, 19 (2): 13–27.

Goodwin, N., Smith, J., Davies, A., Perry, C., Rosen, R., Dixon, A. et al. (2012) *Integrated Care for Patients and Populations: Improving Outcomes by Working Together*, London, King's Fund/Nuffield Trust.

Gorman, H. (1999) *Skills, Knowledge and Continuing Education for Complex Care Management: A Critical Evaluation of the Roles, Tasks and Skills of Care Managers in a Context of Changing Professional Identities and the Commodification of Welfare*, unpublished PhD thesis, Faculty of Education, University of Central England in Birmingham, Birmingham.

Gorman, H. (2000) 'Winning hearts and minds? Emotional labour and learning for care management work', *Journal of Social Work Practice*, 14 (2): 149–58.

Gorman, H. (2003) 'Which skills do care managers need? A research project on skills, competency and continuing professional development', *Social Work Education*, 22 (3): 245–59.

Gorman, H. and Postle, K. (2003) *Transforming Community Care: A Distorted Vision*, Birmingham, Venture Press.

Gorman, H., Gurney, A., Harvey, A., Hutchinson, O., Sylvester, V. and Warburton, J. (1996) 'The value of analysing the interlocking nature of oppression for those involved in working and learning together in community care', *Journal of Interprofessional Care*, 10 (2): 147–57.

Gosling, J. and Martin, J. (2012) *Making Partnerships with Service Users and Advocacy Groups Work*, London, Jessica Kingsley.

Goss, S. and Miller, C. (1995) *From Margin to Mainstream – Developing User and Carer Centred Community Care*, York, Joseph Rowntree Foundation.

Gray, A.M. and Birrell, D. (2013) *Transforming Adult Social Care: Contemporary Policy and Practice*, Bristol, Policy Press.

Griffiths, R. (1988) *Community Care: Agenda for Action*, London, HMSO.

Guardian, The (2012) 'Rich and poor: deserving and undeserving', *The Guardian*, 27 January.

Hadley, R. and Clough, R. (1996) *Care in Chaos. Frustration and Challenge in Community Care*, London, Cassell.

Ham, C., Dixon, A. and Brooke, B. (2012) *Transforming the Delivery of Health and Social Care: The Case for Fundamental Change*, London, The King's Fund.

Harden, I. (1992) *The Contracting State*, Buckingham, Open University Press.

Harris, B. (2004) *The Origins of the Welfare State*, Basingstoke, Palgrave Macmillan.

Harris, J. (1998) 'Scientific management, bureau-professionalism, new managerialism: the labour process of state social work', *British Journal of Social Work*, 28 (6): 839–62.

Harris, J. (1999) 'State social work and social citizenship in Britain: from clientelism to consumerism', *British Journal of Social Work*, 29 (6): 915–37.

Harris, J. (2008) 'State social work: constructing the present from moments in the past', *British Journal of Social Work*, 38 (4): 662–79.

Harris, J. and Roulstone, A. (2011) *Disability, Policy and Professional Practice*, London, Sage.

Harris, J. and Unwin, P. (2009) 'Performance management in modernised social work', in J. Harris and V. White eds *Modernising Social Work: Critical Considerations*, Bristol, Policy Press.

Harris, J. and White, V. (eds) (2009 *Modernising Social Work: Critical Considerations*, Bristol, Policy Press.

Harris, N. (1987) 'Defensive social work', *British Journal of Social Work*, 17 (1): 61–9.

Harrison, S. and Smith, C. (2004) 'Trust and moral motivation: redundant resources in health and social care?' *Policy and Politics*, 31 (3): 371–86.

Hart, V. (2014) 'A view from social work practice', in C. Needham and J. Glasby (eds) *Debates in Personalisation*, Bristol, Policy Press.

Hasler, F. (2004) 'Disability, care and controlling services', in J. Swain, S. French, C. Barnes and C. Thomas (eds) *Disabling Barriers – Enabling Environments*, 2nd edn, London, Sage.

Hawkins, P. and Shohet, R. (2006) *Supervision in the Helping Professions*, 3rd edn, Buckingham, Open University Press.

HCPC (Heath and Care Professions Council) (2007) *Standards of Conduct, Performance and Ethics*, London, HCPC.

HCPC (2012) *Standards of Proficiency: Social Workers in England*, London, HCPC.

Healy, K. (2000) *Social Work Practices: Contemporary Perspectives on Change*, London, Sage.

Healy, K. (2009) 'A case of mistaken identity? The social welfare professions and New Public Management', *Journal of Sociology*, 45 (4): 401–18.

Healy, K. and Meagher, G. (2004) 'The reprofessionalization of social work: collaborative approaches for achieving professional recognition', *British Journal of Social Work*, 34 (2): 243–60.

Henwood, M. (1995) *Making a Difference? Implementation of the Community Care Reforms Two Years On,* London, Nuffield Institute for Health, King's Fund Centre.

Henwood, M. and Hudson, B. (2008) *Lost In the System? The Impact of Fair Access to Care*, London, Commission for Social Care Inspection.

Herod, J. and Lymbery, M. (2002) 'The social work role in multi-disciplinary teams', *Practice*, 14 (4): 17–27.

Hicks, K. (2013) 'Social workers must stand up against councils' false version of personalisation', *Community Care*, 1 July.

HM Government (2007) *Putting People First*, London, HM Government.

HM Government (2008) *The Case for Change – Why England Needs a New Care and Support System*, London, Department of Health.

HM Treasury (2010) *Spending Review 2010*, Cm 7942, London, The Stationery Office.

HM Treasury (2013) *Autumn Statement 2013*, Cm 8747, London, The Stationery Office.

Holman, B. (1993) *A New Deal for Social Welfare,* Oxford, Lion.

Hood, C. (1991) 'A public management for all seasons?' *Public Administration,* 69 (1): 3–19.

Houston, S. (2010) 'Beyond *homo economicus*: recognition and self-realization and social work', *British Journal of Social Work,* 40 (3): 841–57.

Howe, D. (1996) 'Surface and depth in social work practice', in N. Parton (ed.) *Social Theory, Social Change and Social Work,* London, Routledge.

Hoyes, L., Lart, R., Means, R. and Taylor, M. (1994) *Community Care in Transition,* York, Joseph Rowntree Foundation.

Hudson, B. (1990) 'Social policy and the New Right – the strange case of the community care White Paper', *Local Government Studies,* 16 (6): 15–34.

Hudson, B. (1993) *The Busy Person's Guide to Care Management,* Sheffield, Social Services Monographs Research in Practice.

Hudson, B. (1997) 'Michael Lipsky and street level bureaucracy: a neglected perspective' in M. Hill (ed.) *The Policy Process: A Reader,* 2nd edn, Hemel Hempstead, Prentice Hall/Harvester Wheatsheaf.

Hudson, B. and Henwood, M. (2002) 'The NHS and social care: the final countdown?' *Policy and Politics,* 30 (2): 153–66.

Hughes, B., McKie, L., Hopkins, D. and Watson, N. (2005) 'Love's labours lost? Feminism, the disabled people's movement and an ethic of care', *Sociology,* 39 (2): 259–75.

Hugman, R. (1994) 'Social work and case management in the UK: models of professionalism and elderly people', *Ageing and Society,* 14 (2): 237–53.

Hugman, R. (1998) 'Social work and de-professionalization', in P. Abbott and L. Meerabeau (eds) *The Sociology of the Caring Professions,* 2nd edn, London, UCL Press.

Hutton, W. (2014) 'The Doncaster Care UK strike is about putting values over profit', *The Observer,* 9 August.

Huxley, P. (1993) 'Case management and care management in community care', *British Journal of Social Work,* 23 (4): 365–81.

Ife, J. (2012) *Human Rights and Social Work: Towards Rights-based Practice,* 3rd edn, Cambridge, Cambridge University Press.

IFSW (International Federation of Social Workers) (2014) Global definition of social work, http://ifsw.org/get-involved/global-definition-of-social-work/ IFSW, IASSW and ICSW (International Federation of Social Workers, International Association of Schools of Social Work and International Council on Social Welfare) (2012) *The Global Agenda for Social Work and Social Development: Commitment to Action,* www.globalsocialagenda.org/

Illich, I. (1977) *Disabling Professions,* London, Marion Boyars Publishers Ltd.

Ismail, S., Thorlby, R. and Holder H. (2014) *Focus On: Social Care for Older People. Reductions in Adult Social Services for Older People in England,* London, Quality Watch, Nuffield Trust/The Health Foundation.

Jamous, H. and Peloille, B. (1970) 'Professions or self perpetuating systems? Changes in the French university hospital system', in J.A. Jackson (ed.) *Professions and Professionalization*, Cambridge, Cambridge University Press.

Johns R. (2010) 'Vulnerability, Autonomy, Capacity and Consent' in L.-A. Long, J, Roche and D. Stringer (eds) *The Law and Social Work: Contemporary Issues for Practice*, Basingstoke, Palgrave.

Johnson, T. (1972) *Professions and Power*, London, Macmillan.

Johnson, J., Rolph, S. and Smith, R. (2012) *Residential Care Transformed: Revisiting 'The Last Refuge'*, Basingstoke, Palgrave.

Jones, K. (1988) *Experience in Mental Health: Community Care and Social Policy*, London, Sage.

Jones, R. (2013) 'How to privatise child protection in six easy stages', *The Guardian*, 19 November.

Jones, R. (2014) 'The best of times, the worst of times: social work and its moment', *British Journal of Social Work*, 44 (3): 485–502.

Jordan, B. (1984) *Invitation to Social Work*, Oxford, Martin Robertson.

Jung, T. (2010) 'Citizens, co-producers, customers, clients, captives? A critical review of consumerism and public services', *Public Management Review*, 12 (3): 439–46.

Kerrison, S. and Pollock, A. (2001) 'Caring for older people in the private sector in England', *British Medical Journal*, 323 (7312): 566–9.

King, N. and Ross, A. (2003) 'Professional identities and interprofessional relations: evaluation of collaborative community schemes', *Social Work in Health Care*, 38 (2): 51–72.

Kitwood, T. (1993) 'Towards a theory of dementia care: the interpersonal process', *Ageing and Society*, 13 (1): 51–67.

Kitwood, T. and Bredin, K. (1992) 'Towards a theory of dementia care: personhood and well-being', *Ageing and Society*, 12 (3): 269–87.

Knapp, M., Hardy, B. and Forder, J (2001) 'Commissioning for quality: ten years of social care markets in England', *Journal of Social Policy*, 30 (2): 283–306.

Koprowska, J. (2007) 'Communication skills in social work', in M. Lymbery and K. Postle (eds) *Social Work: A Companion for Learning*, London, Sage.

Larson, M.S. (1977) *The Rise of Professionalism: A Sociological Analysis*, Berkeley, CA, University of California Press.

Lass, F. (2001) 'Today's choices: life of grime special: Mr Trebus', *Radio Times*, 28 April–4 May: 104.

Le Grand, J. (2003) *Motivation, Agency and Public Policy*, Oxford, Oxford University Press.

Le Grand, J. (2007a) *The Other Invisible Hand: Delivering Public Services through Choice and Competition*, Princeton, NJ, Princeton University Press.

Le Grand, J. (2007b) *Consistent Care Matters: Exploring the Potential of Social Work Practices*, London, Department for Education and Skills.

Le Grand, J. and Bartlett, W. (1993) *Quasi-Markets and Social Policy*, London, Macmillan.

Leadbeater, C. (2004) *Personalisation through Participation: A New Script for Public Services*, London, Demos.

Leadbeater, C., Bartlett, J. and Gallagher, N. (2008) *Making it Personal*, London: Demos.

Leece, D. and Leece, J. (2006) 'Direct payments: creating a two-tiered system in social care?' *British Journal of Social Work*, 36 (8): 1379–93.

Leece, J. and Peace, S. (2010) 'Developing new understandings of independence and autonomy in the personalised relationship', *British Journal of Social Work*, 40 (6): 1847–65.

Levick, P. (1992) 'The Janus face of community care legislation: an opportunity for radical possibilities', *Critical Social Policy*, 12 (3/4): 75–92.

Lewis, J. (1995) *The Voluntary Sector, the State and Social Work in Britain*, Aldershot, Edward Elgar.

Lewis, J. (1996) 'Women, social work and social welfare in twentieth-century Britain: from (unpaid) influence to (paid) oblivion?' in M. Daunton (ed.) *Charity, Self-interest and Welfare*, London, Routledge.

Lewis, J. (2001) 'Older people and the health–social care boundary in the UK: half a century of hidden policy conflict', *Social Policy and Administration*, 35 (4): 343–59.

Lewis, J. and Glennerster, H. (1996) *Implementing the New Community Care*, Buckingham, Open University Press.

Lewis, J., Bernstock, P., Bovell, V. and Wookey, F. (1997) 'Implementing care management: issues in relation to the new community care', *British Journal of Social Work*, 27 (1): 5–24.

LEWRG (London Edinburgh Weekend Return Group) (1980) *In and Against the State*, London, Pluto Press.

LGA (Local Government Association) (2014) *LGA Adult Social Care Efficiency Programme: The Final Report*, London, Local Government Association.

Lipsky, M. (1980) *Street Level Bureaucracy. Dilemmas of the Individual in Public Service*, New York, NY: Russel Sage Foundation.

Lloyd, L. (2014) 'Can personalisation work for older people?' in C. Needham and J. Glasby (eds) *Debates in Personalisation*, Bristol, Policy Press.

Lloyd, M. (2002) 'Care management', in R. Adams, L. Dominelli and M. Payne (eds) *Critical Practice in Social Work*, Basingstoke, Palgrave.

Loader, B. (1998) 'Welfare direct: informatics and the emergence of self-service welfare?' in J. Carter (ed.) *Postmodernity and the Fragmentation of Welfare*, London, Routledge.

Lombard, D. (2011) 'Employers "using personalisation to shed social workers"', *Community Care*, 5 April.

Longmate, N. (1974) *The Workhouse*, London, Temple Smith.

Lymbery, M. (1998) 'Care management and professional autonomy: the impact of community care legislation on social work with older people', *British Journal of Social Work*, 28 (6): 863–78.

Lymbery, M. (2001) 'Social work at the crossroads', *British Journal of Social Work*, 31 (3): 369–84.

Lymbery, M. (2003) 'Negotiating the contradictions between competence and creativity in social work education', *Journal of Social Work*, 3 (1): 99–117.

Lymbery, M. (2004) 'Managerialism and care management practice with older people', in M. Lymbery and S. Butler (eds) *Social Work Ideals and Practice Realities*, Basingstoke, Palgrave.

Lymbery, M. (2005) *Social Work with Older People: Context, Policy and Practice*, London, Sage.

Lymbery, M. (2006) 'United we stand? Partnership working in health and social care and the role of social work in services for older people', *British Journal of Social Work*, 36 (7): 1119–34.

Lymbery, M. (2007) 'Social work in its organisational context', in M. Lymbery and K. Postle (eds) *Social Work: A Companion for Learning*, London, Sage.

Lymbery, M. (2008) *Social Work with Older People: Context, Policy and Professional Status*, Submitted towards the Award of PhD by Published Work, University of Nottingham.

Lymbery, M. (2009) 'Troubling times for British social work education?' *Social Work Education*, 28 (8): 902–18.

Lymbery, M. (2010) 'A new vision for adult social care? Continuities and change in the care of older people', *Critical Social Policy*, 30 (1): 5–26.

Lymbery, M. (2011) '*Building a Safe and Confident Future: One Year On* – reflections from the world of higher education in England', *Social Work Education* 30 (4): 465–71.

Lymbery, M. (2012) 'Critical commentary: Social work and personalisation', *British Journal of Social Work* 42 (4): 783–92.

Lymbery, M. (2013) 'Reconciling radicalism, relationship and role: priorities for social work with adults in England', *Critical and Radical Social Work*, 1 (2): 201–15.

Lymbery, M. (2014a) 'Understanding personalisation: implications for social work', *Journal of Social Work*, 14 (3): 295–312.

Lymbery, M. (2014b) 'How the market fails social care', in I. Ferguson and M. Lavalette *Adult Social Care*, Bristol, Policy Press.

Lymbery, M. (2014c) 'Austerity, personalisation and older people: the prospects for creative social work practice in England', *European Journal of Social Work*, 17 (3): 367–82.

Lymbery, M. (2014d) 'Social work and personalisation: fracturing the bureau–professional compact?' *British Journal of Social Work*, 44 (4): 795–811.

Lymbery, M. and Morley, K. (2012) 'Self-directed support and social work', *Practice*, 24 (5): 315–27.

Lymbery, M. and Postle, K. (2010) 'Social work in the context of adult social care in England and the resultant implications for social work education', *British Journal of Social Work* 40 (8): 2502–22.

McDonald, A. (1997) *Challenging Local Authority Decisions*, Birmingham, Venture Press.

McDonald, A. (2010) *Social Work with Older People*, Oxford, Polity.

McDonald, A., Postle, K. and Dawson, C. (2008) 'Barriers to retaining and using professional knowledge in local authority social work practice with adults in the UK', *British Journal of Social Work*, 38 (7): 1370–87.

McDonald, C. (2006) 'Institutional transformation: the impact of performance measurement on professional practice in social work', *Social Work and Society*, 4 (1): 26–37.

McDonald, C., Harris, J. and Wintersteen, R. (2003) 'Contingent on context? Social work and the state in Australia, Britain, and the USA', *British Journal of Social Work*, 33 (2): 191–208.

McIntyre, M. (2003) 'Dignity in dementia: person-centered care in community', *Journal of Aging Studies*, 17 (4): 473–84.

McKitterick, B. (2014) 'The recent education reviews demonstrate the limited impact of the Social Work Reform Board's proposals', *Community Care*, 3 March.

McLeod, E. and Bywaters, P. (2000) *Social Work, Health and Equality*, London, Routledge.

McNicoll, A. (2014) '10 ways councils are targeting savings from adult social care in 2014–15', *Community Care*, 9 April.

Malin, N. (ed.) (1995) *Services for People with Learning Disabilities*, London, Routledge.

Mandelstam, M. (2005) *Community Care Practice and the Law*, London, Jessica Kingsley.

Manthorpe, J., Rapaport, J. and Stanley, N. (2008) 'The Mental Capacity Act and its influence on social work practice: debate and synthesis', *Practice*, 20 (3): 151–62.

Manthorpe, J., Harris, J., Hussain, S., Cornes, M. and Moriarty, J. (2014) *Evaluation of the Social Work Practices with Adults Pilots: Final Report*, King's College London, Social Care Workforce Research Unit.

Marshall, M. (1989) 'The sound of silence: who cares about quality of social work with older people?' in C. Rojek, G. Peacock and S. Collins (eds) *The Haunt of Misery: Critical Essays in Social Work and Helping*, London: Routledge.

Marshall, T.H. (2006) 'Citizenship and social class', in C. Pierson and F.G Castles (eds) *The Welfare State Reader*, 2nd edn, Cambridge, Polity Press.

Martin, G.P., Phelps, K. and Katbamna, S. (2004) 'Human motivation and professional practice: of knights, knaves and social workers', *Social Policy and Administration*, 38 (5): 470–87.

Means, R. (2012) 'A brave new world of personalized care? Historical perspectives on social care and older people in England', *Social Policy and Administration* 46 (3): 302–20.

Means R. and Smith R. (1998) *From Poor Law to Community Care*, 2nd edn, Bristol, Policy Press.

Means R., Morbey H. and Smith R. (2002) *From Community Care to Market Care?* Bristol, Policy Press.

Means, R., Richards, S. and Smith, R. (2008) *Community Care: Policy and Practice*, 4th edn, Basingstoke, Palgrave Macmillan.

Midgeley, J. (2001) 'Issues in international social work: resolving critical debates in the profession', *Journal of Social Work*, 1 (1): 21–35.

Midwinter, E. (1994) *The Development of Social Welfare in Britain*, Buckingham, Open University Press.

Milne, A., Sullivan, M.P., Tanner, D., Richards, S., Ray, M., Lloyd, L. et al. (2014) *Future Directions for Investment: Social Work with Older People (Part of the TCSW business case for social work with adults)*, London, The College of Social Work.

Milner, J. and O'Byrne, P. (2009) *Assessment in Social Work*, 3rd edn, Basingstoke, Palgrave Macmillan.

Mitchell, W., Brooks, J. and Glendinning, C. (2014) 'Carers' roles in personal budgets: tensions and dilemmas in front line practice', *British Journal of Social Work* published online 30 March, doi: 10.1093/bjsw/bcu018.

Morris, S. (2013) 'Crisis-hit city council cuts 1,000 more jobs', *The Guardian*, 10 December: 11.

Morrison, J. (2014) 'Our love of a free NHS ignores the gaping hole in social care finances', *The Guardian*, 11 September.

Mowat, C.L. (1961) *The Charity Organisation Society*, London, Methuen.

Munro, E. (2004) 'The impact of audit on social work practice', *British Journal of Social Work*, 34 (8): 1075–95.

Murray, P. and Penman, J. (Compilers) (1996), *Let our Children be*, Sheffield, Parents with Attitude.

Narey, M. (2014) *Making the Education of Social Workers Consistently Effective*, London, Department of Education.

Needham, C. (2011) *Personalising Public Services: Understanding the Personalisation Narrative*, Bristol, Policy Press.

Needham, C. and Carr, S. (2009) *Co-production: an emerging evidence base for adult social care transformation*, Research Briefing 31, London, Social Care Institute for Excellence.

Needham, C. and Glasby, J. (eds) (2014a) *Debates in Personalisation*, Bristol, Policy Press.

Needham, C. and Glasby, J. (2014b) 'Taking stock of personalisation', in C. Needham and J. Glasby (eds) *Debates in Personalisation*, Bristol, Policy Press.

Nocon, A. and Quereshi, H. (1996) *Outcomes of Community Care for Users and Carers*, Buckingham: Open University Press.

Nottingham Post (2014) 'Protests as £83m cuts at Nottinghamshire County Council formally approved' *Nottingham Evening Post*, 28 February.

Oakland, J. (1989) *Total Quality Management*, London, Butterworth and Heinemann.

ODI (Office for Disability Issues) (2008) *Independent Living: A Cross-government Strategy about Independent Living for Disabled People*, London: Office for Disability Issues.

O'Leary, P., Tsui, M.-S. and Ruch, G. (2012) 'The boundaries of the social work relationship revisited: towards a connected, inclusive and dynamic conceptualisation', *British Journal of Social Work*, 43 (1): 135–53.

Oliver, M. (1996) *Understanding Disability*, Basingstoke, Macmillan.

Oliver, M. (2004) 'If I had a hammer: the social model in action', in J. Swain, S. French, C. Barnes and C. Thomas (eds) *Disabling Barriers – Enabling Environments*, 2nd edn, London, Sage.

Oliver, M. and Sapey, B. (2006) *Social Work with Disabled People*, 3rd edn, Basingstoke, Palgrave.

Øvretveit, J. (1993) *Coordinating Community Care, Multidisciplinary Teams and Care Management,* Buckingham, Open University Press.

Parton, N. (ed.) (1996) *Social Theory, Social Change and Social Work,* London, Routledge.

Parton, N. (2000) 'Some thoughts on the relationship between theory and practice in and for social work', *British Journal of Social Work*, 30 (4): 449–63.

Payne, M. (1995) *Social Work and Community Care*, Basingstoke, Macmillan.

Payne, M. (2005) *The Origins of Social Work*, Basingstoke, Palgrave.

Payne, M. (2006) *What is Professional Social Work?* 2nd edn, Bristol, Policy Press.

Pease, B. and Fook, J. (1999) 'Postmodern critical theory and emancipatory social work practice', in B. Pease and J. Fook (eds) *Transforming Social Work Practice: Postmodern Critical Perspectives*, London, Routledge.

Pithouse, A. (1998) *Social Work: The Social Organisation of an Invisible Trade*, 2nd edn, Aldershot, Ashgate.

Plant, R. (1998) 'Citizenship, rights, welfare', in J. Franklin (ed.) *Social Policy and Social Justice: The IPPR Reader*, Cambridge, Polity Press.

Poldervaart, H. and Malenczuk, L. (2013) *Direct Payments for Social Care: Options for Managing the Cash. How local authorities and financial institutions can make managing the finances easier for older people*, London, Age UK.

Pollitt, C. (1990) *Managerialism and the Public Services*, Oxford, Basil Blackwell.

Postle, K. (1999) *Care Managers' Responses to Working under Conditions of Postmodernity*, unpublished PhD thesis, Department of Social Work Studies, University of Southampton, Southampton.

Postle, K. (2001) '"The social work side is disappearing. I guess it started with us being called care managers"', *Practice*, 13 (1): 13–26.

Postle, K. (2002) 'Working "between the idea and the reality": ambiguities and tensions in care managers' work', *British Journal of Social Work*, 32 (3): 335–51.

Postle, K. (2007) 'Value conflicts in practice', in M. Lymbery and K. Postle (eds) *Social Work: A Companion for Learning*, London, Sage.

Postle, K. and Beresford, P. (2007) 'Capacity building and the reconception of political participation: a role for social care workers?' *British Journal of Social Work*, 37 (1): 143–58.

Postle, K. and Ford, P. (2000) 'Using mediation skills in family work', in A. Wheal (ed.) *Working with Parents: Learning from Other People's Experience*, Lyme Regis, Russell House.

Postle, K., Wright, P. and Beresford, P. (2005) 'Older people's participation in political activity – making their voices heard: a potential support role for welfare professionals in countering ageism and social exclusion', *Practice*, 17 (3): 173–89.

Power, M. (1997) *The Audit Society*, Oxford, Oxford University Press.

Preston-Shoot, M. (2000) 'What if? Using the Law to Uphold Practice Values and Standards', *Practice: Social work in action*, 12 (4): 49–63.

Rabiee, P. and Glendinning, C. (2011) 'Organisation and delivery of home care re-ablement: what makes a difference?' *Health and Social in the Community*, 19 (5): 495–503.

Rachman, R. (1995) 'Community care: changing the role of hospital social work', *Health and Social Care in the Community*, 3 (3): 163–72.

Reid, P.N. and Edwards, R.L. (2006) 'The purpose of a school of social work – an American perspective', *Social Work Education*, 25 (5): 461–84.

Richards, S. (2000) 'Bridging the divide: elders and the assessment process', *British Journal of Social Work*, 30 (1): 37–49.

Rogowski, S. (2010) *Social Work: The Rise and Fall of a Profession*, Bristol, Policy Press.

Rooff, M. (1969) *A hundred years of family welfare*, London: Michael Joseph.

Rose, N. (1999) *Powers of Freedom: Reframing Political Thought*, Cambridge, Cambridge University Press.

Roulstone, A. and Morgan, H. (2009) 'Neo-liberal Individualism or Self-directed Support: Are We All Speaking the Same Language on Modernising Adult Social Care?', *Social Policy and Society*, 8 (3): 333–45.

Rummery, K. (2002) *Disability, Citizenship and Community Care: A Case for Welfare Rights?* Aldershot, Ashgate.

Salter, B. (1998) *The Politics of Change in the Health Service*, Basingstoke, Macmillan.

Samuel, M. (2011) 'The rise of non-qualified social care staff under personalisation', *Community Care*, 20 May.

Samuel, M. (2013a) 'Red tape and lack of funding limit choice for people on council-managed personal budgets', *Community Care*, 8 October.

Samuel, M (2013b) 'NHS continuing care assessment failings causing great distress and expense for clients, finds inquiry', *Community Care*, 28 November.

Samuel, M. (2013c) 'Councils losing ability to protect adult social care from significant cuts, says finance watchdog', *Community Care*, 28 November.

Samuel, M. (2013d) 'Castlebeck sold to fellow care provider, saving 850 jobs', *Community Care*, 5 September.

Satyamurti, C. (1981) *Occupational Survival*, Oxford, Basil Blackwell.

Schön, D. (1987) *Educating the Reflective Practitioner: How Professionals Think in Action*, New York, Basic Books.

Schön, D. (1991) *The Reflective Practitioner. How Professionals Think in Action*, New York, Basic Books.

Schön, D. (1992) 'The crisis of professional knowledge and the pursuit of an epistemology of practice', *Journal of Interprofessional Care*, 6 (1): 49–63.

Schorr, A. (1992) *The Personal Social Services: An Outside View*, York, Joseph Rowntree Foundation.

Schraer, R. (2014) 'Report evaluating outsourced adult social work is met with radio silence', *Community Care*, 8 August.

SCIE (Social Care Institute for Excellence) (2010a) *Personalisation Briefing: Implications for Social Workers in Adults' Services*, London, SCIE.

SCIE (2010b) *Improving Personal Budgets for Older People: A Research Overview*, London, SCIE.

Scourfield, P. (2007a) 'Are there reasons to be worried about the "caretelization" of residential care?' *Critical Social Policy*, 27 (2): 155–80.

Scourfield, P. (2007b) 'Social Care and the Modern Citizen: Client, Consumer, Service User, Manager and Entrepreneur', *British Journal of Social Work*, 37 (1): 107–22.

Scourfield, P. (2012) 'Caretelization revisited and the lessons of Southern Cross', *Critical Social Policy* 32 (1): 137–48.

Scourfield, P. (2013) 'Even further beyond street-level bureaucracy: the dispersal of discretion exercised in decisions made in older people's care home reviews', *British Journal of Social Work*, published online 13 November, doi: 10.1093/bjsw/bct175 .

Seebohm Report (1968) *Report of the Committee on Local Authority and Allied Personal Social Services*, London, HMSO.

Seed, P. (1973) *The Expansion of Social Work in Britain*, London, Routledge & Kegan Paul.

Series, L. and Clements, L. (2013) 'Putting the cart before the horse: resource allocation systems and community care', *Journal of Social Welfare and Family Law*, 35 (2): 207–26.

Servian, R. (1996) *Theorising Empowerment: Individual Power and Community Care*, Bristol, Policy Press.

Shakespeare, T. (2000) *Help*, Birmingham, Venture Press.

Sheldrick, D. (2014) '"Get off the sofa and get a job": Council chief blasts Benefits Street welfare claimants', *Daily Express*, 15 January.

Simiç, P. (1995) 'What's in a word? From social "worker" to care "manager"', *Practice,* 7 (3): 5–18.

Simpkin, M. (1983) *Trapped within Welfare*, 2nd edn, London, Macmillan.

Slasberg, C., Beresford, P. and Schofield, P. (2012a) 'How self directed support is failing to deliver personal budgets and personalisation', *Research Policy and Planning*, 29 (3): 161–77.

Slasberg, C., Beresford, P. and Schofield, P. (2012b) 'Can personal budgets really deliver better outcomes for all at no cost? Reviewing the evidence, costs and quality', *Disability and Society*, 27 (7): 1029–34.

Smale, G. (1998) *Managing Change through Innovation*, London, The Stationery Office.

Smale, G., Tuson, G., with Biehal, N. and Marsh, P. (1993) *Empowerment, Assessment, Care Management and the Skilled Worker,* London, HMSO.

Smale, G., Tuson, G. and Statham, D. (2000) *Social Work and Social Problems: Working Towards Social Inclusion and Social Change*, Basingstoke, Macmillan.

Smith, C. (2001) 'Trust and confidence: possibilities for social work in "high modernity"', *British Journal of Social Work*, 31 (2): 287–305.

Social Work Studies, University of Southampton (2003) *Centre for Evaluative and Developmental Research (CEDR): Public Lectures*, www.cedr.soton.ac.uk/lecture. htm, Accessed 21st May 2014.

Specht, H. and Courteney, M. (1994) *Unfaithful Angels: How Social Work has Abandoned its Mission,* New York, Free Press.

Spicker, P. (2000) *The Welfare State: A General Theory*, London, Sage.

Spicker, P. (2013) 'Personalisation falls short', *British Journal of Social Work*, 43 (7): 1259–75.

Stanley, N., Austerberry, H., Bilson, A., Farrelly, N., Hargreaves, K., Hollingworth, K. et al. (2012) *Social Work Practices: Report of the National Evaluation*, London, Department for Education.

Stanley, N., Austerberry, N., Bilson, A., Farrelly, N., Hussein, S., Larkins, C. et al. (2013) 'Turning away from the public sector in children's out-of-home care: an English experiment', *Children and Youth Services Review*, 35: 33–39.

Stewart, J. and Walsh, K. (1992) 'Change in the management of public services', *Public Administration,* 70 (4): 499–518.

Stevens, M., Glendinning, C., Jacobs, S., Moran, N., Challis, D., Manthorpe, J. et al. (2011) 'Assessing the role of increasing choice in English social care services', *Journal of Social Policy*, 40 (2): 257–74.

Stevenson, O. (2005) 'Genericism and specialization: the story since 1970', *British Journal of Social Work*, 35 (5): 569–86.

Stevenson, O. and Parsloe, P. (1993) *Community Care and Empowerment,* York, Joseph Rowntree Foundation.

SWAN (Social Work Action Network) (n.d.) www.socialworkfuture.org/

Swinkels, A., Albarran, J.W., Means, R.I., Mitchell, T. and Stewart, M.C. (2002) 'Evidence-based practice in health and social care: where are we now?' *Journal of Interprofessional Care*, 16 (4): 335–47.

SWRB (Social Work Reform Board) (2009) *Building a Safe and Confident Future*, London, Social Work Reform Board.

SWRB (2010) *Building a Safe and Confident Future: One Year On*, London, Social Work Reform Board.

Syrett, V., Jones, M. and Sercombe, N. (1997) 'Implementing community care: the congruence of manager and practitioner cultures', *Social Work and Social Sciences Review,* 7 (3): 154–69.

Tanner, D. (2003) 'Older people and access to care', *British Journal of Social Work*, 33 (4): 499–515.

Tanner, D. (2013) 'Identity, selfhood and dementia: messages for social work', *European Journal of Social Work*, 16 (2): 155–70.

Taylor-Gooby, P. (2009) *Reframing Social Citizenship*, Oxford, Oxford University Press.

Taylor-Gooby, P. and Stoker, G. (2011) 'The Coalition Programme: A new vision for Britain or politics as usual?', *The Political Quarterly*, 82(1): 4–15.

Taylor-Gooby, P. (2012) 'Root and branch restructuring to achieve major cuts: the social policy programme of the 2010 UK coalition government', *Social Policy and Administration*, 46 (1): 61–82.

Taylor-Gooby, P., Larsen, T. and Kananen, J. (2004) 'Market means and welfare ends: the UK welfare state experiment', *Journal of Social Policy*, 33 (4): 573–92.

TCSW (The College of Social Work) (2012) *The Business Case for Social Work with Adults: A Discussion Paper*, London, The College of Social Work.

TCSW (2013) *The Professional Capabilities Framework (PCF)*, London, The College of Social Work.

Thompson, N. (2012) *Anti-Discriminatory Practice: Equality, Diversity and Social Justice*, 5th edn, Basingstoke, Palgrave.

Timmins, N. (1996) *The Five Giants*, London, Fontana.

Toren, N. (1972) *Social Work: The Case of a Semi-Profession*, London, Sage.

Townsend, P. (1962) *The Last Refuge*, London, Routledge & Kegan Paul.

Townsend, P. and Gebhardt, J. (1990) *Commit to Quality*, New York, John Wiley and Sons.

Tronto, J.C. (2010) 'Creating caring institutions: politics, plurality, and purpose', *Ethics and Social Welfare* 4 (2): 158–71.

Turner, A. (2014) 'Independent sector hit by cut in fees for non-statutory social work placements', *Community Care*, 20 May.

Wanless, D. (2006) *Securing Good Care for Older People: Taking a Long-term View*, London, King's Fund.

Ware, P., Matosevic, T., Forder, J., Hardy, B., Kendall, J., Knapp M. et al. (2001) 'Movement and change: independent sector domiciliary care providers between 1995 and 1999', *Health and Social Care in the Community*, 9 (6): 334–40.

Ware, P., Matosevic, T., Hardy, B., Knapp M., Kendall J. and Forder, J. (2003) 'Commissioning care services for older people in England: the view from care managers, users and carers', *Ageing and Society*, 23 (4): 411–28.

Watt, N. (2014) 'Most deprived local authorities face worst cuts, figures show', *The Guardian*, 30 January: 10.

Webb, A. and Wistow, G. (1987) *Social Work, Social Care and Social Planning*, London, Longman.

Webb, B. (1971 [1926]) *My Apprenticeship*, Harmondsworth, Penguin.

Webb, S.A. (2001) 'Some considerations on the validity of evidence-based practice in social work', *British Journal of Social Work*, 31 (1): 57–79.

Webb, S.A. (2006) *Social Work in a Risk Society: Social and Political Perspectives*, Basingstoke, Palgrave.

Weiss-Gal, I. and Welbourne, P. (2008) 'The professionalisation of social work: a cross-national exploration', *International Journal of Social Welfare*, 17 (4): 281–90.

Welsh Assembly (2011) *Sustainable Social Services for Wales: A Framework for Action* WAG10-11806, Cardiff, Welsh Assembly Government, http://wales.gov.uk/docs/dhss/publications/110216frameworken.pdf, Accessed 25th November 2014.

West, K. (2013) 'The grip of personalization in adult social care: between managerial domination and fantasy', *Critical Social Policy*, 33 (4): 638–57.

Wilding, P. (1982) *Professional Power and Social Welfare*, London, Routledge & Kegan Paul.

Wilkinson, R. and Pickett, K. (2009) *The Spirit Level*, Harmondsworth, Penguin.

Williams, B. and Tyson, A. (2010) 'Self-direction, place and community – re-discovering the emotional depths: a conversation with social workers in a London borough', *Journal of Social Work Practice*, 24 (3): 319–33.

Williams, R. (1975) *Keywords: A Vocabulary of Culture and Society*, London, Fontana.

Williams, Z. (2014) 'Moving beyond left and right could save the public sector', *The Guardian*, 8 September.

Wintour, P. and Booth, R. (2014) 'UK floods: David Cameron pledges unlimited public funds', *The Guardian*, 11 February.

Wistow, G. (2012) 'Still a fine mess? Local government and the NHS 1962 to 2012', *Journal of Integrated Care*, 20 (2): 101–14.

Wistow, G., Knapp, M., Hardy, B. and Allen, C. (1994) *Social Care in a Mixed Economy* Buckingham, Open University Press.

Woodroofe, K. (1962) *From Charity to Social Work*, London, Routledge & Kegan Paul.

Woolham, J. and Benton, C. (2013) 'The costs and benefits of personal budgets for older people: evidence from a single local authority', *British Journal of Social Work*, 43 (8): 1472–91.

Wootton, B. (1959) *Social Science and Social Pathology*, London, George Allen & Unwin.

Younghusband, E. (1955) 'Conclusion', in C. Morris (ed.) *Social Case-work in Great Britain*, 2nd edn, London, Faber & Faber.

Subject index

Author index